Harold W. Kaser
1st Presbyterian Church
Saginaw, Mi.
1982

The Art of Biblical
Narrative

Books by Robert Alter

Rogue's Progress: Studies in the Picaresque Novel

Fielding and the Nature of the Novel

After the Tradition

Modern Hebrew Literature

Partial Magic: The Novel as a Self-Conscious Genre

Defenses of the Imagination

A Lion for Love: A Critical Biography of Stendhal

THE ART OF BIBLICAL NARRATIVE

ROBERT ALTER

BASIC BOOKS, INC., PUBLISHERS
NEW YORK

Library of Congress Cataloging in Publication Data

Alter, Robert.
The art of biblical narrative.

Includes bibliographical references and index.
  1. Bible. O.T.—Language, Style. I. Title.
BS1171.2.A45   221.4'4   80–68958
ISBN: 0–465–00424–5   AACR2

For Alfred Appel

another kind of plexed artistry

CONTENTS

Dec. 14.

Jan. 13.

Feb. 15.

mon 15

PREFACE

THIS BOOK is intended to be a guide to the intelligent reading of biblical narrative. In the first two chapters I shall try to explain both the need for such a guide and its conceptual rationale, but here a few words may be in order about the procedures I shall follow and the origins of this project.

The aim throughout is to illuminate the distinctive principles of the Bible's narrative art. Numerous examples, both brief and extended, are analyzed, but always with the purpose of illustrating general principles, not to provide a commentary, comprehensive or otherwise, on any particular passage. The term Bible here will refer only to the Hebrew Bible. I adhere to the traditional Jewish practice of not using the Christian designation, Old Testament, which implies that the Old is completed only in the New and that together they comprise one continuous work. There are, of course, certain literary as well as theological continuities between the Hebrew Bible and the New Testament, but the narratives of the latter were written in a different language, at a later time, and, by and large, according to different literary assumptions. It therefore does not seem to me that these two bodies of ancient literature can be comfortably set in the same critical framework, and, in any case, I would not have the linguistic and scholarly competence to deal with the New Testament. The Hebrew Bible itself is a collection of works written at intervals over a stretch of seven or eight centuries; and since the narrative books like Esther and Daniel composed in the latter part of this period, during or after the Babylonian Exile, generally reflect rather new literary practices, I have concentrated on the great body of works first formulated in the pre-exilic age, that is, the Pentateuch and the Former Prophets.

As far as possible, I have tried to make my argument intelligible to the general reader and at the same time precise enough to be instructive to those who may have a more specialized knowledge of the Bible. When I began this study, I hoped I might be able to throw some new light on the Bible by bringing a literary perspective to bear on it. It is an aspiration I have not relinquished, but I also discovered for myself something unanticipated in the course of minutely examining many biblical texts: that the Bible on its part has a great deal to teach anyone interested in narrative because its seemingly simple, wonderfully complex art offers such splendid illustrations of the primary possibilities of narrative. This book, then, is directed to anyone concerned with the Bible, whether out of cultural or religious motives, and also to students of narrative. Readers in this last category will find no more than a couple of passing allusions to the new narratology that has flourished in France and America over the last decade because, quite frankly, I find its usefulness limited, and I am particularly suspicious of the value of elaborate taxonomies and skeptical as to whether our understanding of narrative is really advanced by the deployment of bristling neologisms like *analepsis, intradiegetic, actantial.* Occasionally, it has seemed necessary to use an established technical term in order to describe exactly a particular feature of style, syntax, or grammar, but I cling to the belief that it is possible to discuss complex literary matters in a language understandable to all educated people. Beyond such considerations of formulation, my approach differs from that of the new narratologists in my sense that it is important to move from the analysis of formal structures to a deeper understanding of the values, the moral vision embodied in a particular kind of narrative. Precisely for that reason, I think this study may have something to say to readers trying to make sense of the Bible as a momentous document of religious history.

The shape and meaning of any literary text will naturally be dependent to some extent on its linguistic fashioning. Because of that fact, I refer intermittently to matters of word-choice, sound-play, and syntax perceptible in the original Hebrew, occasionally even offering alternative translations to indicate a significant pun. All of this, I think, should be fairly easy for a reader to follow without any knowledge of Hebrew; and the main topics I have chosen are features of biblical narrative that for the most part can be observed reasonably well in translation. (For this reason, I decided not to include a chapter on style, which I had originally contemplated, because it would not have been of much use to readers without Hebrew.) I have done my own translations of all biblical texts cited. The King James Version, of course, remains the magisterial rendering in English, but even in its modern revised form it lacks a good deal in the way of clarity and philological precision, while the various contemporary translations, in striving for just those two qualities, tend to obliterate literary features of the original like expressive syntax, deliberate ambiguity, and purposeful repetition of words. My own versions at times may seem willfully awkward, but at least they have the virtue of making evident certain aspects of the original that play an important role in the artistry of biblical narrative.

The earliest idea for this project began with an invitation in 1971 from the Department of Religion at Stanford University to give an informal colloquium on the literary study of the Bible. That session, devoted to Genesis 38 and 39 (echoes of which will be found in chapters 1 and 5 here), turned out to be rather more successful than the carefully meditated public lectures on modern Jewish writing I was giving that week at Stanford. I put my notes for the colloquium away in a drawer, and some four years later, on an impulse, I asked the editors of *Commentary* whether they would be interested in an article on the need for a literary approach to the Bible. I am grateful to them for their receptivity, and especially to Neal Kozodoy, who encouraged me to make this backward leap of almost three millennia from my usual period of critical specialization. I am even more grateful to the readers of *Commentary*, so many of whom wrote me or the magazine after the appearance in December 1975 of the first article (in revised form, it now constitutes chapter 1) and convinced me that this was a subject eminently worth pursuing. Three subsequent articles were published in *Commentary*, in May 1976, October 1978, and November 1980; these now form part of chapter 5 and all of chapter 6 and chapter 8. Slightly shorter versions of chapters 2 and 3 appeared, respectively, in *Poetics Today* (Spring 1980) and in *Critical Inquiry* (Winter 1978). I would like to thank the editors of all three journals for their openness to a subject that might have seemed outside the chiefly modern purview of their publications, and I want to express my appreciation for their willingness to place the articles in question at my disposal for this book.

Preliminary versions of some of the material were tried out in the Buckstein Memorial Lectures at Trent University, Ontario, at the Indiana University Institute on Teaching the Bible in Literature Courses, and at a conference on biblical literature sponsored by the University of California at San Diego; and in each case the intelligent responsiveness of the audience helped improve the final version. I have also learned much from the keenness of my students in two graduate seminars on biblical narrative taught at the University of California at Berkeley. My colleague Tom Rosenmeyer was kind enough to respond in critical detail to the published segments of this study and, though he may not agree with everything I finally say, his good judgment and learning have saved me more than once from invidious simplifications of the Greeks.

Typing and incidental research costs were covered through the assistance of the Committee on Research of the University of California at Berkeley. The typing itself was done by Florence Myer with her usual meticulous care. Finally, I would also like to thank the many biblical scholars who have encouraged me in this undertaking, a few of them old friends, others whom I came to know through the publication of the first two articles. In my polemic beginning, I imagined, as I suppose most of us sometimes like to imagine, that I was going to ruffle a lot of feathers; instead, what I have discovered for the most part among professionals in the field is a generous receptivity to my ideas.

Berkeley
August 1980

The Art of Biblical

Narrative

1

A Literary Approach
to the Bible

WHAT ROLE does literary art play in the shaping of biblical narrative? A crucial one, I shall argue, finely modulated from moment to moment, determining in most cases the minute choice of words and reported details, the pace of narration, the small movements of dialogue, and a whole network of ramified interconnections in the text. Before we weigh the theoretical considerations that may explain why this should be so, and also the circumstances of intellectual history that have prevented this essential literary dimension from being sufficiently observed, it would be well to follow the sustained operation of narrative art in a biblical text.

Let me propose for analysis a supposedly interpolated story because it will give us an opportunity to observe both how it works in itself and how it interacts with the surrounding narrative material. I should like to discuss, then, the story of Tamar and Judah (Genesis 38), which is set in between the selling of Joseph by his brothers and Joseph's appearance as a slave in the household of Potiphar. This story is characterized by E. A. Speiser, in his superb Genesis volume in the Anchor Bible series, as "a completely independent unit," having "no connection with the drama of Joseph, which it interrupts at the conclusion of Act I."[1] The interpolation does, of course, as Speiser and others have recognized, build

---

[1] *Genesis,* The Anchor Bible (New York, 1964), p. 299.

a sense of suspense about the fate of Joseph and a feeling of time elapsed until Joseph shows up in Egypt, but Speiser's failure to see its intimate connections through motif and theme with the Joseph story suggests the limitations of conventional biblical scholarship even at its best. I shall begin with the last five verses of Genesis 37 in order to make clear the links between frame-narrative and interpolation. My translation will at a number of points be awkwardly literal to reproduce verbal repetitions or syntactic peculiarities of the original for the purposes of analysis.

Joseph's brothers, one recalls, after selling him into slavery, dip his cherished tunic in goat's blood to show to their father.

"They had the ornamented tunic brought to their father [note the indirection of their approach to Jacob, even more marked in the Hebrew syntax], and they said: 'This [*zot*] have we found. Please recognize [*hakerna*], is it your son's tunic or not?' " (Gen. 37:32). The brothers are careful to let the contrived object, "this [*zot*]," do their lying for them—it goes before them literally and syntactically—and of course they appropriately refer to Joseph as "your son," not by name nor as their brother. Jacob now has his prop, and from here on he can improvise his own part: "He recognized it [*vayakirah*], and he said: 'My son's tunic! An evil beast has devoured him,/ Joseph has fallen prey" (Gen. 37:33). *Haker*, the verb for recognition (which we will be seeing more of), stated by the brothers in the imperative, immediately recurs in the perfect tense, Jacob responding at once as the puppet of his sons' manipulation.

It should be observed (I am not sure the scholars have) that when Jacob goes on here to invent a disastrous explanation, left unstated by his sons, for the bloodied tunic, his speech ("An evil beast . . .") switches into formal verse, a neat semantic parallelism that scans with three beats in each hemistich: *ḥayáh ra῾áh ʾakhaláthu / taróf toráf Yoséf.* Poetry is heightened speech, and the shift to formal verse suggests an element of self-dramatization in the way Jacob picks up the hint of his son's supposed death and declaims it metrically before his familial audience. If this seems fanciful, I would direct attention to how Jacob's bereavement is described in the next two verses: "Jacob tore his clothes, put sackcloth on his loins, and mourned his son many days. All his sons and daughters tried to console him but he refused to be consoled, saying, 'No, I will go down to my son in the underworld mourning,' thus did his father bewail him" (Gen. 37:34–35). In two brief verses half a dozen different activities of mourning are recorded, including the refusal to be consoled and direct speech in which the father expresses the wish to mourn until he joins his son in death. (Later, ironically, he will "go down" to his son not to Sheol, the underworld, but to Egypt.) One can hardly dismiss all these gestures of mourning as standard Near Eastern practice, since the degree of specification and synonymity is far beyond the norms of the narrative itself. Thus, just a few verses earlier (Gen. 37:29), when Reuben imagines Joseph is dead, his sincere sense of bereavement is expressed quite simply with "He tore his clothes"—in the Hebrew only two words and a particle.

Finally, the extravagance of Jacob's mourning is pointed up by the verse that immediately follows it and concludes the episode: "And the Midianites sold him in Egypt to Potiphar, courtier of Pharaoh, his chief steward" (Gen. 37:36). Modern translations usually render the initial *vav* of this verse with something like "meanwhile," but that loses the artful ambiguity of the Bible's parataxis. In this cunningly additive syntax, on the same unbroken narrative continuum in which Jacob is mourning his supposedly devoured son, Midianites are selling the living lad: "And his father bewailed him and the Midianites sold him"—for even the sentence break would not have been evident in the ancient text. The original syntax, to be sure, does indicate some opposition and perhaps a past perfect sense of the verb by placing the subject before the verb ("and the Midianites sold him"), not the normal Hebrew order, and by switching the verb form when the Midianites are introduced. In any case, the transition from Jacob mourning to Joseph sold is more nearly seamless, less relationally marked, than modern translations make it seem.

At this point (Genesis 38), with an appropriately ambiguous formulaic time indication, *vayehi baᶜet hahi*, "at about that time," the narrative leaves Joseph and launches on the enigmatic story of Tamar and Judah. From the very beginning of the excursus, however, pointed connections are made with the main narrative through a whole series of explicit parallels and contrasts:

1. At about that time Judah parted from his brothers and camped with an Adullamite named Hirah. 2. There Judah saw the daughter of a Canaanite named Shua, married her, and lay with her. 3. She conceived and bore a son, whom they named Er. 4. She conceived again and bore a son, whom she called Onan. 5. Then she bore still another son, whom she called Shelah; he was in Chezib when she bore him. 6. Judah got a wife for Er his firstborn, and her name was Tamar. 7. Er, Judah's firstborn, displeased God, and God took his life. 8. Judah said to Onan: "Lie with your brother's wife and fulfill your duty as a brother-in-law, providing seed for your brother." 9. But Onan, knowing the seed would not be his, let it go to waste on the ground whenever he lay with his brother's wife, in order not to give seed for his brother. 10. What he did displeased God and He took his life, too. 11. Then

Judah said to Tamar his daughter-in-law, "Stay as a widow in your father's house until Shelah my son grows up," for he thought, "He, too, might die like his brothers." And Tamar went off to dwell in her father's house.

The story begins with Judah parting from his brothers, an act conveyed with a rather odd locution, *vayered m'et*, literally, "he went down from," and which undoubtedly has the purpose of connecting this separation of one brother from the rest with Joseph's, transmitted with the same verb-root (see, for example, the very beginning of the next chapter: "Joseph was brought down [*hurad*] to Egypt"). There is thematic justification for the connection since the tale of Judah and his offspring, like the whole Joseph story, and indeed like the entire Book of Genesis, is about the reversal of the iron law of primogeniture, about the election through some devious twist of destiny of a younger son to carry on the line. There is, one might add, genealogical irony in the insertion of this material at this point of the story, for while Joseph, next to the youngest of the sons, will eventually rule over his brothers in his own lifetime as splendidly as he has dreamed, it is Judah, the fourthborn, who will be the progenitor of the kings of Israel, as the end of Genesis 38 will remind us.

In any case, the preceding block of narrative had ended with a father bemoaning what he believed to be the death of his son. Genesis 38 begins with Judah fathering three sons, one after another, recorded in breathless pace. Here, as at other points in the episode, nothing is allowed to detract our focused attention from the primary, problematic subject of the proper channel for the seed (since this is thought of both figuratively and in the most concretely physical way, I have translated it literally throughout). In a triad of verbs that admits nothing adventitious, Judah sees, takes, lies with a woman; and she, responding appropriately, conceives, bears, and—the necessary completion of the genealogical process—gives the son a name. Then, with no narrative indication of any events at all in the intervening time, we move ahead an entire generation to the inexplicable death ("he displeased God") of Er, Judah's firstborn, after his marriage to Tamar. The firstborn very often seem to be losers in Genesis by the very condition of their birth—the epithet "firstborn," hardly needed as identification, is asserted twice here, almost as though it explained why Er displeased God—while an inscrutable, unpredictable principle of election other than the "natural" one works itself out. The second son, Onan, however, makes the mistake of rebelling by *coitus interruptus* against the legal obligations of the system of primogeniture, refusing to act as his dead brother's proxy by impregnating the widow in the brother's name, and so he, too, dies. Interestingly, after we have been exposed to Jacob's extravagant procedures of mourning over the imagined death of one son, Judah's reaction to the actual death in quick sequence of two sons is passed over in complete silence: he is only reported delivering pragmatic instructions having to do with the next son in line. If this striking contrast underscores Jacob's excesses, it surely also makes us wonder whether there is a real lack of responsiveness in Judah, and thus indicates how parallel acts or situations are used to comment on each other in biblical narrative.

After the death of the second son, the narrator gives us (Gen. 38:11) Judah's direct speech to Tamar as well as Judah's interior speech explaining his motive, but no response on the part of Tamar is recorded. This may suggest silent submission, or at least her lack of any legal options as a childless young widow, and it certainly leaves us wondering about what she is feeling—something which her actions will presently elucidate. There is one small but tactically effective hint that Judah is in the wrong: when he addresses Tamar, she is identified as "Tamar his daughter-in-law," an otherwise superfluous designation that reminds us of his legal obligation to provide her a husband from among his sons.

At this point we are given another time indication to mark the next stage of the story, in which the tempo of narration will slow down drastically to attend to a crucial central action:

12. A long time afterward, Judah's wife, the daughter of Shua, died; after being consoled, he went up toward Timnah to his sheepshearers, together with his friend Hirah the Adullamite.

All the information in this verse is essential for what follows. Tamar has been allowed to linger mateless "a long time," so that her own perception, reported two verses later, that she has been deliberately neglected is given an objective grounding. Judah has been widowed and the official period of mourning has passed—that is the meaning of "being consoled," but it is worth translating literally because it stands in contrast to Jacob's previous refusal to be consoled—so Tamar can plausibly infer that Judah is in a state of sexual neediness. Here begins her bold plan:

13. And Tamar was told, "Your father-in-law is coming up to Timnah for the sheepshearing." 14. Then she took off her widow's garments, covered her face with a veil, wrapped herself up, and sat down at the entrance to Eynaim on the road to Timnah, for she saw that Shelah

7

was grown up and she had not been given to him as a wife. 15. Judah saw her and took her for a harlot because she had covered her face. 16. So he turned aside to her by the road and said, "Look here, let me lie with you," for he did not realize that she was his daughter-in-law. She answered, "What will you pay me for lying with me?" 17. He replied, "I'll send you a kid from my flock." She said, "Only if you leave a pledge until you send it." 18. And he said, "What pledge should I leave you?" She replied, "Your seal and cord, and the staff you carry." He gave them to her and he lay with her and she conceived by him. 19. Then she got up, went away, took off her veil, and put on her widow's garments. 20. Judah sent the kid by his friend the Adullamite to redeem the pledge from the woman, but he could not find her. 21. He inquired of the men of the place, "Where is the cult prostitute, the one at Eynaim by the road?" and they answered, "There has been no cult prostitute here." 22. So he went back to Judah and told him, "I couldn't find her, and the men of the place even said, 'There has been no cult prostitute here.'" 23. Judah said, "Let her keep the things, or we shall become a laughingstock. I did, after all, send her this kid, but you could not find her."

Until this point Tamar had been a passive object, acted upon—or, alas, not acted upon—by Judah and his sons. The only verbs she was the subject of were the two verbs of compliance and retreat, to go off and dwell, at the end of verse 11. Now, a clear perception of injustice done her is ascribed to Tamar (verse 14), and she suddenly races into rapid, purposeful action, expressed in a detonating series of verbs: in verse 14 she quickly takes off, covers, wraps herself, sits down at the strategic location, and after the encounter, in verse 19, there is another chain of four verbs to indicate her brisk resumption of her former role and attire. (One might usefully compare this to the rapid series of verbs attached to Rebekah's activities [Gen. 27:14–17] as she prepares through another kind of deception to wrest the blessing from Isaac for her son Jacob.) Judah takes the bait—his sexual appetite will not tolerate postponement though he has been content to let Tamar languish as a childless widow indefinitely—and here we are given the only extended dialogue in the story (verses 16–18). It is a wonderfully businesslike exchange, reinforced in the Hebrew by the constant quick shifts from the literally repeated "he said" *(vayomer)* to "she said" *(vatomer)*. Wasting no time with preliminaries, Judah immediately tells her, "Let me lie with you" (literally, "let me come to you," or even, "let me enter you"), to which Tamar responds like a hard-headed businesswoman, finally exacting the rather serious pledge of Judah's seal and cord and staff, which as the legal surrogate of the bearer would have been a kind of ancient Near Eastern equivalent of all a person's major credit cards.

The agreement completed, the narrative proceeds in three quick verbs (the end of verse 18)—he gave, he lay, she conceived—to Tamar's single-minded purpose, which, from her first marriage, has been to become the channel of the seed of Judah. When the Adullamite comes looking for Tamar, he asks, decorously enough, for a cult prostitute *(qedeshah)*, though Judah had in fact thought he was dealing with an ordinary whore *(zonah)*.[2] The local people answer quite properly that there has been no *qedeshah* in that place, an assertion which receives special emphasis through the narrative contrivance by which it is repeated verbatim in Hirah's report to Judah. Nor, we may be led to think, has there been a *zonah* in that place, but only a wronged woman taking justice into her own hands. We are now prepared for the climax of the story.

24. About three months later, Judah was told, "Tamar your daughter-in-law has played the harlot [*zantah*] and what is more she is with child by harlotry [*zenunim*]." And Judah said, "Take her out and let her be burned."

The naked unreflective brutality of Judah's response to the seemingly incriminating news is even stronger in the original, where the synthetic character of biblical Hebrew reduces his deadly instructions to two words: *hotzi'uha vetisaref.* As elsewhere, nothing adventitious is permitted to intervene between intention and fulfilled purpose, and so the next two words of the text go on from Judah's command almost as if there had been no time lapse, as though there were no perceptible interval between magically powerful speech and the results of speech: Judah says, *hotzi'uha,* take her out, and the next two words, in a rare present passive participle, are *vehi mutz'et,* literally, "And she is being taken out." But this is the last instant before Tamar's triumphant revelation:

25. As she was being taken out, she sent word to her father-in-law, "By the man to whom these belong, by him am I with child." And she added, "Please recognize [*haker-na*], to whom do these belong, this

[2] In ancient Near Eastern pagan religion, there were special temple prostitutes with whom male worshippers consorted as part of a fertility cult. Their activity would not have had the base mercenary motives that impelled common prostitutes.

seal and cord and staff?" 26. Judah recognized [*vayaker*] them and he said, "She is more in the right than I for I did not give her to my son Shelah." And he had no carnal knowledge of her again.

The whole inset of Genesis 38 then concludes with four verses devoted to Tamar's giving birth to twin boys, her aspiration to become the mother of male offspring realized twofold. Confirming the pattern of the whole story and of the larger cycle of tales, the twin who is about to be second-born somehow "bursts forth" *(parotz)* first in the end, and he is Peretz, progenitor of Jesse from whom comes the house of David.

If some readers may have been skeptical about the intentionality of the analogies I have proposed between the interpolation and the frame-story, such doubts should be laid to rest by the exact recurrence at the climax of Tamar's story of the formula of recognition, *haker-na* and *vayaker*, used before with Jacob and his sons. The same verb, moreover, will play a crucial thematic role in the dénouement of the Joseph story when he confronts his brothers in Egypt, he recognizing them, they failing to recognize him. This precise recurrence of the verb in identical forms at the ends of Genesis 37 and 38 respectively is manifestly the result not of some automatic mechanism of interpolating traditional materials but of careful splicing of sources by a brilliant literary artist. The first use of the formula was for an act of deception; the second use is for an act of unmasking. Judah with Tamar after Judah with his brothers is an exemplary narrative instance of the deceiver deceived, and since he was the one who proposed selling Joseph into slavery instead of killing him (Gen. 37:26–27), he can easily be thought of as the leader of the brothers in the deception practiced on their father. Now he becomes their surrogate in being subject to a bizarre but peculiarly fitting principle of retaliation, taken in by a piece of attire, as his father was, learning through his own obstreperous flesh that the divinely appointed process of election cannot be thwarted by human will or social convention. In the most artful of contrivances, the narrator shows him exposed through the symbols of his legal self given in pledge for a kid *(gedi ʿizim)*, as before Jacob had been tricked by the garment emblematic of his love for Joseph which had been dipped in the blood of a goat *(seʿir ʿizim)*. Finally, when we return from Judah to the Joseph story (Genesis 39), we move in pointed contrast from a tale of exposure through sexual incontinence to a tale of seeming defeat and ultimate triumph through sexual continence—Joseph and Potiphar's wife.

It is instructive that the two verbal cues indicating the connection between the story of the selling of Joseph and the story of Tamar and

Judah were duly noted more than 1500 years ago in the Midrash: "The Holy One Praised be He said to Judah, 'You deceived your father with a kid. By your life, Tamar will deceive you with a kid'. . . The Holy One Praised be He said to Judah, 'You said to your father, *haker-na*. By your life, Tamar will say to you, *haker-na*' " (*Bereshit Rabba* 84:11,12). This instance may suggest that in many cases a literary student of the Bible has more to learn from the traditional commentaries than from modern scholarship. The difference between the two is ultimately the difference between assuming that the text is an intricately interconnected unity, as the midrashic exegetes did, and assuming it is a patchwork of frequently disparate documents, as most modern scholars have supposed. With their assumption of interconnectedness, the makers of the Midrash were often as exquisitely attuned to small verbal signals of continuity and to significant lexical nuances as any "close reader" of our own age.

There are, however, two essential distinctions between the way the text is treated in the Midrash and the literary approach I am proposing. First, although the Midrashists did assume the unity of the text, they had little sense of it as a real narrative continuum, as a coherent unfolding story in which the meaning of earlier data is progressively, even systematically, revealed or enriched by the addition of subsequent data. What this means practically is that the Midrash provides exegesis of specific phrases or narrated actions but not continuous *readings* of the biblical narratives: small pieces of the text become the foundations of elaborate homiletical structures that have only an intermittent relation to the integral story told by the text.

The second respect in which the midrashic approach to the biblical narratives does not really recognize their literary integrity is the didactic insistence of midrashic interpretation. One might note that in the formulation recorded in the passage just cited from *Bereshit Rabba,* God Himself administers a moral rebuke to the twice-sinning Judah, pointing out to him the recurrence of the kid and of the verb "to recognize" that links his unjust deception of his father with his justified deception by Tamar. That thematic point of retaliation, as we have seen, is intimated in the biblical text, but without the suggestion that Judah himself is conscious of the connections. That is, in the actual literary articulation of the story, we as audience are privileged with a knowledge denied Judah, and so the link between kid and kid, recognize and recognize, is part of a pattern of dramatic irony, in which the spectator knows something the protagonist doesn't and should know. The preservation of Judah's ignorance here is important, for the final turn of his painful moral education must be withheld for the quandary in which he will find himself later when he encounters Joseph as viceroy of Egypt without realizing his brother's identity. The Midrash, on the other hand, concentrating on the present moment in the text and on underscoring a moral point, must make things more explicit than the biblical writer intended.

Indeed, an essential aim of the innovative technique of fiction worked out by the ancient Hebrew writers was to produce a certain indeterminacy of meaning, especially in regard to motive, moral character, and psychology. (Later we shall look at this indeterminacy in detail when we consider characterization in the Bible.) Meaning, perhaps for the first time in narrative literature, was conceived as a *process*, requiring continual revision—both in the ordinary sense and in the etymological sense of seeing-again—continual suspension of judgment, weighing of multiple possibilities, brooding over gaps in the information provided. As a step in the process of meaning of the Joseph story, it is exactly right that the filial betrayal of Genesis 37 and the daughter-in-law's deception of Genesis 38 should be aligned with one another through the indirection of analogy, the parallels tersely suggested but never spelled out with a thematically unambiguous closure, as they are in the Midrash.

These notes on the story of Judah and Tamar are not, of course, by any means an exhaustive analysis of the material in question, but they may illustrate the usefulness of trying to look carefully into the literary art of a biblical text. This sort of critical discussion, I would contend, far from neglecting the Bible's religious character, focuses attention on it in a more nuanced way. The implicit theology of the Hebrew Bible dictates a complex moral and psychological realism in biblical narrative because God's purposes are always entrammeled in history, dependent on the acts of individual men and women for their continuing realization. To scrutinize biblical personages as fictional characters is to see them more sharply in the multifaceted, contradictory aspects of their human individuality, which is the biblical God's chosen medium for His experiment with Israel and history. Such scrutiny, however, as I hope I have shown, cannot be based merely on an imaginative impression of the story but must be undertaken through minute critical attention to the biblical writer's articulations of narrative form.

It is a little astonishing that at this late date literary analysis of the Bible of the sort I have tried to illustrate here in this preliminary fashion is only in its infancy. By literary analysis I mean the manifold varieties of minutely discriminating attention to the artful use of language, to the shifting play of ideas, conventions, tone, sound, imagery, syntax, narrative viewpoint, compositional units, and much else; the kind of disciplined attention, in other words, which through a whole spectrum of critical approaches has illuminated, for example, the poetry of Dante, the plays of Shakespeare, the novels of Tolstoy. The general absence of such critical discourse on the Hebrew Bible is all the more perplexing when one recalls that the masterworks of Greek and Latin antiquity have in recent decades enjoyed an abundance of astute literary analysis, so that we have learned to perceive subtleties of lyric form in Theocritus as in Marvell, complexities of narrative strategy in Homer or Virgil as in Flaubert.

In making such a sweeping negative assertion about biblical criticism, I may be suspected of polemical distortion impelled by the animus of a modern literary person against antiquarian scholarship, but I do not think this is the case. There has been, of course, a vast amount of scholarly work on the Bible over the past hundred years or more. It would be easy to make light of the endless welter of hypotheses and counter-hypotheses generated in everything from textual criticism to issues of large historical chronology; but the fact is that, however wrong-headed or extravagantly perverse many of the scholars have been, their enterprise as a whole has enormously advanced our understanding of the Bible. Virtually all this activity has been what we might call "excavative"—either literally, with the archeologist's spade and reference to its findings, or with a variety of analytic tools intended to uncover the original meanings of biblical words, the life situations in which specific texts were used, the sundry sources from which longer texts were assembled. Although much remains debatable—necessarily so, when we are separated from the origins of the texts by three millennia—the material unearthed by scholarship has clearly dispelled many confusions and obscurities.

Let me offer one brief example. The ancient city of Ugarit at the site of Ras Shamra on the Syrian coast, first excavated in 1929, has yielded a wealth of texts in a Semitic language closely cognate to biblical Hebrew, some of them strikingly parallel in style and poetic convention to familiar biblical passages. Among other things, the Ugaritic texts report in epic detail a battle between the regnant land god, Baal, and the sea god, Yamm. Suddenly, a whole spate of dimly apprehended allusions in Psalms and Job came into focus: an antecedent epic tradition had been assimilated into the recurrent imagery of God's breaking the fury of the elemental sea or shackling a primordial sea monster. Thus, when Job cries out (Job 7:12), *ha-yam ʾani ʾim tanin*, he is not asking rhetorically whether he is the sea *(yam)*, but, with a pointed sardonic allusion to the Canaanite myth, he is saying: "Am I Yamm, am I the Sea Beast, that you should set a guard over me?"

Excavative scholarship, then, demonstrably has its place as a necessary first step to the understanding of the Bible, but until the last few years there was little evidence that much more than excavation was going on, except, of course, for the perennial speculations of the theologians built on biblical texts. A systematic survey of the state of knowledge in the field, Herbert F. Hahn's *The Old Testament in Modern Research*,[3] delineates source analysis, anthropology, sociology, comparative religion, form criticism, archeology, and theology as the relevant major areas of professional study—but nothing at all that any literary person would recognize as literary inquiry. The uneven but sometimes valuable literary commentary occasionally provided by such scholars as Umberto Cassuto and Luis Alonso-Schökel (the former writing mainly in Hebrew, the latter in Spanish and German) was apparently deemed so peripheral to the discipline as not to be worthy of categorization.

Still more revealing as a symptom of the need for a literary perspective is Otto Eissfeldt's massive *The Old Testament: An Introduction*,[4] widely regarded as one of the most authoritative general reference works in the field. Most of Eissfeldt's considerations, of course, are purely excavative, but when the nature of the biblical materials confronts him with literary categories, his apparent authoritativeness begins to look shaky. Thus, he divides biblical narrative into myths, fairy tales, sagas, legends, anecdotes, and tales, using these problematic terms with a casualness and a seeming indifference to their treatment in other disciplines that are quite dismaying. Or again, his eight-page summary of conflicting scholarly theories on biblical prosody painfully illustrates how the scholars have read biblical poetry with roughly the intellectual apparatus appropriate to the decipherment of cuneiform inscriptions, multiplying confusion by the invention of elaborate pseudo-mathematical systems of scansion or by the wholesale importation of terms and concepts from Greek prosody. The latest trend, moreover, in describing biblical prosody is a system of syllable-counting proposed by the American scholar David Noel Freedman, which reflects the most unlikely conception of how lines of poetry operate and also requires a dubious hypothetical reconstruction of the "original" Hebrew vowel-system. The inadequacy of all this becomes transparent when one compares it to the wonderfully incisive analysis of biblical verse as a "semantic-syntactic-accentual" rhythm by Benjamin Hrushovski—not a Bible scholar but a leading authority in the field of poetics and comparative literature—in his synoptic article on Hebrew prosody for the 1971 edition of the *Encyclopedia Judaica*. In a few packed paragraphs, Hrushovski manages to cut through generations of confusion

[3] New York, 1954, 1st ed.; updated to 1970 through an appended bibliographical essay by Horace D. Hummel.
[4] Rev. ed., trans. P. R. Ackroyd, New York, 1965.

and to offer a general account of biblical prosody at once plausible and elegantly simple, avoiding the far-fetched structures and the strained terminology of his predecessors.

Until the mid-1970s, the only book-length study in English by a professional Bible scholar that made a sustained effort to use a literary perspective was Edwin M. Good's *Irony in the Old Testament*.[5] One sympathizes with Good's complaints about the general indifference of his colleagues to literary issues and with the reasonableness of his declared intention merely to make a modest start in the right direction. His book succeeds in doing that, but no more than that. (Good's most recent articles, however, reflect an admirable advance in literary sophistication over this early work.) *Irony in the Old Testament* is an engaging book, and one that offers useful local perceptions, but it has no clearly defined critical method, no way of adequately discriminating the complex distinctive forms of biblical literary art. The concept of irony becomes so elastic that it threatens to lose descriptive value, though perhaps one might argue that this is a problem almost equally perceptible in the work of many literary critics who discuss irony. Elsewhere, of course, we have had sensitive appreciations of the Bible's imaginative power by literary people like Mark Van Doren, Maurice Samuel, and Mary Ellen Chase. Good's book often seems more like such an appreciation than a rigorous literary analysis, though it has the advantage of being supported by a professional knowledge of Hebrew philology, source criticism, and ancient Near Eastern history.

Over the last few years, there has been growing interest in literary approaches among the younger generation of Bible scholars—in this country, especially those associated with the new journal, *Semeia*—but, while useful explications of particular texts have begun to appear, there have been as yet no major works of criticism, and certainly no satisfying overviews of the poetics of the Hebrew Bible. As elsewhere in the academy, the manifest influence of the vogue of Structuralism on these Bible scholars has not been a very fruitful one; and one too often encounters in their work rather simple superimpositions of one or another modern literary theory on ancient texts that in fact have their own dynamics, their own distinctive conventions and characteristic techniques. One sometimes gets the impression that scholars of this sort are trying manfully, perhaps almost too conscientiously, to make a start, but that literary analysis, after all those seminars in graduate school on Sumerian law and Ugaritic cult terms, remains for them a foreign language laboriously learned, whose accents and intonations they have not yet gotten right.

Three recent first books by Bible scholars may be partly exempted,

[5] Philadelphia, 1965.

though only partly, from these strictures. Michael Fishbane's *Text and Texture*[6] provides a series of sensitive close readings of a variety of biblical texts, but it does not propose any general critical method; it is often a little ponderous in its formulations and in its application of Structuralist or ethnopoetic notions; and it seems finally less concerned with poetics than with homiletics. The Dutch scholar, J. P. Fokkelman, in *Narrative Art in Genesis*,[7] a book strongly influenced by the Swiss-German *Werkinterpretation* school of literary criticism (an approximate analogue to the American New Criticism), gives us some brilliant analyses of formal patterns in the Hebrew prose and of how they function thematically; but he also shows a certain tendency to interpretive overkill in his explications, at times discovering patterns where they may not be, and assuming with a noticeable degree of strain that form must always be significantly expressive. Finally, the Israeli Bible scholar, Shimon Bar-Efrat, has attempted in *The Art of the Biblical Story* the first serious book-length introduction in any language to the distinctive poetics of biblical narrative.[8] He makes a valuable beginning, offering some splendid readings of individual scenes and nicely observing certain general principles of biblical narrative; but whether out of an uncertain sense of audience or because of his own relation to the subject, rather too much space is devoted to belaboring the obvious, especially in regard to basic matters of how literary narratives work. These recent publications, then, indicate that things may be in the early stages of changing within the field of biblical studies proper, but also that the discipline still has a considerable way to go.

The one obvious reason for the absence of scholarly literary interest in the Bible for so long is that, in contrast to Greek and Latin literature, the Bible was regarded for so many centuries by both Christians and Jews as the primary, unitary source of divinely revealed truth. This belief still makes itself profoundly felt, in both reactions against and perpetuations of it. The first several waves of modern biblical criticism, beginning in the nineteenth century, were from one point of view a sustained assault on the supposedly unitary character of the Bible, an attempt to break it up into as many pieces as possible, then to link those pieces to their original life contexts, thus rescuing for history a body of texts that religious tradition had enshrined in timelessness, beyond precise historical considerations. The momentum of this enterprise continues unabated, so that it still seems to most scholars in the field much more urgent to inquire, say, how a particular psalm might have been used in a hypothetically

[6] New York, 1979.
[7] Assen and Amsterdam, 1975.
[8] (Hebrew) Tel Aviv, 1979.

reconstructed temple ritual than how it works as an achieved piece of poetry. At the same time, the potent residue of the older belief in the Bible as the revelation of ultimate truth is perceptible in the tendency of scholars to ask questions about the biblical view of man, the biblical notion of the soul, the biblical vision of eschatology, while for the most part neglecting phenomena like character, motive, and narrative design as unbefitting for the study of an essentially religious document. The fact that such a substantial proportion of academic biblical studies goes on in theological seminaries, both here and in Europe, institutionally reinforces this double-edged pursuit of analyzed fragments and larger views, with scarcely any literary middle ground.

The rare exceptions to this general rule have often occurred, as in the case of the Hrushovski article, when a literary scholar with a grasp of biblical Hebrew has addressed himself to biblical materials, approaching them from some larger literary perspective. The one celebrated instance is the immensely suggestive first chapter of Erich Auerbach's *Mimesis*,[9] in which the antithetical modes of representing reality in Genesis and the Odyssey are compared at length. Auerbach must be credited with showing more clearly than anyone before him how the cryptic conciseness of biblical narrative is a reflection of profound art, not primitiveness, but his insight is the result of penetrating critical intuition unsupported by any real method for dealing with the specific characteristics of biblical literary forms. His key notion of biblical narrative as a purposefully spare text "fraught with background" is at once resoundingly right and too sweepingly general. Distinctions have to be made for narratives by different authors, of different periods, and written to fulfill different generic or thematic requirements. An arresting starkness of foreground, an enormous freight of background, are beautifully illustrated in the story of the binding of Isaac which Auerbach analyzes, but those terms would have to be seriously modified for the psychologically complex cycle of stories about David, for the deliberately schematic folktale frame of the Book of Job, or for a late (in part, satirical) narrative like Esther, where in fact there is a high degree of specification in the foreground of artifacts, costume, court customs, and the like.

Moving beyond Auerbach toward the definition of a specific poetics of biblical narrative are four important articles by Menakhem Perry and Meir Sternberg, two young Israeli literary scholars, which appeared in the Hebrew quarterly, *Ha-Sifrut*. The first of these, "The King through Ironic Eyes,"[10] is a brilliant verse-by-verse analysis of the story of David

---

[9] Trans. Willard Trask, Princeton, 1953.
[10] *Ha-Sifrut* 1:2 (Summer 1968), pp. 263–292.

and Bathsheba demonstrating—to my mind, conclusively—that an elaborate system of gaps between what is told and what must be inferred has been artfully contrived to leave us with at least two conflicting, mutually complicating interpretations of the motives and states of knowledge of the principal characters. This reading, which insists on a structural analogy between the story in 2 Samuel and Henry James's deliberate ambiguity in *The Turn of the Screw,* stirred up a hornet's nest of protest after its initial publication. The most recurrent theme of the article's critics was that the biblical story was, after all, religious, moral, and didactic in intention, and so would hardly indulge in all this fancy footwork of multiple ironies that we moderns so love. (Implicit in such a contention is a rather limiting notion of what a "religious" narrative is, or of how the insight of art might relate to a religious vision. This is a central question to which we shall return.) Perry and Sternberg responded with a rejoinder of over 50,000 words in which they convincingly argued that they had not imposed modern literary criteria on the Bible but rather had meticulously observed what were the general norms of biblical narrative itself and in what significant ways the story in question diverged from those norms.[11]

More recently, Sternberg, writing alone, has provided a shrewdly perceptive analysis of the story of the rape of Dinah, concluding his discussion with a general description of the spectrum of rhetorical devices, from explicit to (predominantly) oblique, through which biblical narrative conveys moral judgments of its characters.[12] Finally, Sternberg, in still another lengthy article, has catalogued with apt illustrative explications the repertory of repetitive devices used by the biblical writers.[13] Anyone interested in the narrative art of the Bible has much to learn from all four of these articles. The rigor and subtlety of Perry and Sternberg's readings in themselves lend support to the programmatic assertion they make at the end of their response to their critics: "The perspective of literary studies is the only relevant one to the consideration of the Bible *as literature.* Any other discipline, real or imagined, runs the danger of inventing groundless hypotheses and losing touch with the literary *power* of the actual biblical story."

Having been taught so much by Perry and Sternberg, I would like to express two small reservations about their approach, one perhaps just a quibble over formulation, the other an issue of method. The notion of "the Bible as literature," though particularly contaminated in English by

[11] *Ha-Sifrut* 2:3 (August 1970), pp. 608–663.
[12] *Ha-Sifrut* 4:2 (April 1973), pp. 193–231.
[13] *Ha-Sifrut* 25 (October 1977), pp. 110–150.

its use as a rubric for superficial college courses and for dubious publishers' packages, is needlessly concessive and condescending toward literature in any language. (It would at the very least be gratuitous to speak of "Dante as literature," given the assured literary status of Dante's great poem, though the *Divine Comedy* is more explicitly theological, or "religious," than most of the Bible.) Perry and Sternberg, answering their critics, characterize the biblical story as "a junction of purposes which generate relations of complementarity and tension." "One such purpose," they go on to say, "is the 'aesthetic' aim" to which at least one of their critics makes a gesture of concession. Rather than viewing the literary character of the Bible as one of several "purposes" or "tendencies" (*megamot* in the original), I would prefer to insist on a complete interfusion of literary art with theological, moral, or historiosophical vision, the fullest perception of the latter dependent on the fullest grasp of the former. This point has been aptly made by Joel Rosenberg, a young American scholar and poet, in an admirably intelligent general rationale for a literary perspective on the Bible published in *Response:* "The Bible's value as a religious document is intimately and inseparably related to its value as literature. This proposition requires that we develop a different understanding of what literature is, one that might—and should—give us some trouble."[14] One could add that the proposition also requires, conversely, that we develop a somewhat more troublesome understanding of what a religious document might be.

One leading emphasis of the Rosenberg essay points to what I think is a methodological deficiency in Perry and Sternberg's otherwise apt analyses. They tend to write about biblical narrative as though it were a unitary production just like a modern novel that is entirely conceived and executed by a single independent writer who supervises his original work from first draft to page proofs. They turn their backs, in other words, on what historical scholarship has taught us about the specific conditions of development of the biblical text and about its frequently composite nature. Rosenberg, by contrast, is keenly aware of historical scholarship, and he sees its findings, in a way the historical scholars themselves do not, as aspects of the distinctive artistic medium of the biblical authors. Here is his comment on the Pentateuch, the set of biblical narratives most thoroughly analyzed into antecedent sources by the scholars: "It may actually improve our understanding of the Torah to remember that it is *quoting* documents, that there is, in other words, a purposeful documentary *montage* that must be perceived as a unity, regardless of the

---

[14] "Meanings, Morals, and Mysteries: Literary Approaches to the Torah," *Response* 9:2 (Summer 1975), pp. 67–94.

number and types of smaller units that form the building blocks of its composition. Here, the weight of literary interest falls upon the activity of the *final* redactor, whose artistry requires far more careful attention than it has hitherto been accorded." The last clause if anything understates the case, since biblical critics frequently assume, out of some dim preconception about the transmission of texts in "primitive" cultures, that the redactors were in the grip of a kind of manic tribal compulsion, driven again and again to include units of traditional material that made no connective sense, for reasons they themselves could not have explained.

There is no point, to be sure, in pretending that all the contradictions among different sources in the biblical texts can be happily harmonized by the perception of some artful design. It seems reasonable enough, however, to suggest that we may still not fully understand what would have been perceived as a real contradiction by an intelligent Hebrew writer of the early Iron Age, so that apparently conflicting versions of the same event set side by side, far from troubling their original audience, may have sometimes been perfectly justified in a kind of logic we no longer apprehend. (We shall be considering this phenomenon more closely later, in chapter 7.) In any case, the validity of Rosenberg's general claim can, I think, be demonstrated by a careful reading of countless biblical narratives. Genesis 38, which we have examined in detail, is generally ascribed by scholars to the so-called Yahwistic or *J* Document after a mingling of *J* and *E* (the Elohistic Document) in the previous episode. But even if the text is really composite in origin, I think we have seen ample evidence of how brilliantly it has been woven into a complex artistic whole.

Accustomed as we are to reading narratives in which there is a much denser specification of fictional data, we have to learn, as Perry and Sternberg have shown, to attend more finely to the complex, tersely expressive details of the biblical text. (Traditional exegesis in its own way did this, but with far-reaching assumptions about the text as literal revelation which most of us no longer accept.) Biblical narrative is laconic but by no means in a uniform or mechanical fashion. Why, then, does the narrator ascribe motives to or designate states of feeling in his characters in some instances, while elsewhere he chooses to remain silent on these points? Why are some actions minimally indicated, others elaborated through synonym and detail? What accounts for the drastic shifts in the time-scale of narrated events? Why is actual dialogue introduced at certain junctures, and on what principle of selectivity are specific words assigned to characters? In a text so sparing in epithets and relational designations, why are particular identifications of characters noted by the narrator at specific points in the story? Repetition is a familiar feature of the Bible, but it is in no way an automatic device: when does literal repetition occur, and what are the significant variations in repeated verbal formulas?

Finally, to understand a narrative art so bare of embellishment and explicit commentary, one must be constantly aware of two features: the repeated use of narrative analogy, through which one part of the text provides oblique commentary on another; and the richly expressive function of syntax, which often bears the kind of weight of meaning that, say, imagery does in a novel by Virginia Woolf or analysis in a novel by George Eliot. Attention to such features leads not to a more "imaginative" reading of biblical narrative but to a more precise one; and since all these features are linked to discernible details in the Hebrew text, the literary approach is actually a good deal *less* conjectural than the historical scholarship that asks of a verse whether it contains possible Akkadian loanwords, whether it reflects Sumerian kinship practices, whether it may have been corrupted by scribal error.

In any case, the fact that the text is ancient and that its characteristic narrative procedures may differ in many respects from those of modern texts should not lead us to any condescending preconception that the text is therefore bound to be crude or simple. Tzvetan Todorov has shrewdly argued that the whole notion of "primitive narrative" is a kind of mental mirage engendered by modern parochialism, for the more closely you look at a particular ancient narrative, the more you are compelled to recognize the complexity and subtlety with which it is formally organized and with which it renders its subjects, and the more you see how it is conscious of its necessary status as artful discourse. It is only by imposing a naive and unexamined aesthetic of their own, Todorov proposes, that modern scholars are able to declare so confidently that certain parts of the ancient text could not belong with others: the supposedly primitive narrative is subjected by scholars to tacit laws like the law of stylistic unity, of noncontradiction, of nondigression, of nonrepetition, and by these dim but purportedly universal lights is found to be composite, deficient, or incoherent. (If just these four laws were applied respectively to *Ulysses, The Sound and the Fury, Tristram Shandy,* and *Jealousy,* each of those novels would have to be relegated to the dustbin of shoddily "redacted" literary scraps.) Attention to the ancient narrative's consciousness of its own operations, Todorov proposes, will reveal how irrelevant these complacently assumed criteria generally are.[15] Todorov bases his argument on examples from the *Odyssey;* but his questioning the existence of primi-

---

[15] *The Poetics of Prose,* trans. Richard Howard (Ithaca, New York, 1977), pp. 53–65.

tive narrative could be equally well supported by a consideration of the Hebrew Bible.

What we need to understand better is that the religious vision of the Bible is given depth and subtlety precisely by being conveyed through the most sophisticated resources of prose fiction. In the example we have considered, Judah and Jacob-Israel are not simple eponymic counters in an etiological tale (this is the flattening effect of some historical scholarship) but are individual characters surrounded by multiple ironies, artfully etched in their imperfections as well as in their strengths. A histrionic Jacob blinded by excessive love and perhaps loving the excess; an impetuous, sometimes callous Judah, who is yet capable of candor when confronted with hard facts; a fiercely resolved, steel-nerved Tamar—all such subtly indicated achievements of fictional characterization suggest the endlessly complicated ramifications and contradictions of a principle of divine election intervening in the accepted orders of society and nature. The biblical tale, through the most rigorous economy of means, leads us again and again to ponder complexities of motive and ambiguities of character because these are essential aspects of its vision of man, created by God, enjoying or suffering all the consequences of human freedom. Different considerations would naturally have to be explored for biblical poetry. Almost the whole range of biblical narrative, however, embodies the basic perception that man must live before God, in the transforming medium of time, incessantly and perplexingly in relation with others; and a literary perspective on the operations of narrative may help us more than any other to see how this perception was translated into stories that have had such a powerful, enduring hold on the imagination.

2

Sacred History and the
Beginnings of Prose Fiction

THE HEBREW BIBLE is generally perceived, with considerable justice, as sacred history, and both terms of that status have often been invoked to argue against the applicability to the Bible of the methods of literary analysis. If the text is sacred, if it was grasped by the audiences for whom it was made as a revelation of God's will, perhaps of His literal words, how can one hope to explain it through categories developed for the understanding of such a fundamentally secular, individual, and aesthetic enterprise as that of later Western literature? And if the text is history, seriously purporting to render an account of the origins of things and of Israelite national experience as they actually happened, is it not presumptuous to analyze these narratives in the terms we customarily apply to prose fiction, a mode of writing we understand to be the arbitrary invention of the writer, whatever the correspondences such a work may exhibit with quotidian or even historical reality? In a novel by Flaubert or Tolstoy or Henry James, where we are aware of the conscious fashioning of a fictional artifice, sometimes with abundant documentation from the writer's notebooks and letters, it is altogether appropriate to discuss techniques of characterization, shifts of dialogue, the ordering of larger compositional elements; but are we not coercing the Bible into being "literature" by attempting to transfer such categories to a set of texts that are theologically motivated, historically oriented, and perhaps to some extent collectively composed?

At least some of these objections will be undercut by recognizing, as several recent analysts have argued, that history is far more intimately related to fiction than we have been accustomed to assume. It is important to see the common ground shared by the two modes of narrative, ontologically and formally, but it also strikes me as misguided to insist that writing history is finally identical with writing fiction. The two kinds of literary activity obviously share a whole range of narrative strategies, and the historian may seem to resemble the writer of fiction in employing, as in some ways he must, a series of imaginative constructs. Yet there remains a qualitative difference, for example, between G. M. Trevelyan's portrait of Robert Walpole, which, though an interpretation and so in some degree an imaginative projection, is closely bound to the known historical facts, and Fielding's Jonathan Wild, a character that alludes satirically to Walpole but clearly has its own dynamics as an independent fictional invention.

The case of the Bible's sacred history, however, is rather different from that of modern historiography. There is, to begin with, a whole spectrum of relations to history in the sundry biblical narratives, as I shall try to indicate later, but none of these involves the sense of being bound to documentable facts that characterizes history in its modern acceptation. It is often asserted that the biblical writer is bound instead to the fixed materials, whether oral or written, that tradition has transmitted to him. This is a claim difficult to verify or refute because we have no real way of knowing what were the precise contents of Hebrew tradition around the beginning of the first millennium B.C.E. A close inspection, however, of the texts that have been passed down to us may lead to a certain degree of skepticism about this scholarly notion of the tyrannical authority of ancient tradition, may lead us, in fact, to conclude that the writers exercised a good deal of artistic freedom in articulating the traditions at their disposal.

As odd as it may sound at first, I would contend that prose fiction is the best general rubric for describing biblical narrative. Or, to be more precise, and to borrow a key term from Herbert Schneidau's speculative, sometimes questionable, often suggestive study, *Sacred Discontent*, we can speak of the Bible as *historicized* prose fiction. To cite the clearest example, the Patriarchal narratives may be composite fictions based on national traditions, but in the writers' refusal to make them conform to the symmetries of expectation, in their contradictions and anomalies, they suggest the unfathomability of life in history under an inscrutable God. "What we are witnessing in Genesis, and in parts of the David story," Schneidau observes, "is the birth of a new kind of historicized fiction, moving steadily away from the motives and habits of the world of legend and myth."[1] This generalization can, I think, be extended beyond Genesis and the David story to most of biblical narrative, even where, as in parts of the Book of Kings, an abundance of legendary material is evident. Because the central thesis of Schneidau's book is the rebellion of biblical literature against the pagan world-view, which is locked into an eternal cyclical movement, his stress falls on the historicizing, though the fiction deserves equal attention. Indeed, as we shall have occasion to see, it may often be more precise to describe what happens in biblical narrative as fictional- ized history, especially when we move into the period of the Judges and Kings. But before we pursue the theme of either history or fiction, we should pause over the prose component of prose fiction, which is far more than a matter of convenience in classification for the librarian.

It is peculiar, and culturally significant, that among ancient peoples only Israel should have chosen to cast its sacred national traditions in prose. Among many hazily conceived literary terms applied to the Bible, scholars have often spoken of it as the "national epic" of ancient Israel, or, more specifically, they have conjectured about an oral Creation epic and Exodus epic upon which the authors of the Pentateuch drew. But, as the Israeli Bible scholar Shemaryahu Talmon has shrewdly argued, what by all appearance we have in the Bible is, quite to the contrary, a deliberate avoidance of epic, and the prose form of Hebrew narrative is the chief evidence for this avoidance:

> The ancient Hebrew writers purposefully nurtured and developed prose narration to take the place of the epic genre which by its content was intimately bound up with the world of paganism, and appears to have had a special standing in the polytheistic cults. The recitation of the epics was tantamount to an enactment of cosmic events in the manner of sympathetic magic. In the process of total rejection of the polytheistic religions and their ritual expressions in the cult, epic songs and also the epic genre were purged from the repertoire of the Hebrew authors.[2]

What is crucial for the literary understanding of the Bible is that this reflex away from the polytheistic genre had powerfully constructive consequences in the new medium which the ancient Hebrew writers fash- ioned for their monotheistic purposes. Prose narration, affording writers

---

[1] *Sacred Discontent* (Baton Rouge, La., 1977), p. 215.
[2] "The 'Comparative Method' in Biblical Interpretation—Principles and Problems," *Göttingen Congress Volume* (Leiden, 1978), p. 354.

a remarkable range and flexibility in the means of presentation, could be utilized to liberate fictional personages from the fixed choreography of timeless events and thus could transform storytelling from ritual rehearsal to the delineation of the wayward paths of human freedom, the quirks and contradictions of men and women seen as moral agents and complex centers of motive and feeling.

The underlying impulse of this whole portentous transition in literary modes is effectively caught, though with certain imprecisions I shall try to correct, by Herbert Schneidau in an anthropological generalization that nicely complements Talmon's historical proposal. Schneidau speaks of a "world of linked analogies and correspondences" manifested in the primitive imagination and in the divinitory mode of expression. "A cosmology of hierarchical continuities, as in mythological thought, exhibits strong metaphorical tendencies. The enmeshing and interlocking of structures are coherently expressed in poetic evocation of transferable, substitutable qualities and names. In this world, movement tends to round itself into totalization, impelled by the principle of closure." In contrast to this mythological world dominated by metaphor, Schneidau sees metonymy— the linking of things through mere contact rather than through likeness, as in metaphor—with its point-to-point movement suggesting the prosaic modes of narrative and history, as the key to the literature of the Bible. Because it is a literature that breaks away from the old cosmic hierarchies, the Bible switches from a reliance on metaphor to a reliance on metonymy. Schneidau attempts to summarize this whole contrast in an aphorism: "Where myth is hypotactic metaphors, the Bible is paratactic metonymies."[3] That is, where myth involves a set of equivalencies arranged in some system of subordination, the Bible offers a series of contiguous terms arranged in sequence without a clear definition of the link between one term and the next.[4]

This general comparison provides an important insight into the innovative nature of the Bible's literary enterprise, but some of the concepts invoked are a little misleading. There are, to begin with, a good many ancient Near Eastern narratives which are sophisticated, fundamentally

[3] *Sacred Discontent,* p. 292.
[4] Parataxis, we should recall, means placing the main elements of a statement in a sequence of simple parallels, connected by "and," while hypotaxis arranges statements in subordinate and main clauses, specifying the relations between them with subordinate conjunctions like "when," "because," "although." Thus, the sentence "Joseph was brought down to Egypt and Potiphar bought him" is paratactic. The same facts would be conveyed hypotactically as follows: "When Joseph was brought down to Egypt, Potiphar bought him." (My example is actually an abbreviated version of Gen. 38:1. The first version is the way the original reads, the second version, the way some modern translations, avoiding parataxis, render it.)

secular literary works, though for Schneidau as for Talmon the mythological poems would appear to be the paradigm of pagan literature from
which the Bible swerves. The paradigmatic function of this particular
kind of pre-Israelite narrative may well justify the stress on the Hebrew
literary rejection of myth, but other terms that Schneidau adopts remain
problematic. Hypotaxis and parataxis may be logically coordinated with
metaphor and metonymy respectively, but in actual syntactic patterns,
the Near Eastern mythological verse narratives would appear to be mainly
paratactic, while biblical narrative prose exhibits a good deal of variation
from parataxis to hypotaxis, according to the aims of the writer and
the requirements of the particular narrative juncture. Roman Jakobson's
schematic distinction, moreover, between metaphor and metonymy fits
the case under discussion only in a loose figurative sense because actual
metaphor (rather than inferable metaphysical "correspondences") is by
no means predominant in the extant ancient Near Eastern mythological
epics. Schneidau's most valuable perception, in any case, is not dependent
on these terms, for his main point is the vigorous movement of biblical
writing away from the stable closure of the mythological world and toward
the indeterminacy, the shifting causal concatenations, the ambiguities
of a fiction made to resemble the uncertainties of life in history. And
for that movement, I would add, the suppleness of prose as a narrative
medium was indispensable, at least in the Near Eastern setting.

One final qualification should be added to this instructive if somewhat
overdrawn opposition between myth and "historicized fiction." Different
cultures often take different routes to what is substantially the same
end; and if one moves beyond the ancient Fertile Crescent to the Greek
sphere, one can find in sophisticated mythographic verse-narratives, such
as Hesiod and the mythological episodes in Homer, a good deal in the
treatment of motive, character, and causation that is analogous to the
biblical sense of indeterminacy and ambiguity. The Hebrew writers, however, made a special virtue in this regard out of the newly fashioned
prose medium in which they worked, and this deserves closer attention
than it has generally received.

As an initial illustration of how the modalities of prose fiction operate
in biblical narrative, I should like to consider a passage from the so-
called primeval history, the creation of Eve (Genesis 2). It may serve as
a useful test case because with its account of origins, its generalized human
figures, its anthropomorphic deity, and the Mesopotamian background
of the version of creation in which it occurs, it has been variously classified
by modern commentators as myth, legend, and folklore, and would seem
quite unlike what we usually think of as artfully conceived fiction. In

the immediately preceding verse, one recalls, God had warned Adam under the penalty of death not to eat from the Tree of Knowledge. Man's response to this injunction is not recorded. Instead, the narrative moves on—perhaps making that hiatus itself a proleptic intimation of the link between Adam's future mate and the seizing of forbidden knowledge— to an expression in direct speech of God's concern for the solitary condition of His creature:

18. The Lord God said, "It is not good for man to be alone. I shall make him an aid fit for him." 19. And the Lord God formed from the earth every beast of the field and every bird of the sky and He brought them to the man to see what he would call them; and whatever the man called a living creature would be its name. 20. The man called names to all the cattle and the birds of the sky and to every beast of the field, but for the man no fit aid was found. 21. And the Lord God cast a deep slumber upon the man and he slept; and He took one of his ribs and closed up the flesh at that place. 22. And the Lord God fashioned the rib he had taken from the man into a woman and He brought her to the man. 23. The man said:

This one at last
bone of my bones
and flesh of my flesh.
This one shall be called woman
for from man was this one taken.

24. Thus does a man leave his father and mother and cling to his woman, and they become one flesh. 25. And the two of them were naked, the man and his woman, and they were not ashamed.

The usual taxonomic approach to the Bible would explain the whole passage as a piece of ancient folklore, an etiological tale intended to account for the existence of woman, for her subordinate status, and for the attraction she perennially exerts over man. The inset of formal verse (a common convention in biblical narrative for direct speech that has some significantly summarizing or ceremonial function) in fact looks archaic, and could conceivably have been a familiar etiological tag in circulation for centuries before the making of this passage. Folkloric traditions may very well be behind the text, but I don't think that in themselves they provide a very satisfactory sense of the artful complex which the writer has shaped out of his materials. Our first ancestors of course cannot be allowed much individuality and so they are not exactly "fictional characters" in the way that later figures in Genesis like Jacob and Joseph and Tamar will be. Nevertheless, the writer, through a subtle manipulation of language and narrative exposition, manages to endow Adam and Eve with a degree of morally problematic interiority one would hardly expect in a primitive folktale explaining origins. Before we look at some of the details, we might contrast the general impression of this passage with the account of the creation of mankind (there is no separate creation of woman) in the *Enuma Elish,* the Babylonian creation epic. The god Marduk, after triumphing over the primeval mother Tiamat, announces:

> Blood I will mass and cause bones to be.
> I will establish a savage, "man" shall be his name.
> Verily, savage-man I will create.
> He shall be charged with the service of the gods
>   That they might be at ease.[5]

Marduk shares with the God of Israel the anthropomorphic métier of a sculptor in the medium of flesh and bone, but man in the Akkadian verse narrative is merely an object acted upon, his sole reason for existence to supply the material wants of the gods. Humanity is conceived here exclusively in terms of ritual function—man is made in order to offer sacrifices to the gods—and so the highly differentiated realms of history and moral action are not intimated in the account of man's creation. This is a signal instance of what Schneidau means by humanity's being locked into a set of fixed hierarchies in the mythological world-view. Man so conceived cannot be the protagonist of prose fiction: the appropriate narrative medium is that of mythological epic, in which the stately progression of parallelistic verse—in fact, predominantly paratactic and unmetaphorical here—emphatically rehearses man's eternal place in an absolute cosmic scheme. (Of course, few mythological epics will correspond so neatly to these notions of fixity and closure. But the model of the *Enuma Elish* is decisive for our text because it reflects the prevalent norm of sacred narrative with which the Hebrew writer was breaking.) If we now return to Genesis 2, we can clearly see how the monotheistic writer works not only with very different theological assumptions but also with a radically different sense of literary form.

In contrast to the hortatory diction of Marduk and his fellow members of the Babylonian pantheon, God expresses His perception of man's condition and His own intention with a stark directness: "It is not good for man to be alone. I shall make him an aid fit for him." (His utterance,

[5] J. B. Pritchard, ed., *Ancient Near Eastern Texts Relating to the Old Testament* (Princeton, 1969), p. 68.

nevertheless, is close enough to a scannable verse of complementary parallelism to give it a hint of formal elevation.) Then there occurs a peculiar interruption. We have been conditioned by the previous version of cosmogony to expect an immediate act of creation to flow from the divine utterance that is introduced by the formula, "And God said." Here, however, we must wait two verses for the promised creation of a helpmate while we follow the process of man giving names to all living creatures. These verses (Gen. 2:19–20) are marked, as a formal seal of their integration in the story, by an envelope structure, being immediately preceded by the thematically crucial phrase, ʿezer kenegdo (literally, "an aid alongside him") and concluding with that same phrase. A concise comment on these two verses in the classical Midrash nicely reflects their strategic utility: "He made them pass by in pairs. He said, 'Everything has its partner but I have no partner' " (*Bereshit Rabba* 17:5). What is especially interesting about this miniature dramatization in the Midrash is where it might have come from in the text, for the literary insights of the midrashic exegetes generally derive from their sensitive response to verbal clues—in the recurrence of a key-word, the nuanced choice of a particular lexical item, significant sound-play, and so forth. Here, however, it seems that the Midrash is responding not to any particular word in the passage but to an aspect of the text continuum which today we would call a strategy of narrative exposition. Eve has been promised. She is then withheld for two carefully framed verses while God allows man to perform his unique function as the bestower of names on things. There is implicit irony in this order of narrated events. Man is superior to all other living creatures because only he can invent language, only he has the level of consciousness that makes him capable of linguistic ordering. But this very consciousness makes him aware of his solitude in contrast to the rest of the zoological kingdom. (It is, perhaps, a solitude mitigated but not entirely removed by the creation of woman, for that creation takes place through the infliction of a kind of wound on him, and afterward, in historical time, he will pursue her, strain to become "one flesh" with her, as though to regain a lost part of himself.) The contrast between mateless man calling names to a mute world of mated creatures is brought out by a finesse of syntax not reproducible in translation. Verse 20 actually tells us that man gave names "to all cattle . . . to birds . . . to beast . . . to the man," momentarily seeming to place Adam in an anaphoric prepositional series with all living creatures. This incipient construal is then reversed by the verb "did not find," which sets man in opposition to all that has preceded. One could plausibly argue, then, that the Midrash was not merely indulging in a flight of fancy when it imagined Adam making that confession of loneliness as he named the creatures passing before him.

When God at last begins to carry out His promise at the beginning of verse 21, man, with the intervention of divine anaesthetic, is reduced from a conscious agent to an inert object acted upon, for the moment much like man in the *Enuma Elish.* The thematic difference, of course, is that this image of man as passive matter is bracketed on both sides by his performances as master of language. As soon as the awakened man discovers woman, he proceeds—as natural births elsewhere in the Bible are regularly followed by the ceremony of naming—to name her, adopting the formal emphasis of a poem. The poem (verse 23), whether or not it was the writer's original composition, fits beautifully into the thematic argument of his narrative. Written in a double chiastic structure, it refers to the woman just being named by an indicative, *zot*, "this [feminine] one," which is the first and last word of the poem in the Hebrew as well as the linchpin in the middle. Man names the animals over whom he has dominion; he names woman, over whom he ostensibly will have dominion. But in the poem, man and his bone and flesh are syntactically surrounded by this new female presence, a rhetorical configuration that makes perfect sense in the light of their subsequent history together.

The explanatory verse 24, which begins with "thus" *(ᶜal-ken),* a fixed formula for introducing etiological assertions, might well have been part of a proverbial statement adopted verbatim by the writer, but even if this hypothesis is granted, what is remarkable is the artistry with which he weaves the etiological utterance into the texture of his own prose. The splendid image of desire fulfilled and, by extension, of the conjugal state—"they become one flesh"—is both a vivid glimpse of the act itself and a bold hyperbole. The writer, I would suggest, is as aware of the hyperbolic aspect of the image as later Plato will be when in *The Symposium* he attributes to Aristophanes the notion that lovers are the bifurcated halves of a primal self who are trying to recapture that impossible primal unity. For as soon as the idea of one flesh has been put forth (and "one" is the last word of the verse in the Hebrew), the narration proceeds as follows: "And the two of them were naked, the man and his woman, and they were not ashamed." After being invoked as the timeless model of conjugal oneness, they are immediately seen as two, a condition stressed by the deliberately awkward and uncharacteristic doubling back of the syntax in the appositional phrase, "the man and his woman"—a small illustration of how the flexibility of the prose medium enables the writer to introduce psychological distinctions, dialectical reversals of thematic direction, that would not have been feasible in the verse narratives of the ancient Near East. So the first man and woman are now two, vulnerable in their twoness to the temptation of the serpent, who will be able to seduce first one, and through the one, the other: naked *(ˤarumim)*, unashamed, they are about to be exposed to the most cunning *(ˤarum)* of the beasts of the field, who will give them cause to feel shame.

From this distance in time, it is impossible to determine how much of this whole tale was sanctified, even verbally fixed, tradition; how much was popular lore perhaps available in different versions; how much the original invention of the writer. What a close reading of the text does suggest, however, is that the writer could manipulate his inherited materials with sufficient freedom and sufficient firmness of authorial purpose to define motives, relations, and unfolding themes, even in a primeval history, with the kind of subtle cogency we associate with the conscious artistry of the narrative mode designated prose fiction. (Here and in what follows, I assume when I say "conscious artistry" that there is always a complex interplay between deliberate intention and unconscious intuition in the act of artistic creation; but the biblical writer is no different from his modern counterpart in this regard.) Throughout these early chapters of Genesis, Adam and Eve are not the fixed figures of legend or myth but are made to assume contours conceived in the writer's particularizing imagination through the brief but revealing dialogue he invents for them and through the varying strategies of presentation he adopts in reporting their immemorial acts.

Let me hasten to say that in giving such weight to fictionality, I do not mean to discount the historical impulse that informs the Hebrew Bible. The God of Israel, as so often has been observed, is above all the God of history: the working out of His purposes in history is a process that compels the attention of the Hebrew imagination, which is thus led to the most vital interest in the concrete and differential character of historical events. The point is that fiction was the principal means which the biblical authors had at their disposal for realizing history.[6] Under scrutiny, biblical narrative generally proves to be either fiction laying claim to a place in the chain of causation and the realm of moral consequentiality that belong to history, as in the primeval history, the tales of the Patriarchs and much of the Exodus story, and the account of the early Conquest, or history given the imaginative definition of fiction,

---

[6] A recent book by Jacob Licht, *Storytelling in the Bible* (Jerusalem, 1978), proposes that the "historical aspect" and the "storytelling" or "aesthetic" aspect of biblical narrative be thought of as entirely discrete functions that can be neatly peeled apart for inspection— apparently, like the different colored strands of electrical wiring. This facile separation of the inseparable suggests how little some Bible scholars have thought about the role of literary art in biblical literature.

as in most of the narratives from the period of the Judges onward. This schema, of course, is necessarily neater than the persistently untidy reality of the variegated biblical narratives. What the Bible offers us is an uneven continuum and a constant interweaving of factual historical detail (especially, but by no means exclusively, for the later periods) with purely legendary "history"; occasional enigmatic vestiges of mythological lore; etiological stories; archetypal fictions of the founding fathers of the nation; folktales of heroes and wonder-working men of God; verisimilar inventions of wholly fictional personages attached to the progress of national history; and fictionalized versions of known historical figures. All of these narratives are presented as history, that is, as things that really happened and that have some significant consequence for human or Israelite destiny. The only evident exceptions to this rule are Job, which in its very stylization seems manifestly a philosophic fable (hence the rabbinic dictum, "There was no such creature as Job; he is a parable") and Jonah, which, with its satiric and fantastic exaggerations, looks like a parabolic illustration of the prophetic calling and of God's universality.

Despite the variegated character of these narratives, composed as they were by many different hands over a period of several centuries, I would like to attempt a rough generalization about the kind of literary project they constitute. The ancient Hebrew writers, as I have already intimated, seek through the process of narrative realization to reveal the enactment of God's purposes in historical events. This enactment, however, is continuously complicated by a perception of two, approximately parallel, dialectical tensions. One is a tension between the divine plan and the disorderly character of actual historical events, or, to translate this opposition into specifically biblical terms, between the divine promise and its ostensible failure to be fulfilled; the other is a tension between God's will, His providential guidance, and human freedom, the refractory nature of man.

If one may presume at all to reduce great achievements to a common denominator, it might be possible to say that the depth with which human nature is imagined in the Bible is a function of its being conceived as caught in the powerful interplay of this double dialectic between design and disorder, providence and freedom. The various biblical narratives in fact may be usefully seen as forming a spectrum between the opposing extremes of disorder and design. Toward the disorderly end of things, where the recalcitrant facts of known history have to be encompassed, including specific political movements, military triumphs and reversals, and the like, would be Judges, Samuel, and Kings. In these books, the narrators and on occasion some of the personages struggle quite explicitly to reconcile their knowledge of the divine promise with their awareness of what is actually happening in history. At the other end of the spectrum, near the pole of design, one might place the Book of Esther. This post-exilic story, which presents itself as a piece of political history affecting the main diaspora community, is in fact a kind of fairytale—the lovely damsel, guided by a wise godfather, is made queen and saves her people—richly embellished with satiric invention; its comic art departs from historical verisimilitude in ways that pre-exilic Hebrew narrative seldom does, and the story demonstrates God's providential power in history with a schematic neatness unlike that of earlier historicized fiction in the Bible.

Somewhere toward the middle of this spectrum would be Genesis, where the sketchiness of the known historical materials allows considerable latitude for the elucidation of a divine plan, with, however, this sense of design repeatedly counterbalanced by the awareness of man's unruly nature, the perilous and imperious individuality of the various human agents in the divine experiment. Individuality is played against providential design in a rather different fashion in the Book of Ruth. Ruth, Naomi, and Boaz are fictional inventions, probably based on no more than names, if that, preserved in national memory. In the brief span of this narrative, they exhibit in speech and action traits of character that make them memorable individuals in a way that the more schematically conceived Esther and Mordecai are not. But in their plausible individuality they also become exemplary figures, thus earning themselves a place in the national history; Ruth, through her steadfastness, and Boaz, through his kindness and his adherence to the procedures of legitimate succession, make themselves the justified progenitors of the line of David. The Book of Ruth, then, which we might place near Genesis toward the pole of design in our imaginary spectrum, is, because of its realistic psychology and its treatment of actual social institutions, a verisimilar historicized fiction, while the Book of Esther seems more a comic fantasy utilizing pseudo-historical materials.

Let me risk a large conjecture, if only because it may help us get a clearer sighting on the phenomenon we are considering. It may be that a sense of some adequate dialectical tension between these antitheses of divine plan and the sundry disorders of human performance in history served as an implicit criterion for deciding which narratives were to be regarded as canonical. It would be an understatement to say we possess only scanty information about the now lost body of uncanonical ancient Hebrew literature, but the few hints which the Bible itself provides would seem to point in two opposite directions. On the one hand, in Kings we are repeatedly told that details skimped in the narrative at hand can be discovered by referring to the Chronicles of the Kings of Judea and the Chronicles of the Kings of Israel. Those books, one may assume, were excluded from the authoritative national tradition and hence not preserved because they were court histories, probably partisan in character, and erred on the side of the cataloguing of historical events without an informing vision of God's design working through history. On the other hand, brief and enigmatic allusion with citation is made in Numbers, Joshua, and Samuel to the Book of Yashar and the Book of the Battles of Yahweh. The latter sounds as though it was a list of military triumphs with God as principal actor; the former, to judge by the two fragments quoted (Josh. 10:13; 2 Sam. 1:18–19), was probably a verse narrative, perhaps a martial epic with miraculous elements. I would venture to guess that both books were felt to be too legendary, too committed to the direct narrative tracing of God's design, without a sufficient counterweight of the mixed stuff of recognizable historical experience.

Let us direct our attention now to the Bible's historical narratives proper in order to understand more concretely what is implied by the fictional component in describing them as historicized fiction. The large cycle of stories about David, which is surely one of the most stunning imaginative achievements of ancient literature, provides an instructive central instance of the intertwining of history and fiction. This narrative, though it may have certain folkloric embellishments (such as David's victory over Goliath), is based on firm historical facts, as modern research has tended to confirm: there really was a David who fought a civil war against the house of Saul, achieved undisputed sovereignty over the twelve tribes, conquered Jerusalem, founded a dynasty, created a small empire, and was succeeded by his son Solomon. Beyond these broad outlines, it is quite possible that many of the narrated details about David, including matters bearing on the complications of his conjugal life and his relations with his children, may have been reported on good authority.

Nevertheless, these stories are not, strictly speaking, historiography, but rather the imaginative reenactment of history by a gifted writer who organizes his materials along certain thematic biases and according to his own remarkable intuition of the psychology of the characters. He feels entirely free, one should remember, to invent interior monologue for his characters; to ascribe feeling, intention, or motive to them when he chooses; to supply verbatim dialogue (and he is one of literature's masters of dialogue) for occasions when no one but the actors themselves could have had knowledge of exactly what was said. The author of the David stories stands in basically the same relation to Israelite history as Shakespeare stands to English history in his history plays. Shakespeare was obviously not free to have Henry V lose the battle of Agincourt, or to allow someone else to lead the English forces there, but, working from the hints of historical tradition, he could invent a kind of *Bildungsroman* for the young Prince Hal; surround him with invented characters that would serve as foils, mirrors, obstacles, aids in his development; create a language and a psychology for the king which are the writer's own achievement, making out of the stuff of history a powerful projection of human possibility. That is essentially what the author of the David cycle does for David, Saul, Abner, Joab, Jonathan, Absalom, Michal, Abigail, and a host of other characters.

One memorable illustration among many of this transmutation of history into fiction is David's great confrontation with Saul at the cave in the wilderness of Ein Gedi (1 Samuel 24). The manic king, one recalls, while in pursuit of the young David, has gone into a cave to relieve himself, where by chance David and his men have taken refuge. David sneaks up to Saul and cuts off a corner of his robe. Then he is smitten with remorse for having perpetrated this symbolic mutilation on the anointed king, and he sternly holds his men in check while the unwitting Saul walks off from the cave unharmed. Once the king is at a distance, David follows him out of the cave. Holding the excised corner of the robe, he hails Saul and shouts out to his erstwhile pursuer one of his most remarkable speeches, in which he expresses fealty and reverence to the Lord's anointed one, disavows any evil intention toward him (with the corner of the robe as evidence of what he could have done but did not do), and proclaims his own humble status: "After whom did the king of Israel set out?" he says in verse-like symmetry, "After whom are you chasing? After a dead dog, after a single flea?" (1 Sam. 24:15).

At the end of this relatively lengthy speech, the narrator holds us in suspense for still another moment by choosing to preface Saul's response with a chain of introductory phrases: "And it came to pass when David finished speaking these words, that Saul said"—and then what he says has a breathtaking brevity after David's stream of words, and constitutes one of those astonishing reversals that make the rendering of character in these stories so arresting: " 'Is it your voice, David, my son?' and Saul raised his voice and wept" (1 Sam. 24:17). The point is not merely that the author has made up dialogue to which he could have had no "documentary" access; Thucydides, after all, does that as a stylized technique of representing the various positions maintained by different historical personages. In the biblical story the invented dialogue is an expression of the author's imaginative grasp of his protagonists as distinctive moral and psychological figures, of their emotion-fraught human intercourse dramatically conceived; and what that entire process of imagination essentially means is the creation of fictional character.

As elsewhere in biblical narrative, the revelation of character is effected with striking artistic economy: the specification of external circumstances, setting, and gesture is held to a bare minimum, and dialogue is made to carry a large part of the freight of meaning. To David's impassioned, elaborate rhetoric of self-justification, Saul responds with a kind of choked cry: "Is it your voice, David, my son?" Perhaps he asks this out of sheer amazement at what he has just heard, or because he is too far off to make out David's face clearly, or because his eyes are blinded with tears, which would be an apt emblem of the condition of moral blindness that has prevented him from seeing David as he really is. In connection with this last possibility, one suspects there is a deliberate if approximate echo of the blind Isaac's words to his son Jacob (after asking, "Who are you my son?" [Gen. 27:18] Isaac proclaims, "The voice is the voice of Jacob" [Gen. 27:22]). The allusion, which complicates the meaning of the present encounter between an older and a younger man in a number of ways, is not one that a historical Saul would have been apt to make on the spot, but which a writer with the privilege of fictional invention could brilliantly contrive for this shadow-haunted king whose own firstborn son will not reign after him.

Perhaps it might be objected that the David stories are merely the exception that proves the rule—a sunburst of imaginative literary activity in a series of historical books which are, after all, chronicles of known events variously embroidered with folklore and underscored for theological emphasis. Let us consider, then, a passage from that long catalogue of military uprisings, the Book of Judges, where no serious claims could be made for complexity of characterization or for subtlety of thematic development, and see if we can still observe the modalities of prose fiction in what is told and how it is told. I should like to take the story of the assassination of Eglon, King of Moab, by Ehud, the son of Gera (Judges 3). In the absence of convincing evidence to the contrary, let us assume the historical truth of the story, which seems plausible enough: that a tough, clever guerrilla leader named Ehud, from the tribe of Benjamin (known for its martial skills), cut down Eglon more or less in the manner described, then mustered Israelite forces in the hill country of Ephraim for a successful rebellion, which was followed by a long period of relief from Moabite domination. Only the formulaic number of twice forty at the end ("And the land was quiet eighty years" [Judg. 3:30]) would patently appear not to correspond to historical fact. Where, then, in this succinct political chronicle, is there room to talk about prose fiction? Here is how the main part of the story reads:

15. The Israelites cried out to the Lord, and he raised up a champion for them, Ehud the son of Gera the Benjaminite, a left-handed man. Now the Israelites sent tribute through him to Eglon, King of Moab. 16. Ehud made himself a double-edged dagger a *gomed* long and strapped it under his garments on his right thigh. 17. He brought the tribute to Eglon, King of Moab—and this Eglon was a very stout man. 18. And it came about that after he had finished presenting the tribute, he dismissed the people who had carried it. 19. And he had come from Pesilim near Gilgal. Then he said, "A secret word I have for you, King." "Silence!" he replied, and all his attendants went out. 20. Ehud came to him as he was sitting in his cool upper chamber all alone, and Ehud said, "A word of God I have for you," and he rose from his seat. 21. And Ehud reached with his left hand and took the dagger from his right thigh and thrust it into Eglon's belly. 22. The hilt went in after the blade and the fat closed over the blade, for he did not withdraw the dagger from the belly and [the filth burst out].[7] 23. Ehud came out through the vestibule, closing the doors of the upper chamber on him and locking them. 24. He had just gone out when the courtiers came and saw that the doors were locked. "He is just relieving himself in the cool chamber," they said. 25. They waited a long time, and still he did not open the doors of the chamber. So they took the key and opened them, and, look, their lord was sprawled on the floor, dead.

It will be observed at once that the detailed attention given here to the implement and technique of killing, which would be normal in the *Iliad*, is rather uncharacteristic of the Hebrew Bible. One may assume that Ehud's bold resourcefulness in carrying out this assassination, which threw the Moabites into disarray and enabled the insurrection to succeed, was remarkable enough for the chronicler to want to report it circumstantially. Each of the details, then, contributes to a clear understanding of just how the thing was done (clearer, of course, for the ancient audience than for us since we no longer know much about the floor plan of the sort of Canaanite summer residence favored by Moabite kings and therefore may have a little difficulty in reconstructing Ehud's entrances and exits). The left-handed Benjaminite warriors were known for their prowess, but Ehud also counts on his left-handedness as part of his strategy of surprise: a sudden movement of the left hand will not instantaneously be construed by the king as a movement of a weapon hand. Ehud also

---

[7] There is a textual ambiguity here in the Hebrew. In subsequent text citations, ambiguities will be indicated by brackets.

counts on the likelihood that Eglon will be inclined to trust him as a vassal bringing tribute and that the "secret" he promises to confide to the king will thus be understood as a piece of intelligence volunteered by an Israelite collaborator. The dagger or short sword *(ḥerev)* is of course strapped to Ehud's right thigh for easy drawing with the left hand; it is short enough to hide under his clothing, long enough to do Eglon's business without the killer's having to be unduly close to his victim, and double-edged to assure the lethalness of one quick thrust. Eglon's encumbrance of fat will make him an easier target as he awkwardly rises from his seat, and perhaps Ehud leaves the weapon buried in the flesh in order not to splatter blood on himself, so that he can walk out through the vestibule unsuspected and make his escape. One commentator has ingeniously proposed that even the sordid detail of the release of the anal sphincter in the death spasm has its role in the exposition of the mechanics of the assassination: the courtiers outside, detecting the odor, assume that Eglon has locked the door because he is performing a bodily function, and so they wait long enough to enable Ehud to get away safely.[8]

Yet if all this is the scrupulous report of a historical act of political terrorism, the writer has given his historical material a forceful thematic shape through a skillful manipulation of the prose narrative medium. What emerges is not simply a circumstantial account of the Moabite king's destruction but a satiric vision of it, at once shrewd and jubilant. The writer's imagination of the event is informed by an implicit etymologizing of Eglon's name, which suggests the Hebrew *ʿegel,* calf. The ruler of the occupying Moabite power turns out to be a fatted calf readied for slaughter, and perhaps even the epithet *bari,* "stout," is a play on *meri,* "fatling," a sacrificial animal occasionally bracketed with calf. Eglon's fat is both the token of his physical ponderousness, his vulnerability to Ehud's sudden blade, and the emblem of his regal stupidity. Perhaps it may also hint at a kind of grotesque feminization of the Moabite leader: Ehud "comes to" the king, an idiom also used for sexual entry, and there is something hideously sexual about the description of the dagger-thrust. There may also be a deliberate sexual nuance in the "secret thing" Ehud brings to Eglon, in the way the two are locked together alone in a chamber, and in the sudden opening of locked entries at the conclusion of the story.[9]

Ehud's claim to have a secret message for the king is accepted immediately and without qualification by Eglon's confidential "Silence!" (or per-

---

[8] Yehezkel Kaufmann, *The Book of Judges* (Hebrew) (Jerusalem, 1968), p. 109.

[9] The possible significance of locking and unlocking in the story was brought to my attention by George Savran.

haps one might translate the onomatopoeic term as *sssh!*), the Moabite either failing to notice that Ehud has brusquely addressed him as "King" without the polite "My lord" (*ʾadoni*) or construing this omission simply as evidence of Ehud's urgency. When the two are alone and Ehud again turns to Eglon, he drops even the bare title, flatly stating, "A word of God I have for you." This statement is a rather obvious but nevertheless effective piece of dramatic irony: the secret thing—the Hebrew term *davar*, can mean word, message, or thing—hidden beneath Ehud's garment is in fact the word of God that the divinely "raised" Benjaminite champion is about to bring home implacably to the corpulent king. Hearing that the promised political secret is actually an oracle, Eglon rises, perhaps in sheer eagerness to know the revelation, perhaps as an act of accepted decorum for receiving an oracular communication, and now Ehud can cut him down.

The courtiers' erroneous assumption that their bulky monarch is taking his leisurely time over the chamber pot is a touch of scatological humor at the expense of both king and followers, while it implicates them in the satiric portrayal of the king's credulity. This last effect is heightened by the presentation of their direct speech at the end of verse 24, and the switch of the narrative to their point of view in verses 23 and 24. Let me retranslate these clauses literally to reproduce the immediate effect of seeing the scene through their eyes that one experiences in the Hebrew: "The courtiers came and saw, look, the doors of the upper chamber are locked. . . . They waited a long time and, look, he's not opening the doors of the upper chamber, and they took the keys and opened them, and, look, their lord is sprawled on the floor, dead." The syntax of the concluding clause nicely follows the rapid stages of their perception as at last they are disabused of their illusion: first they see their king prostrate, and then they realize, climactically, that he is dead. An enemy's obtuseness is always an inviting target for satire in time of war, but here the exposure of Moabite stupidity has a double thematic function: to show the blundering helplessness of the pagan oppressor when faced with a liberator raised up by the all-knowing God of Israel, and to demonstrate how these gullible Moabites, deprived of a leader, are bound to be inept in the war that immediately ensues.

In fact, great numbers of the Moabites are slaughtered at the fords of the Jordan, the location of the debacle perhaps suggesting that they allowed themselves to be drawn into an actual ambush, or at any rate, that they foolishly rushed into places where the entrenched Israelites could hold them at a terrific strategic disadvantage. Ehud's assassination of Eglon, then, is not only connected causally with the subsequent Moabite defeat but it is also a kind of emblematic prefiguration of it. The link between the regicide and the war of liberation is reinforced by two punning verbal clues. Ehud thrusts *(tq')* the dagger into Eglon's belly (verse 21), and as soon as he makes good his escape (verse 27), he blasts the ram's horn—the same verb, *tq'*—to rally his troops.[10] The Israelites kill 10,000 Moabites, "everyone a lusty man and a brave man" (verse 29), but the word for "lusty," *shamen,* also means "fat," so the Moabites are "laid low [or subjugated] under the hand of Israel" (verse 30) in a neat parallel to the fate of their fat master under the swift left hand of Ehud. In all this, as I have said, it is quite possible that the writer faithfully represents the historical data without addition or substantive embellishment. The organization of the narrative, however, its lexical and syntactic choices, its small shifts in point of view, its brief but strategic uses of dialogue, produce an imaginative reenactment of the historical event, conferring upon it a strong attitudinal definition and discovering in it a pattern of meaning. It is perhaps less historicized fiction than fictionalized history—history in which the feeling and the meaning of events are concretely realized through the technical resources of prose fiction.

To round out this overview of the spectrum of fictional modalities in the Bible's sacred history, I should like to return to Genesis for a concluding illustration—this time, from the patriarchal narratives, which, unlike the story of the first ancestors of mankind, are firmly linked to Israelite national history. The linkage, to be sure, would appear to be more the writers' attribution than the result of any dependable historical traditions. Many modern scholars have assumed that the patriarchs are the invented figures of early Hebrew folklore elaborated on by later writers, particularly in order to explain political arrangements among the twelve tribes generations after the Conquest. But even if one follows the inclination of some contemporary commentators to see a historical kernel in many of these tales, it is obvious that, in contrast to our examples from Judges and the David story, the authors, writing centuries after the supposed events, had scant historical data to work with. To what degree they believed the various traditions they inherited were actually historical is by no means clear, but if caution may deter us from applying a term like "invention" to their activity, it still seems likely that they exercised a good deal of shaping power over their materials as they articulated them. The point I should like to stress is that the immemorial inventions, fabrications,

---

[10] The pun has been observed by Luis Alonso-Schökel, who also comments on the play of *'egel* in Eglon's name, "Erzählkunst im Buche der Richter," *Biblica* 42 (1961), pp. 148–158.

or projections of folk tradition are not in themselves fiction, which depends on the particularizing imagination of the individual writer. The authors of the patriarchal narratives exhibit just such an imagination, transforming archetypal plots into the dramatic interaction of complex, probingly rendered characters. These stories are "historicized" both because they are presented as having a minute causal relation to known historical circumstances and because (as Schneidau argues) they have some of the irregular, "metonymic" quality of real historical concatenation; they are fiction because the national archetypes have been made to assume the distinctive lineaments of individual human lives.

Biblical narrative in fact offers a particularly instructive instance of the birth of fiction because it often exhibits the most arresting transitions from generalized statement, genealogical lists, mere summaries of characters and acts, to defined scene and concrete interaction between personages. Through the sudden specifications of narrative detail and the invention of dialogue that individualizes the characters and focuses their relations, the biblical writers give the events they report a fictional time and place.

Let us consider a single succinct example, Esau's selling of the birthright to Jacob (Genesis 25):

27. As the lads grew up, Esau became a skilled hunter, a man of the field, and Jacob was a mild man, who kept to his tents. 28. Isaac loved Esau because he had a taste for game, but Rebekah loved Jacob. 29. Once when Jacob was cooking a stew, Esau came in from the field, famished. 30. Esau said to Jacob, "O, give me a swallow of this red red stuff for I am famished."—Thus is his name called Edom. 31. Jacob said, "First sell your birthright to me." 32. And Esau said, "Look, I am at the point of death, so what good to me is a birthright?" 33. And Jacob said, "Swear to me first," and he swore to him and sold his birthright to Jacob. 34. Then Jacob gave Esau bread and lentil stew, and he ate and he drank and he rose and he went off and Esau spurned the birthright.

Now Esau or Edom and Jacob or Israel are the eponymous founders of two neighboring and rival peoples, as the text has just forcefully reminded us in the oracle preceding their birth ("Two nations are in your womb. / Two peoples apart while still in your belly. / One people will outdo the other, / The older will serve the younger." [Gen. 25:23]). The story of the two rival brothers virtually asks us to read it as a political allegory, to construe each of the twins as an embodiment of his descendants' national characteristics, and to understand the course of their struggle as an outline of their future national destinies. The ruddy Esau, hungry for the red stew, is the progenitor of Edom, by folk etymology associated with *ʾadom,* the color red, so that the people are given a kind of national emblem linked here with animality and gross appetite. This negative characterization is probably sharpened, as E. A. Speiser has proposed, by a borrowing from Near Eastern literary tradition: the red Esau, born with "a mantle of hair all over," would appear to allude to Enkidu of the Akkadian Gilgamesh Epic, whose birth is described in just this manner, and who is also an uncouth man of the field.[11] What happens, however, when the story is read entirely as a collision of national archetypes is strikingly illustrated by the commentaries of the early rabbis who—tending to interpret Edom as the typological forerunner of Rome—are relentless in making Esau out to be a vicious brute, while Jacob the tent-dweller becomes the model of pious Israel pondering the intricacies of God's revelation in the study of the Law. The anachronism of such readings concerns us less than the way they project onto the text, from their national-historical viewpoint, a neat moral polarity between the brothers. The text itself, conceiving its personages in the fullness of a mature fictional imagination, presents matters rather differently, as even this brief passage from the larger Jacob–Esau story will suggest.

The episode begins with a schematic enough contrast between Esau the hunter and the sedentary Jacob. This apparently neat opposition, however, contains a lurking possibility of irony in the odd epithet *tam* attached to Jacob in verse 27. Most translators have rendered it, as I have, by following the immediate context, and so have proposed something like "mild," "plain," or even "retiring" as an English equivalent. Perhaps this was in fact one recognized meaning of the term, but it should be noted that *all* the other biblical occurrences of the word—and it is frequently used, both in adjectival and nominative forms—refer to innocence or moral integrity. A little earlier in Genesis (20:5–6) Abraham professed the "innocence of his heart" *(tom-levav);* in contrast to this collocation, Jeremiah will announce (Jer. 17:9) that the "heart is treacherous" *(ʿaqov ha-lev),* using the same verbal root that Esau sees in Jacob's name *(Ya ʿaqov)* as an etymological signature of his treachery. This usage opens the possibility that we are dealing here with recognized antonyms, both of them commonly bound in idiomatic compounds to the word for heart. Jacob, *Ya ʿaqov,* whose name will soon be interpreted as the one who deceives (the Hebrew could be construed as "he will deceive"), is about to carry out an act if not of deception at least of shrewd calculation, and the choice of an epithet suggesting innocence as an introduction to the episode is bound to give us pause, to make us puzzle over the moral

[11] *Genesis,* The Anchor Bible (New York, 1964), p. 196.

nature of Jacob—an enigma we shall still be trying to fathom twenty chapters later when he is an old man worn by experience, at last reunited with his lost son Joseph and received in the court of Pharaoh.

The next verse (Gen. 25:28) provides an almost diagrammatic illustration of the Bible's artful procedure of variously stipulating or suppressing motive in order to elicit moral inferences and suggest certain ambiguities.[12] Isaac's preference for Esau is given a causal explanation so specific that it verges on satire: he loves the older twin because of his own fondness for game. Rebekah's love for Jacob is contrastively stated without explanation. Presumably, this would suggest that her affection is not dependent on a merely material convenience that the son might provide her, that it is a more justly grounded preference. Rebekah's maternal solicitude, however, is not without its troubling side, for we shall soon see a passive and rather timid Jacob briskly maneuvered about by his mother so that he will receive Isaac's blessing. This brief statement, then, of parental preferences is both an interesting characterization of husband and wife and an effectively reticent piece of exposition in the story of the two brothers.

The twins then spring to life as fictional characters when the narration moves into dialogue (Gen. 25:30–33). Biblical Hebrew, as far as we can tell, does not incorporate in direct speech different levels of diction, deviations from standard grammar, regional or class dialects; but the writers, even in putting "normative" Hebrew in the mouths of their personages, find ways of differentiating spoken language according to character. Esau asks for the stew with a verb used for the feeding of animals (hilʿit)— one might suggest the force of the locution in English by rendering it as "let me cram my maw"—and, all inarticulate appetite, he cannot even think of the word for stew but only points to it pantingly, calling it "this red red stuff." His explanation, however, "for I am famished," is factually precise, as it echoes verbatim what the narrator has just told us. In the first instance, that is, Esau does not choose an exaggeration, like that of verse 32, but states his actual condition: a creature of appetite, he is caught by the pangs of a terrible appetite. Esau speaks over the rumble of a growling stomach with the whiff of the cooking stew in his nostrils. Jacob speaks with a clear perception of legal forms and future consequences, addressing his brother twice in the imperative—"First sell . . . swear to me first"—without the deferential particle of entreaty, na, that Esau used in his own initial words to his twin. When Jacob asks Esau to sell the birthright, he withholds the crucial "to me" till the end of his proposal with cautious rhetorical calculation. Fortunately for him, Esau is too absorbed in his own immediate anguish—"I am at the point

[12] For a detailed discussion of this central aspect of biblical narrative, see chapter 6.

of death"—to pay much attention to Jacob's self-interest. After the trans-action is completed, as we move back from dialogue to uninterrupted narration, Esau's precipitous character is mirrored stylistically in the rapid chain of verbs—"and he ate and he drank and he rose and he went off"—that indicates the uncouth dispatch with which he "spurned," or held in contempt, his birthright.

What is one to make of this vivid fictional realization of the scene in regard to its evident national-historical signification? The two are not really at cross-purposes, but certain complications of meaning are intro-duced in the process of fictional representation. Esau, the episode makes clear, is not spiritually fit to be the vehicle of divine election, the bearer of the birthright of Abraham's seed. He is altogether too much the slave of the moment and of the body's tyranny to become the progenitor of the people promised by divine covenant that it will have a vast historical destiny to fulfill. His selling of the birthright in the circumstances here described is in itself proof that he is not worthy to retain the birthright.

As the author, however, concretely imagines Jacob, what emerges from the scene is more than simple Israelite (and anti-Edomite) apologetics. Jacob is a man who thinks about the future, indeed, who often seems worried about the future, and we shall repeatedly see him making prudent stipulations in legal or quasi-legal terms with God, with Laban, with his mysterious adversary, about future circumstances. This qualifies him as a suitable bearer of the birthright: historical destiny does not just happen; you have to know how to make it happen, how to keep your eye on the distant horizon of present events. But this quality of wary calculation does not necessarily make Jacob more appealing as a character, and, indeed, may even raise some moral questions about him. The contrast in this scene between the impetuous, miserably famished Esau and the shrewdly businesslike Jacob may not be entirely to Jacob's advantage, and the episode is surely a little troubling in light of the quality of "inno-cence" which the narrator has just fastened as an epithet to the younger twin. His subsequent stealing of his blind father's blessing by pretending to be Esau (Genesis 27) sets him in a still more ambiguous light; and the judgment that Jacob has done wrong in taking what is, in a sense, his, is later confirmed in the narrative, as Umberto Cassuto and other commentators have noted: Jacob becomes the victim of symmetrical poetic justice, deceived in the blindness of the night by having Leah passed off on him as Rachel, and rebuked in the morning by the deceiver, his father-in-law Laban: "It is not done thus in our region to give the younger daughter before the firstborn" (Gen. 29:26).

If one insists on seeing the patriarchal narratives strictly as paradigms for later Israelite history, one would have to conclude that the authors and redactor of the Jacob story were political subversives raising oblique but damaging questions about the national enterprise. Actually, there may be some theological warrant for this introduction of ambiguities into the story of Israel's eponymous hero, for in the perspective of ethical monotheism, covenantal privileges by no means automatically confer moral perfection, and that monitory idea is perhaps something the writers wanted to bring to the attention of their audiences. I do not think, though, that every nuance of characterization and every turning of the plot in these stories can be justified in either moral-theological or national-historical terms. Perhaps this is the ultimate difference between any hermeneutic approach to the Bible and the literary approach that I am proposing: in the literary perspective there is latitude for the exercise of pleasurable invention for its own sake, ranging from "microscopic" details like sound-play to "macroscopic" features like the psychology of individual characters.

This need not imply a blurring of necessary distinctions between sacred and secular literature. The biblical authors are of course constantly, urgently conscious of telling a story in order to reveal the imperative truth of God's works in history and of Israel's hopes and failings. Close attention to the literary strategies through which that truth was expressed may actually help us to understand it better, enable us to see the minute elements of complicating design in the Bible's sacred history. But it also seems to me important to emphasize that the operation of the literary imagination develops a momentum of its own, even for a tradition of writers so theologically intent as these. Genesis is not *Pale Fire*, but all fiction, including the Bible, is in some sense a form of play. Play in the sense I have in mind enlarges rather than limits the range of meanings of the text. For the classics of fiction, ancient and modern, embody in a vast variety of modes the most serious playfulness, endlessly discovering how the permutations of narrative conventions, linguistic properties, and imaginatively constructed personages and circumstances can crystalize subtle and abiding truths of experience in amusing or arresting or gratifying ways. The Bible presents a kind of literature in which the primary impulse would often seem to be to provide instruction or at least necessary information, not merely to delight. If, however, we fail to see that the creators of biblical narrative were writers who, like writers elsewhere, took pleasure in exploring the formal and imaginative resources of their fictional medium, perhaps sometimes unexpectedly capturing the fullness of their subject in the very play of exploration, we shall miss much that the biblical stories are meant to convey.

3

Biblical Type-Scenes and

the Uses of Convention

A COHERENT READING of any art work, whatever the medium, requires some detailed awareness of the grid of conventions upon which, and against which, the individual work operates. It is only in exceptional moments of cultural history that these conventions are explicitly codified, as in French neoclassicism or in Arabic and Hebrew poetry of the Andalusian Golden Age, but an elaborate set of tacit agreements between artist and audience about the ordering of the art work is at all times the enabling context in which the complex communication of art occurs. Through our awareness of convention we can recognize significant or simply pleasing patterns of repetition, symmetry, contrast; we can discriminate between the verisimilar and the fabulous, pick up directional clues in a narrative work, see what is innovative and what is deliberately traditional at each nexus of the artistic creation.

One of the chief difficulties we encounter as modern readers in perceiving the artistry of biblical narrative is precisely that we have lost most of the keys to the conventions out of which it was shaped. The professional Bible scholars have not offered much help in this regard, for their closest approximation to the study of convention is form criticism, which is set on finding recurrent regularities of pattern rather than the manifold variations upon a pattern that any system of literary convention elicits; moreover, form criticism uses these patterns for excavative ends—to sup-

47

port hypotheses about the social functions of the text, its historical evolution, and so forth. Before going on to describe what seems to me a central and, as far as I know, unrecognized convention of biblical narrative, I would like to make clearer by means of an analogy our dilemma as moderns approaching this ancient literary corpus which has been so heavily encrusted with nonliterary commentaries.

Let us suppose that some centuries hence only a dozen films survive from the whole corpus of Hollywood westerns. As students of twentieth-century cinema screening the films on an ingeniously reconstructed archaic projector, we notice a recurrent peculiarity: in eleven of the films, the sheriff-hero has the same anomalous neurological trait of hyperreflexivity—no matter what the situation in which his adversaries confront him, he is always able to pull his gun out of its holster and fire before they, with their weapons poised, can pull the trigger. In the twelfth film, the sheriff has a withered arm and, instead of a six-shooter, he uses a rifle that he carries slung over his back. Now, eleven hyperreflexive sheriffs are utterly improbable by any realistic standards—though one scholar will no doubt propose that in the Old West the function of sheriff was generally filled by members of a hereditary caste that in fact had this genetic trait. The scholars will then divide between a majority that posits an original source-western (designated Q) which has been imitated or imperfectly reproduced in a whole series of later versions (Q_1, Q_2, etc.— the films we have been screening) and a more speculative minority that proposes an old California Indian myth concerning a sky-god with arms of lightning, of which all these films are scrambled and diluted secular adaptations. The twelfth film, in the view of both schools, must be ascribed to a different cinematic tradition.

The central point, of course, that these strictly historical hypotheses would fail even to touch upon is the presence of convention. We contemporary viewers of westerns back in the twentieth century immediately recognize the convention without having to name it as such. Much of our pleasure in watching westerns derives from our awareness that the hero, however sinister the dangers looming over him, leads a charmed life, that he will always in the end prove himself to be more of a man than the bad guys that stalk him, and the familiar token of his indomitable manhood is his invariable, often uncanny, quickness on the draw. For us, the recurrence of the hyperreflexive sheriff is not an enigma to be explained but, on the contrary, a necessary condition for telling a western story in the film medium as it should be told. With our easy knowledge of the convention, moreover, we naturally see a point in the twelfth, exceptional film that would be invisible to the historical scholars. For in this case, we recognize that the convention of the quick-drawing hero is present through its deliberate suppression. Here is a sheriff who seems to lack the expected equipment for his role, but we note the daring assertion of manly will against almost impossible odds in the hero's learning to make do with what he has, training his left arm to whip his rifle into firing position with a swiftness that makes it a match for the quickest draw in the West.

Some of the analogous conventions through which biblical narrators variously worked out their tacit contract with their contemporary audiences are perhaps, after three millennia, no longer recoverable. Let me be perfectly candid about the inherent difficulty of our project. The key problem is not only the centuries elapsed since this body of literature was created but the small corpus of works that has survived. Within this small corpus, certain narrative conventions that are observable on the "microscopic" level of the text, like the formulas for beginning and ending narrative units, can be identified with considerable confidence because one can locate fifteen, twenty, or even more instances in the Hebrew Bible. Other conventions, however, which determine larger patterns of recurrence in the "macroscopic" aspects of the stories and which are not strictly tied to stylistic formulas, like the convention I shall now attempt to investigate, are bound to be more conjectural because, given the limited corpus with which we have to work, we may be able to locate confidently no more than five or six signal occurrences. Nevertheless, I think that we may be able to recuperate some essential elements of ancient convention, and thus to understand biblical narrative more precisely, if the questions we ask of it assume a fairly high degree of literary purposefulness.

The most crucial case in point is the perplexing fact that in biblical narrative more or less the same story often seems to be told two or three or more times about different characters, or sometimes even about the same character in different sets of circumstances. Three times a patriarch is driven by famine to a southern region where he pretends that his wife is his sister, narrowly avoids a violation of the conjugal bond by the local ruler, and is sent away with gifts (Gen. 12:10–20; Gen. 20; Gen. 26:1–12). Twice Hagar flees into the wilderness from Sarah's hostility and discovers a miraculous well (Gen. 16; Gen. 21:9–21), and that story itself seems only a special variation of the recurrent story of bitter rivalry between a barren, favored wife and a fertile co-wife or concubine. That situation, in turn, suggests another oft-told tale in the Bible, of a woman long barren who is vouchsafed a divine promise of progeny, whether by God himself or through a divine messenger or oracle, and who then gives birth to a hero.

Different repeated episodes have elicited different explanations, but

The Art of Biblical Narrative

the most common strategy among scholars is to attribute all ostensible duplication in the narratives to a duplication of sources, to a kind of recurrent stammer in the process of transmission, whether written or oral. The latest explanatory word of this sort is a monograph by Robert C. Culley, *Studies in the Structure of Hebrew Narrative*,[1] which first surveys some recent ethnographic studies of oral storytelling in the West Indies and Africa and then tentatively proposes that the same mechanism is present in biblical narrative. Since the students of oral narration have observed that as a tale is told over and over changes occur in it and even the identities of its personages shift, Culley suggests that the Bible may reflect the same phenomenon and that the somewhat distorted duplications of narratives in Scripture could well be evidence of oral transmission. To make his point graphically, he even lays out a series of tables with parallel episodes in which more or less the same elements of plot occur in different circumstances with different characters. As I stared at Culley's schematic tables, it gradually dawned on me that he had made a discovery without realizing it. For what his tables of parallels and variants actually reveal are the lineaments of a purposefully deployed literary convention. The variations in the parallel episodes are not at all *random*, as a scrambling by oral transmission would imply, and the repetitions themselves are no more "duplications" of a single *ur*-story than our eleven films about a fast-shooting sheriff were duplications of a single film.

In order to define this basic convention of biblical narrative, I am going to borrow a concept from Homer scholarship, though a couple of major modifications of the concept will have to be made. Students of Homer have generally agreed that there are certain prominent elements of repetitive compositional pattern in both Greek epics that are a conscious convention, one which has been designated "type-scene."[2] The notion was first worked out by Walter Arend in 1933 *(Die typischen Szenen bei Homer)* before the oral-formulaic nature of the Homeric poems was understood. Since then, the type-scene has been plausibly connected with the special needs of oral composition, and a good deal of recent scholarship has been devoted to showing the sophisticated variations on the set patterns of the various type-scenes in the Homeric epics. Very briefly, Arend's notion is that there are certain fixed situations which the poet is expected to include in his narrative and which he must perform according to a set order of motifs—situations like the arrival, the message, the voyage, the assembly, the oracle, the arming of the hero, and some half-dozen others.

[1] Philadelphia, 1976.
[2] For bibliographical advice on Homeric type-scenes, I am indebted to my friend and colleague Thomas G. Rosenmeyer.

The type-scene of the visit, for example, should unfold according to the following fixed pattern: a guest approaches; someone spots him, gets up, hurries to greet him; the guest is taken by the hand, led into the room, invited to take the seat of honor; the guest is enjoined to feast; the ensuing meal is described. Almost any description of a visit in Homer will reproduce more or less this sequence not because of an overlap of sources but because that is how the convention requires such a scene to be rendered.

Some of this obviously cannot apply to biblical narrative because the epic type-scene involves descriptive detail, while the Bible is not descriptive, and, concomitantly, the type-scene is a performance of a quotidian situation, and the Bible touches on the quotidian only as a sphere for the realization of portentous actions: if in the Bible someone is brewing up a mess of lentil stew, the reader can rest assured that it is not to exhibit the pungency of ancient Hebrew cuisine but because some fatal transaction will be carried out with the stew, which even proves to have a symbolically appropriate color (see chapter 2).

Nevertheless, I should like to propose that there is a series of recurrent narrative episodes attached to the careers of biblical heroes that are analogous to Homeric type-scenes in that they are dependent on the manipulation of a fixed constellation of predetermined motifs. Since biblical narrative characteristically catches its protagonists only at the critical and revealing points in their lives, the biblical type-scene occurs not in the rituals of daily existence but at the crucial junctures in the lives of the heroes, from conception and birth to betrothal to deathbed. Not every type-scene will occur for every major hero, though often the absence of a particular type-scene may itself be significant. Some of the most commonly repeated biblical type-scenes I have been able to identify are the following: the annunciation (and I take the term from Christian iconography precisely to underscore the elements of fixed convention) of the birth of the hero to his barren mother; the encounter with the future betrothed at a well; the epiphany in the field; the initiatory trial; danger in the desert and the discovery of a well or other source of sustenance; the testament of the dying hero.

How all of this may bring us closer to an understanding of the artistry of biblical narrative will, I hope, become apparent through an extended analysis of one such type-scene. I shall focus on the betrothal, for it offers some particularly interesting and inventive variations of the set pattern. Conveniently, this is one of the examples of "duplications" that Culley sets out in his tables with schematic clarity. What I would suggest is that when a biblical narrator—and he might have originally been an oral storyteller, though that remains a matter of conjecture—came to the moment of his hero's betrothal, both he and his audience were aware that the scene had to unfold in particular circumstances, according to a fixed order. If some of those circumstances were altered or suppressed, or if the scene were actually omitted, that communicated something to the audience as clearly as the withered arm of our twelfth sheriff would say something to a film audience. The betrothal type-scene, then, must take place with the future bridegroom, or his surrogate, having journeyed to a foreign land. There he encounters a girl—the term "*na*ʿ*arah*" invariably occurs unless the maiden is identified as so-and-so's daughter—or girls at a well. Someone, either the man or the girl, then draws water from the well; afterward, the girl or girls rush to bring home the news of the stranger's arrival (the verbs "hurry" and "run" are given recurrent emphasis at this junction of the type-scene); finally, a betrothal is concluded between the stranger and the girl, in the majority of instances, only after he has been invited to a meal.

The archetypal expressiveness of this whole type-scene is clear enough. The hero's emergence from the immediate family circle—though two of the most famous betrothal scenes stress endogamy (Gen. 24:10–61; Gen. 29:1–20)—to discover a mate in the world outside is figured in the young man's journey to a foreign land; or perhaps the foreign land is chiefly a geographical correlative for the sheer female otherness of the prospective wife. The well at an oasis is obviously a symbol of fertility and, in all likelihood, also a female symbol. The drawing of water from the well is the act that emblematically establishes a bond—male-female, host-guest, benefactor-benefited—between the stranger and the girl, and its apt result is the excited running to bring the news, the gestures of hospitality, the actual betrothal. The plot of the type-scene, then, dramatically enacts the coming together of mutually unknown parties in the marriage. It may have ultimately originated in prebiblical traditions of folklore, but that is a matter of conjecture peripheral to the understanding of its *literary* use. And, in any case, as is true of all original art, what is really interesting is not the schema of convention but what is done in each individual application of the schema to give it a sudden tilt of innovation or even to refashion it radically for the imaginative purposes at hand.

The first occurrence in the Bible of the betrothal type-scene is also by far the most elaborate version of it—the encounter at the well in Aram-Naharaim between Abraham's servant and Rebekah (Gen. 24:10–61). All the elements of the convention we have just reviewed are present here. The servant, as Isaac's surrogate, has been sent by Abraham all the way back to the family home in Mesopotamia to seek a bride for his master's son. The servant, combining, as it were, a knowledge of social custom with the requirements of the literary convention, carefully stations himself by the well toward evening, when each day the local girls come out to draw water. The *na͑arah* who immediately turns up is, of course, Rebekah. She draws water for the stranger and his camels. As soon as he assures himself of her family background, he loads her with jewelry; she runs home with the news of his arrival; her brother Laban comes out to welcome the stranger, sets a meal before him, and negotiations follow, concluding with an agreement to betroth Rebekah to Isaac.

The most striking feature of this version of the type-scene is its slow, stately progress, an effect achieved by the extensive use of dialogue, by a specification of detail clearly beyond the norm of biblical narrative, and, above all, by a very elaborate use of the device of verbatim repetition, which is a standard resource of the biblical writers.[3] These strategies of retardation are important because in this particular instance the betrothal is conceived *ceremoniously,* as a formal treaty between two branches of the Nahor clan, and so the bestowal of gifts is specified here, and we are given the precise diplomatic language in which the betrothal negotiations are carried out. We also get a concise, devastating characterization of Laban—"Seeing the nose-ring and the bracelets on his sister's arms, . . . he said, 'Come in, O blessed of the Lord' " (Gen. 24:30–31)—because his canny, grasping nature will be important when a generation later Jacob comes back to Aram-Naharaim to find *his* bride at a nearby rural well.

All these features are merely elaborations of or accretions to the conventional constellation of motifs. The role played here, on the other hand, by bridegroom and bride is a pointed divergence from the convention. Isaac is conspicuous by his absence from the scene: this is in fact the only instance where a surrogate rather than the man himself meets the girl at the well. That substitution nicely accords with the entire career of Isaac, for he is manifestly the most passive of the patriarchs. We have already seen him as a bound victim for whose life a ram is substituted; later, as a father, he will prefer the son who can go out to the field and bring him back provender, and his one extended scene will be lying in bed, weak and blind, while others act on him.

As a complement to this absence of the bridegroom, it is only in this betrothal scene that the girl, not the stranger, draws water from the well. Indeed, the narrator goes out of his way to give weight to this act by presenting Rebekah as a continuous whirl of purposeful activity. In four

---

[3] We shall consider the device of verbatim repetition at length in chapter 5.

short verses (Gen. 24:16, 18–20) she is the subject of eleven verbs of action and one of speech, going down to the well, drawing water, filling the pitcher, pouring, giving drink. One might note that the two verbs of rushing and hurrying (*rutz* and *maher*) generally reserved for the bringing of the news of the stranger's arrival are here also repeatedly attached to Rebekah's actions at the well, and the effect of rapid bustling activity is reinforced by the verbatim recapitulation of this moment with its verbs (verses 45–46) in the servant's report to Laban. Later, Rebekah will take the initiative at a crucial moment in the story in order to obtain the paternal blessing for her favored son, Jacob, and again she will be the subject of a rapid chain of verbs, hurriedly taking and cooking and dressing and giving before Esau can return from the field. Rebekah is to become the shrewdest and the most potent of the matriarchs, and so it is entirely appropriate that she should dominate her betrothal scene. She is immediately identified (verse 16) with unconventional explicitness as the suitable bride for both her beauty and her unimpeachable virginity. Then in her actions and speech we see her energy, her considerate courtesy, her sense of quiet self-possession. Exceptionally and aptly, the future matriarch's departure at the end of the type-scene is marked by the ceremonial flourish of a formal verse inset, the blessing conferred on her by the members of her family: "O sister, / may you become / thousands of myriads, / may your offspring take / the gates of its foes" (Gen. 24:60).

How differently the same conventional motifs can be deployed is made clear in the next instance of the betrothal type-scene, Jacob's encounter at the well with Rachel (Gen. 29:1–20). Here the stranger comes not as an official emissary but as a refugee from his brother's wrath, accompanied not by camels and gifts but only, as he will later recall, by his walking-staff. At once, we are taken into the scene literally through Jacob's eyes (verse 2): "He saw, and look [*vehinneh*], there was a well in the field, and, look, three flocks of sheep were lying by it."[4] This particular betrothal is very much Jacob's personal story, one which will involve a deep emotional attachment rather than a family treaty ("Jacob worked for Rachel seven years, and they seemed a few days in his eyes through his love for her" [Gen. 29:20]), and so it is fitting that we come to the well through his point of view. The scene takes place by a well in the fields, not by a well in town as in Genesis 24, for the whole story of Jacob, his two wives, his two concubines, and his scheming father-in-law will unfold

---

[4] J. P. Fokkelman in his remarkable recent book, *Narrative Art in Genesis* (Assen and Amsterdam, 1975), has made the acute observation that the presentative *hinneh* (the familiar "behold" of the King James Version) is often used to mark a shift in narrative point of view from third-person omniscience to the character's direct perception (see pp. 50–51).

against a background of pastoral activity, with close attention to the economics and ethics of sheep and cattle herding.

Jacob questions the shepherds at the well about the name of the place and then about his uncle Laban. In stark contrast to the stately movement of the dialogue in Genesis 24, with its formal modes of address and its ample synonymity, the dialogue here is a rapid exchange of brief questions and answers that seems almost colloquial by comparison; this again is an appropriate prelude to Jacob's quick-paced story of vigorously pursued actions, deceptions, and confrontations. The formula previously used to indicate an immediate concatenation of events in the entrance of the future bride—"[The servant] *had barely finished talking* [to God] *when*, look, out came Rebekah" (Gen. 24:15)—occurs here to interrupt the dialogue between Jacob and the shepherds: *"He was still talking* with them *when* Rachel arrived" (Gen. 29:9).

In this case, not only does the bridegroom take care of the drawing of water, but he has an obstacle to overcome—the stone on the mouth of the well. This minor variation of the convention contributes to the consistent characterization of Jacob, for we already know him, as his name at birth *(Ya'aqov)* has been etymologized, as the "heel-grabber" or wrestler, and we shall continue to see him as the contender, the man who seizes his fate, tackles his adversaries, with his own two hands. If the well of the betrothal scene is in general associated with woman and fertility, it is particularly appropriate that this one should be blocked by an obstacle, for Jacob will obtain the woman he wants only through great labor, against resistance, and even then God will, in the relevant biblical idiom, "shut up her womb" for years until she finally bears Joseph. There is even some point in the fact that the obstacle is a stone, for, as J. P. Fokkelman has noted, stones are a motif that accompanies Jacob in his arduous career: he puts a stone under his head as a pillow at Beth-El; after the epiphany there he sets up a commemorative marker of stones; and when he returns from Mesopotamia, he concludes a mutual nonaggression pact with his father-in-law by setting up on the border between them a testimonial heap of stones. These are not really symbols, but there is something incipiently metaphorical about them: Jacob is a man who sleeps on stones, speaks in stones, wrestles with stones, contending with the hard unyielding nature of things, whereas, in pointed contrast, his favored son will make his way in the world as a dealer in the truths intimated through the filmy insubstantiality of dreams.

In this particular encounter at the well, no direct speech between the stranger and the girl is reported, only a terse summary of the exchange between them. Rachel had been named by the shepherds and identified as Laban's daughter even before she actually reached the well, and for that reason she is not called *na'arah* but by her name, Rachel, throughout. Jacob weeps and embraces her as his kinswoman, revealing his familial tie to her, and she, following the requirements of the type-scene, then runs (the verb *"rutz"*) to tell her father. Laban responds by running back to greet the guest and embrace him, but our memory of Laban's glittering eye on the golden bangles may make us wonder how disinterested this surge of hospitality will prove to be. If his first statement to Jacob (verse 14) is an affirmation of kinship, the next recorded statement (verse 15) is an overture to a bargaining session and reveals incidentally that he has already been extracting labor from his kinsman-guest for a month.

It is only at this point that we get a piece of information about Rachel which in the case of Rebekah was announced as soon as the girl arrived at the well: that the maiden was very beautiful. This small difference in the strategy of exposition between the two versions nicely illustrates how substantially the same materials can be redeployed in order to make different points. Rebekah's beauty is part of her objective identity in a scene that she dominates, an item in her pedigreed nubility along with her virginity, and so it is appropriately announced the moment she enters the scene. Rachel's beauty, on the other hand, is presented as a causal element in Jacob's special attachment to her, and that, in turn, is fearfully entangled in the relationship of the two sisters with each other and in their competition for Jacob. The crucial fact of Rachel's beauty, then, is withheld from us until both Rachel and Leah can be formally introduced (verses 16–17) as a prelude to the agreement on a bride-price, and so it can be ambiguously interwoven with the prerogatives of the elder versus the younger sister and contrastively bracketed with Leah's "tender eyes" (presumably all she had to recommend her looks, or perhaps actually to be construed as a disfigurement, "weak eyes"). One can clearly see that the betrothal type-scene, far from being a mechanical means of narrative prefabrication for conveying the reader from a celibate hero to a married one, is handled with a flexibility that makes it a supple instrument of characterization and foreshadowing.

The next explicit occurrence of this particular type-scene (Exodus 2:15b–21) is the most compact version, but the strength of the convention is attested to by the fact that in six and a half swift verses all the requisite elements appear. Moses, the native of Egypt, has fled to a foreign land, Midian, where he encounters the seven daughters of the Midianite priest Reuel who have come out to draw water from a well. In this case, the stranger is obliged to drive off a gang of hostile shepherds before drawing water and giving drink to the flocks, as the convention requires. The girls hurry off to tell their father, a fact which in this accelerated version of the type-scene is not independently stated by the narrator but touched on by Reuel in the first words of the vivid dialogue between him and his daughters: "Why did you hurry [*miharten*] back today?" (verse 18). With similar economy, the welcoming feast is not directly reported but intimated in Reuel's concluding words in the dialogue: "Why did you leave the man? Call him in to have something to eat" (verse 20). The two immediately following clauses tersely inform us that Moses took up residence with Reuel and was given one of the daughters, Zipporah, as a wife.

These few verses may seem so spare a treatment of the convention as to be almost nondescript, but in fact this is just the kind of betrothal type-scene needed for Moses. To begin with, any presentation that would give more weight to Zipporah than merely one nubile daughter out of seven would throw the episode off balance, for her independent character and her relationship with Moses will play no significant role in the subsequent narrative. (The single enigmatic episode of the Bridegroom of Blood is scarcely an exception.) If this version reads like a succinct summary of the convention, that is fitting, for it holds Moses the man and his personal involvement at a distance, under the perspective of a certain stylization, and throughout his story we shall be excluded from the kind of intimacy of domestic observation we get in the narratives of the patriarchs or in the stories about David. That effect of stylization is surely reinforced by introducing the formulaic number of seven for the maidens, a detail that helps give this narrative by a sophisticated writer a deliberate, archaizing quality of folktale. At the same time, the manner of drawing water here is distinctively appropriate for Moses. He is faced not just with an obstacle but with enemies whom he has to drive off, not surprising for the killer of the Egyptian taskmaster, the future liberator of his people and its military commander in forty years of desert warfare. The narrator uses the verb "*hoshiʿa*," "to save," for Moses' rescue of the seven girls, a lexical clue to his future role of *moshiʿa*, national redeemer. The water drawn from the well in any case has special resonance in Moses' career, and Reuel's daughters seem to stress the physical act of drawing up water. Here is their entire narration of the incident to their father (verse 19): "An Egyptian man saved us from the shepherds, and what is more, he actually drew water for us [*daloh dalah*, the intensifying repetition of the infinitive alongside the perfect verb] and gave drink to the flock." Moses the infant was saved on the water, given a name said to mean "drawn from the water"; Moses the leader will miraculously take his people through an expanse of water that will then close over their enemies;

and in the wilderness he will bring forth water from a rock, but in an outburst of impatience for which he will be condemned. Moses' betrothal type-scene may not tell us a great deal, but it tells us just what we need to know for this protagonist at this point in the narrative.

What I am suggesting is that the contemporary audiences of these tales, being perfectly familiar with the convention, took particular pleasure in seeing how in each instance the convention could be, through the narrator's art, both faithfully followed and renewed for the specific needs of the hero under consideration. In some cases, moreover, the biblical authors, counting on their audience's familiarity with the features and function of the type-scene, could merely allude to the type-scene or present a transfigured version of it. Allusion and transfiguration are not necessarily limited to the later books of the Bible, and other type-scenes, as for example that of the annunciation to the barren wife, appear several times in integral form in post-Pentateuchal stories. But in the instance of the betrothal type-scene which we are considering, it happens that the three full-dress occurrences are all in the Pentateuch, while later narratives—I would be inclined to assume, later in regard to date of composition as well as in historical setting—transform or simply allude to the primary scene. Let me offer two brief examples.

The one biblical narrative that is in a sense entirely devoted to the circumstances leading to a betrothal is the Book of Ruth. Where the whole story is a betrothal narrative, one segment could not very easily be a betrothal type-scene, but the author of Ruth, who is one of the most brilliant masters of formal technique among biblical writers, finds an ingenious way to allude to the type-scene. Ruth's first encounter with her future husband, Boaz, is in the field where she has gone to glean the leavings of the harvest (Ruth 2). Boaz asks one of his retainers, "Whose girl [naʿarah] is that?" and is told that she is Ruth the Moabite, just returned from Moab with Naomi. Boaz then addresses Ruth directly (verses 8–9): "Listen, my daughter. Do not go to glean in another field, and don't go away, but stick here with my maidens [naʿarotai]. Keep your eyes on the field they are reaping and go after them, for I have ordered the lads [neʿarim] not to touch you. When you are thirsty, go to the jars and drink from what the lads draw." In this elliptical version, the author has rotated the betrothal type-scene 180 degrees on the axes of gender and geography. The protagonist is a heroine, not a hero, and her homeland is Moab, so the "foreign soil" on which she meets her future mate near a well is Judea. (Much of the thematic argument of the story as a whole is carried by the complex ambiguities in the repeated use of the verb "to return." Here Ruth is said to have "returned" to Bethlehem, an alien place to her, when it is only her mother-in-law who has really returned. But we get a progressive sense that she is actually coming back to the unknown homeland of her new destiny.) Boaz at first erroneously identifies Ruth as a *naᶜarah*—she is, in fact, a young-looking widow. He enjoins her to follow his *neᶜarot,* who in the traditional type-scene would come out to draw water. Here, since it is a female protagonist who has come to the foreign land to find a spouse, the male counterparts of the maidens, the *neᶜarim,* take over the customary function of water-drawing. The presence of the convention may have even led the audience to wonder temporarily whether Ruth would choose a mate from among the *neᶜarim.*

In the ensuing dialogue between Ruth and Boaz, the reversal of conventional literary gender is reinforced by a pointed allusion (verse 11) to Abraham, when Boaz says, "You have left your father and mother and the land of your birth and gone to a people you never knew" (cf. Genesis 12:1—"Go you from your land and your birthplace and your father's house . . . "). Ruth is conceived by the author as a kind of matriarch by adoption. This particular allusion links her with the movement from the East to Canaan at the beginning of the patriarchal enterprise, while the whole invocation of the betrothal type-scene suggests a certain connection with the matriarchs. In the case of Rebekah and Rachel, considerable importance is attached to ascertaining the genealogy of the maiden at the well. Here, in the exchange with Ruth, Boaz essentially establishes that Ruth's courage and her loyalty to her mother-in-law will amply serve in place of a genealogy. At the end of the dialogue, he invites her (verse 14) to a simple rural repast of roasted grain and bread dipped in vinegar—the hospitable feast which, according to the convention, follows the drawing of water and the conversation between the future spouses at the well. In this version, there is no running to bring the news—and, indeed, the lexicon of the Book of Ruth moves from recurrent verbs of going and returning to a cluster of words that suggest clinging or being at rest—because Ruth is not a young girl dependent on the decisions of her paternal household and also because the actual conclusion of the betrothal must be postponed to the last chapter of the story, where it is preceded by the legal ceremony of the refusal of the levirate obligation by a nearer kinsman of Naomi. In any case, the contemporary audience must have admired the inventiveness and allusive economy with which the betrothal type-scene was brought into Ruth's story and must have taken a certain pleasure in recognizing the thematic clues it provided.

In all this, of course, we must keep in mind that what we are witnessing is not merely the technical manipulation of a literary convention for the sheer pleasure of play with the convention, though, as I argued at the end of the previous chapter, significant playful activity on the part of the Hebrew writers should by no means be discounted, even in these sacred texts. The type-scene is not merely a way of formally recognizing a particular kind of narrative moment; it is also a means of attaching that moment to a larger pattern of historical and theological meaning. If Isaac and Rebekah, as the first man and wife born into the covenant God has made with Abraham and his seed, provide certain paradigmatic traits for the future historical destiny of Israel, any association of later figures with the crucial junctures of that first story—the betrothal, the life-threatening trial in the wilderness, the enunciation of the blessing— will imply some connection of meaning, some further working-out of the original covenant. In the foregoing discussion, I have been stressing the elements of divergence in the various invocations of the convention in order to show how supple an instrument of expression it can be. The fact of recurrence, however, is as important as the presence of innovation in the use of the type-scene; and the convention itself, the origins of which may well antecede biblical monotheism, has been made to serve an eminently monotheistic purpose: to reproduce in narrative the recurrent rhythm of a divinely appointed destiny in Israelite history. In this fashion, the alignment of Ruth's story with the Pentateuchal betrothal type-scene becomes an intimation of her portentous future as progenitrix of the divinely chosen house of David.

A much simpler example of allusion to the betrothal type-scene occurs at the beginning of Saul's career (1 Sam. 9:11–12). Having set out with his servant in search of his lost asses, he decides to consult the local seer, who turns out to be Samuel, the man who will anoint him king. "They were ascending the mountain slope when they met some maidens [*ne'arot*] going out to draw water, and they said, 'Is there a seer here?' " What we have in this verse, I would suggest, is the makings of a betrothal scene: a hero at the outset of his career in a foreign region (Saul has wandered out of his own tribal territory) meeting girls who have come to draw water from a well. As an audience familiar with the convention, we might properly expect that he will draw water for the girls, that they will then run home with the news of the stranger's arrival, and so forth. Instead, this is what ensues: "They answered them saying, 'There is. Straight ahead of you. Hurry [*maher*] now, for he has come to town today, for today the people is offering a sacrifice on the ritual platform.' "

The type-scene has been aborted. The hero swings away from the girls at the well to hurry after the man of God who will launch him on his destiny of disaster. This is probably a deliberate strategy of foreshadowing. The sense of completion implicit in the betrothal of the hero is withheld from this protagonist; the deflection of the anticipated type-scene somehow isolates Saul, sounds a faintly ominous note that begins to prepare us for the story of the king who loses his kingship, who will not be a conduit for the future rulers of Israel, and who ends skewered on his own sword. If this interpretation seems to exert too much pressure on half a dozen words of the Hebrew text, one must keep in mind the rigorous economy of biblical narrative. For the particular detail of an encounter on unfamiliar territory with maidens by a well would otherwise be gratuitous. Saul could have easily been made to proceed directly to find Samuel, or, as happens in other biblical narratives, he could have simply met an anonymous "man" and asked directions of him. The fact that instead the author chose to have him meet girls by a well and to stress the verb "to hurry" as they begin their response to the stranger is in all likelihood a clue of meaning.

Finally, the total suppression of a type-scene may be a deliberate ploy of characterization and thematic argument. The case of David, who has rather complicated relations with at least three of his wives, may be an ambiguous one, for perhaps the author, working closely with observed historical data about David, did not feel free to impose the stylization of a betrothal type-scene when he knew the circumstances of David's marriages to have been otherwise. Be that as it may, we might note that the three discriminated premarital episodes in the David cycle all involve bloodshed, in an ascending order of moral questionability: the two hundred Philistines he slaughters in battle as the bride-price for Michal; his threat to kill Nabal, Abigail's husband, who then conveniently dies of shock; and his murder of the innocent Uriah after having committed adultery with Bathsheba. Are these betrothals by violence a deliberate counterpoint to the pastoral motif of betrothal after the drawing of water? Perhaps, though from this distance in time it is hard to be sure.

More confidently, one can see the likely point of the omitted betrothal scene in the Samson story (Judges 14). At the beginning of his adventures, Samson goes down to Philistine Timnah, and so we have a young hero on foreign soil, but there is no well, no ritual of hospitality. Instead he sees a woman he wants, promptly returns home, and brusquely announces to his parents that he expects them to arrange the marriage for him. Grudgingly, they accompany him back to Timnah for the betrothal negotiations, and on the way he encounters a lion that he tears limb from limb. The awesome destruction of the lion, and the subsequent scooping out of honey from the lion's bleached carcass, may even be a pointed substitution for the more decorous and pacific drawing of water from the well. In any event, the impetuous rush of Samson's career is already communicated in his impatient movement from seeing a woman to taking her without the ceremonious mediation of a betrothal type-scene, and we all know what calamities the marriage itself will engender.

The process of literary creation, as criticism has clearly recognized from the Russian Formalists onward, is an unceasing dialectic between the necessity to use established forms in order to be able to communicate coherently and the necessity to break and remake those forms because they are arbitrary restrictions and because what is merely repeated automatically no longer conveys a message. "The greater the probability of a symbol's occurrence in any given situation," E. H. Gombrich observes in *Art and Illusion,* "the smaller will be its information content. Where we can anticipate we need not listen."[5] Reading any body of literature involves a specialized mode of perception in which every culture trains its members from childhood. As modern readers of the Bible, we need to relearn something of this mode of perception that was second nature to the original audiences. Instead of relegating every perceived recurrence in the text to the limbo of duplicated sources or fixed folkloric archetypes, we may begin to see that the resurgence of certain pronounced patterns at certain narrative junctures was conventionally anticipated, even counted on, and that against that ground of anticipation the biblical authors set words, motifs, themes, personages, and actions into an elaborate dance of significant innovation. For much of art lies in the shifting aperture between the shadowy foreimage in the anticipating mind of the observer and the realized revelatory image in the work itself, and that is what we must learn to perceive more finely in the Bible.

[5] New York, 1961, p. 205.

4

Between Narration and

Dialogue

HOW DO the biblical writers create a narrative event through their report of it? The term "event" as I shall be using it is a significant junction in the narrative continuum that is different in kind from summary, which is a form of narration abundantly used in the Bible both to provide links between events and for the independent presentation of material not deemed suitable for concrete rendering as discrete events. To take an extreme example of summary, one could hardly construe a genealogical list—"And Arpachshad begat Shelah and Shelah begat Eber"—as a narrative event because, though there is a report of something that happened, the notation abstracts a single essential datum from a lifespan of experience, and the ratio between narrating time and time narrated is too drastically disproportionate. A proper narrative event occurs when the narrative tempo slows down enough for us to discriminate a particular scene; to have the illusion of the scene's "presence" as it unfolds; to be able to imagine the interaction of personages or sometimes personages and groups, together with the freight of motivations, ulterior aims, character traits, political, social, or religious constraints, moral and theological meanings, borne by their speech, gestures, and acts. (In some novels, summary may at times shade into event, but in the Bible the two categories tend to be distinct.) These are the moments when the fictional imagination, as I have defined it in chapter 2, is in full operation, however much a particular event may be based on an actual historical occurrence.

The characteristic presentation of such narrative events in the Bible is notably different from that of the Greek epics and romances and of much later Western narrative literature. It is important to keep clearly in mind the peculiarity of the Hebrew mode of presentation because that will help us learn where to look for its revelations of meaning, nuanced and oblique as well as emphatic and overt. The story of David's encounter with Ahimelech at the sanctuary of Nob (1 Samuel 21) is a fairly representative biblical rendering of an event. David, warned by Jonathan of Saul's murderous intentions toward him, has fled unaccompanied to Nob, without provisions or weapons.

2. *Then David came to Nob, to Ahimelech the priest, and Ahimelech rushed out to meet David* and said to him: "Why are you alone, and no one is with you?" 3. And David said to Ahimelech the priest: "The king has charged me with a mission, and said to me, 'Let no one know anything of the mission on which I am sending you and with which I charge you.' And as to my young men, I have set a rendezvous with them at such and such a place. 4. Now then, what do you have at hand? Five loaves of bread, give it to me, or whatever there is." 5. The priest answered David and said, "I have no ordinary bread at hand, but consecrated bread there is, if the young men have kept themselves from women." 6. David answered the priest and said to him, "In fact, women are always kept from us when I am out on a sortie, so that the [vessels] of the young men should be consecrated, and all the more so now may consecrated food be in [their vessels]."[1] 7. *Then the priest gave him consecrated bread, for there was no bread there except the bread of the Presence which had been removed from before the Lord to be replaced by warm bread as soon as it was taken away. 8. And there was a man there of Saul's followers, detained that day before the Lord, and his name was Do'eg the Edomite, chief herdsman of Saul.* 9. And David said to Ahimelech, "Don't you have at hand here a spear or sword? For I have taken with me neither my sword nor my weapons because the king's mission was urgent." 10. The priest said, "The sword of Goliath the Philistine whom you struck down in the Valley of Elah, here it is, wrapped in a cloth behind the ephod. If you will take it, take it, for there is no other beside it here." And David said, "There's none like it; give it to me." 11. *And David rose and fled from Saul on that day, and came to Achish king of Gath.*

---

[1] The meaning of the Hebrew here is not entirely certain. The word "vessels" *(kelei)* might even refer to weapons, the sense in which the same word occurs in verse 9.

I have italicized everything in the episode that can be construed as narration, excluding the strictly formulaic introductions of speech ("and he said," "and he answered and he said") which, by the fixed convention of biblical literature, are required to indicate statement and response in dialogue. What this typographical distinction should make immediately apparent in the passage is the highly subsidiary role of narration in comparison to direct speech by the characters. The episode is framed by an introductory half-verse that tersely reports David's flight to Nob and Ahimelech's reception of him, and by a brief concluding verse that tells how David, now armed and provisioned, continues his flight to the Philistine city of Gath. The ancient Hebrew audience would have immediately recognized this last verse as the end of the episode because it invokes the formula of rising up and going off to a different place which is one of the prevalent biblical conventions for marking the end of a narrative segment.[2]

Within the frame set by these two verses (1 Sam. 21:2 and 11), the flow of dialogue is interrupted just once, in verses 7–8. It should be noted that the first of these two verses repeats almost verbatim Ahimelech's statement in verse 5 about the absence in the sanctuary of any bread except the consecrated loaves, only adding an explanatory comment about the loaves in question having been replaced by fresh shewbread, so we will understand that David is not taking bread actually needed for cultic purposes. In any case, verse 7 illustrates a general trait of biblical narrative: the primacy of dialogue is so pronounced that many pieces of third-person narration prove on inspection to be dialogue-bound, verbally mirroring elements of dialogue which precede them or which they introduce. Narration is thus often relegated to the role of confirming assertions made in dialogue—occasionally, as here, with an explanatory gloss.

In regard to the proportions of the narrative, third-person narration is frequently only a bridge between much larger units of direct speech. In regard to the perspective of the narrative, the third-person restatement of what has been said in dialogue directs our attention back to the speakers, to the emphases they choose, the ways their statements may diverge from the narrator's authoritative report of what occurs. (In the next chapter, we shall look at two especially instructive instances of such divergence, the story of Joseph and Potiphar's wife and the account of Solomon's succession to the throne through the intervention of Bathsheba and Na-

---

[2] Shimon Bar-Efrat has nicely observed how variations of this formula constitute a distinct convention for narrative endings. See his *The Art of the Biblical Story* (Hebrew) (Tel Aviv, 1979), pp. 142–43.

than.) The biblical writers, in other words, are often less concerned with actions in themselves than with how individual character responds to actions or produces them; and direct speech is made the chief instrument for revealing the varied and at times nuanced relations of the personages to the actions in which they are implicated.

If verse 7 of our passage is a dialogue-bound bridge between two moments in the dramatic exchange between David and Ahimelech, completing the question of food and so moving us on to the question of a weapon, verse 8, which reports the presence in the sanctuary of an eavesdropper, Do'eg, is intended as a deliberate intrusion upon the dialogue. Do'eg is not the subject here of any proper narrated action—indeed, in the Hebrew no verb is attached to him, for the verb "to be" has no present or participial form, and the report of Do'eg's being in the sanctuary is cast in the present in what would be the equivalent of a long noun phrase. In this way, attention is focused on the man rather than on anything he might have done. The facts that he is identified as an official of Saul's and that he is an Edomite of course do not augur well for the part he will play in the story as it continues to unfold.

We were not told of Do'eg's presence in the sanctuary when we first heard of David's arrival there. Biblical narrative often withholds pieces of exposition until the moment in the story when they are immediately relevant; but what is the immediate relevance here? There is nothing in the episode itself that makes it clear why Do'eg should be mentioned at this point, so we experience this interruption of the dialogue precisely as an interruption, perhaps merely puzzling, perhaps a bit ominous. The inference of something ominous is strengthened by what directly follows this mention of Do'eg: David's request for a weapon. The giving of Goliath's sword to David will be the most damaging item in Do'eg's subsequent denunciation of Ahimelech to Saul (1 Sam. 22:10), which, in addition to the provision of food, includes a third element that would appear to be the informer's own invention in order to compound the priest's guilt—an alleged inquiry of the oracle by David, which could have been done only through Ahimelech. Do'eg's denunciation will trigger a general massacre of the priests of Nob, with the Edomite acting as executioner as well as informer, so his appearance in our passage just before a discussion of swords and spears is also an apt piece of foreshadowing. (In all this, the writer seems to be playing on the verbal root, d'g, reflected in the Edomite's name, which means "worry.") In any case, the way the report of Do'eg in the sanctuary works in tension with its context of dialogue illustrates how narration in the biblical story is finally oriented toward dialogue.

By and large, the biblical writers prefer to avoid indirect speech. In the passage we have been considering, for example, even Saul's supposed orders to David (1 Sam. 21:3) are not presented in summary or as indirect speech but as an actual quotation imbedded in David's dialogue. The rule of thumb is that when speech is involved in a narrative event, it is presented as direct speech. If, for example, the narrator reports that "David was smitten with remorse for having cut off the corner of Saul's cloak," he does not continue, as a narrator in another tradition might, "And he told his men, God forbid that he should do such a thing to his master, God's anointed one, to raise his hand against him, for he was God's anointed one." Instead, the narrator switches to direct discourse: "God forbid that I should do this thing to my master, God's anointed one, to raise my hand against him, for he is God's anointed one" (1 Sam. 24:5–6). The difference between the two forms of presentation is not trivial, for the version the Bible actually uses has the effect of bringing the speech-act into the foreground, making us keenly conscious of David as a figure addressing his men and using language both to produce a certain effect on them and to define his relation to Saul. Indeed, though I have been careful in my hypothetical version in indirect speech to alter neither the terms of the statement nor their order, even the syntax of David's declaration is shaped by the pressures of the dramatic moment. He begins with a vow, "God forbid that I should do this thing," and then goes on to an additive series that is determined by his groping toward a cumulative effect, a climactic emphasis, quite unlike normative prose syntax for biblical narrative: "to my master, God's anointed one, to raise my hand against him, for he is God's anointed one." The form of the statement makes us feel the urgent presence of David saying: I am the king's vassal, he is my master; he is God's anointed one, the sanctity of whose election is an awesome thing to me; I will not do this thing that you and I see as an imminent possibility here and now; I will not raise this hand that you see gripping the sword-hilt against God's anointed one. The advantage gained by presenting David's address in direct speech is not only immediacy but also a certain complicating ambiguity. An avowal by David to his men reported in the third person would take on some of the authoritativeness of the reliable narrator; as things are actually presented, we find ourselves confronted with David as he makes his public statement, and, as elsewhere, we are led to ponder the different possible connections between his spoken words and his actual feelings or intentions.

The biblical preference for direct discourse is so pronounced that thought is almost invariably rendered as actual speech, that is, as quoted monologue. Attitude, of course—love, hate, fear, jealousy, and so forth—can be merely reported in a single appropriate verb because what is involved is in effect a summary of interior experience rather than a narrative realization of it. But when an actual process of contemplating specific possibilities, sorting out feelings, weighing alternatives, making resolutions, is a moment in the narrative event, it is reported as direct discourse. Here, for example, is the account of how David ponders the danger to which he is exposed because of Saul's persistently erratic behavior toward him (1 Sam. 27:1): "David said to himself, One of these days I will surely perish by the hand of Saul. There is nothing better for me than to escape without delay to Philistine country, so that Saul will despair of hunting me through all the territory of Israel and I shall escape from his hands." The formal similarity between uttered speech and unspoken thought is reinforced by the introductory formula, "David said to himself" (literally, "to his heart"), and in many other instances, the verb "to say" without any qualifier means to think, context alone instructing us as to whether we are encountering interior speech or dialogue.

It is not easy to determine in each instance why thought should be reported as speech. One is tempted to conclude that the biblical writers did not distinguish sharply between the two in their assumptions about how the mind relates to reality. Perhaps, with their strong sense of the primacy of language in the created order of things, they tended to feel that thought was not fully itself until it was articulated as speech. In any case, the repeated translation of thought into speech allows for a certain clarifying stylization, a dramatic vividness and symmetry of effect. These characteristics are observable on a modest scale even in the brief instance of David contemplating flight to Philistia. He begins his interior monologue with a quasi-temporal, quasi-attitudinal indicator of emphasis, ʿatah (King James Version, "now," but probably more with the sense of "now, look here" or "in that case"), which focuses his moment of resolution, places it contrastively at the end of that sequence of time in which he has been on the run from Saul, nearly killed by Saul, and precariously reconciled twice with the manic king. The introductory ʿatah of David's interior monologue dramatically announces the narrative turning-point that sends David away from Saul, whom he will never see again, and that sends Saul to his grim meeting with the ghost of Samuel, and then to his death. David's monologue also exhibits the thematic lucidity of symmetrically articulated speech. His statement begins with the prospect of death at the hands of Saul and concludes with the idea of escape from those same hands. The verb "escape" becomes the governing key-word of this small unit, looming in the middle of David's monologue through the Hebrew rhetorical device of emphatic statement of the infinitive before the conjugated verb (*himmalet 'immalet,* literally, "escape will I escape"), and then concluding the monologue, "I will escape from his hands." A neat antithesis, moreover, is set up in the speech between Philistine country and Israelite territory, underscoring the painful and perhaps ambiguous predicament of the future king of Israel forced to seek refuge among his people's hated enemies.

The bias of stylization in the biblical commitment to dialogue before all else is perhaps most instructively revealed by an extreme instance: the report of inquiry of an oracle as dialogue. Here is a characteristic example (2 Sam. 2:1): "Sometime afterward David inquired of the Lord as follows, 'Shall I go up to one of the towns of Judah?' And God said to him, 'Go up.' And David said, 'To which one shall I go up?' And He said, 'To Hebron.'" Now, it is not clear what particular method of consulting an oracle David used, but the common ones—drawing lots, divining through the gems set in the priestly breastplate—were not verbal, and since David is nowhere presented as a seer vouchsafed direct communication from God, there is no reason to assume that an actual dialogue took place as it seems to be reported. (We might recall that even when God wants to convey to David the divine judgment that not he but his son will build God a house in Jerusalem, He does not address David directly but conveys His detailed message through Nathan the prophet in a dream-vision.) In the case of David's inquiry of the oracle, then, the writer almost certainly counted on his audience's understanding that God did not in fact respond to David in this manner, that the inquiry itself was made not through speech but through some manipulation of cultic objects, and that what is reported is by no means the form but rather the gist of the inquiry. This procedure violates our own general sense of how mimesis should operate: why render an action in terms which are patently not the terms of the action itself?

The answer, I think, must be sought in what I have called the bias of stylization in the Bible's narration-through-dialogue. The mechanical agency of consulting the oracle is in the eyes of the writer a trivial matter and not worthy of narrative representation. What is important to him is human will confronted with alternatives which it may choose on its own or submit to divine determination. Articulated language provides the indispensable model for defining this rhythm of political or historical alternatives, question and response, creaturely uncertainty over against the Creator's intermittently revealed design, because in the biblical view words underlie reality. With words God called the world into being; the capacity for using language from the start set man apart from the other

creatures; in words each person reveals his distinctive nature, his willingness to enter into binding compacts with men and God, his ability to
control others, to deceive them, to feel for them, and to respond to them.
Spoken language is the substratum of everything human and divine that
transpires in the Bible, and the Hebrew tendency to transpose what is
preverbal or nonverbal into speech is finally a technique for getting at
the essence of things, for obtruding their substratum.

In a mode of narration so dominated by speech, visual elements will
necessarily be sparsely represented. And even in the exceptional cases
when a scene is conceived visually, the writer may contrive to report
what is seen through what is spoken. Modern commentators, for example,
have admired the moment when David sits at the gates of the city, await-
ing the outcome of the battle against Absalom's forces (2 Samuel 18),
and sees first one runner then a second overtaking the first, moving toward
him across the plain with the fateful news. What needs to be observed,
though, is that this remarkable dramatic "long shot" is conveyed to us
in dialogue, through two exchanges between David and the keen-sighted
lookout.

Let us return briefly to the encounter between David and Ahimelech
at the Nob sanctuary in order to see how this general principle of getting
at the essence, obtruding the substratum, is manifested in the rendering
of a narrative event as dialogue. To begin with, it is worth underlining
the obvious: that nothing is allowed to enter the scene which will detract
attention from the dialogue itself. We are not informed what David and
Ahimelech are wearing or what they look like; and we are not even
given guidance as to where or behind what Do'eg is lurking so that he
can witness the exchange between David and Ahimelech without, perhaps, being noticed by them. (Later, David will claim to have been aware
of Do'eg's presence in the sanctuary, but why then did he leave this
potential informer untouched?) The biblical scene, in other words, is conceived almost entirely as verbal intercourse, with the assumption that
what is significant about a character, at least for a particular narrative
juncture, can be manifested almost entirely in the character's speech.

I would stress that the speech reported, though dramatically convincing,
is not meant to be altogether naturalistic. We of course have no way of
knowing what ordinary spoken Hebrew was like around the turn of the
first millennium B.C.E., but there is some internal evidence here—and a
good deal more throughout biblical dialogue—that the "bias of stylization" affects the words assigned to the speakers. The symptomatic instance
in our passage is David's telling Ahimelech that he has set a rendezvous
with his men "at such and such a place." A more literally mimetic writer

would have invented a plausible place-name for the rendezvous—and we may note that later in the dialogue Ahimelech mentions a specific place-name, the Valley of Elah, as the site of Goliath's defeat. If it were the writer's intention to indicate that David is concealing the location of the supposed rendezvous from Ahimelech, he could have rendered this naturalistically as "at a place that I told them." To write instead "at such and such a place" is to weave into the texture of David's speech, with no formal indication of transition, a clear signal of authorial abstraction. What the writer seems to have in mind is David's manifest desire to fabricate a story that will allay Ahimelech's suspicions and enable him to get what he wants from the priest. For this purpose, the stylized unspecificity of "such and such"—that is, Location x, which I, David, have invented to pad out my story—serves better than a mimetically faithful place-name.

Stylization, in any case, is present from the very beginning of the dialogue in Ahimelech's first words to David. Narration and especially dialogue in the Bible shift into the formal symmetry of near-verse and actual verse more often than has been generally noticed by readers and even by scholarly specialists. Ahimelech's initial question to David is cast in a perfectly scannable line of Hebrew verse, three beats in each hemistich, with the requisite semantic parallelism of biblical poetry in its paradigmatic form: "Why are you alone, / and no one is with you?" Perhaps the formality of this opening was deemed appropriate for Ahimelech because it reveals him at once as a man speaking *ex cathedra*, out of a sense of the weight and dignity of his priestly authority. At the same time, the repetition, normative for verse, may suggest in the flow of prose dialogue a certain slowness or obtuseness on the part of Ahimelech, the consequences of which will be lethal for him. The priest exhibits a definite tendency to almost leisurely restatement of the obvious: "I have no ordinary bread at hand, but consecrated bread there is," and toward the end of the dialogue, "If you will take it, take it, for there is no other beside it here." David's speech, on the other hand, has something of the breathlessness and lack of shape of words spoken in a moment of urgency. The repetitive elements on his side of the dialogue suggest a speaker groping for an object, and do not reflect the formal symmetry of verse: "Now then, what do you have at hand? Five loaves of bread? Give it to me, or whatever there is." That pattern of dramatically plausible repetition is still more evident as David edges toward the crucial request for a weapon: "Don't you have at hand here a spear or sword? For I have taken with me neither my sword nor my weapons because the king's mission was urgent." David's last words in the dialogue—only four in number in the Hebrew—do move from this sort of syntactic sprawl to succinct symmetry: "There's none like it; give it to me." But the statement is too short to be scannable as a line of verse like Ahimelech's at the beginning. What it perfectly crystalizes at the end of the scene are the qualities of impatience and driving insistence that have characterized David's words throughout the encounter, joined now as he departs from Nob with a note of iron resolution.

The dialogue, then, oscillating between the poles of formal stylization and dramatic mimesis, reveals individual character caught in the fullness of portentous action. The whole episode, of course, could have been reported as narrative summary in a single verse, but by rendering it through dialogue as a proper narrative event, the writer is able to trace the fateful intersection of two disparate human types: the young David, cunning for the purposes of his own survival, tense with the consciousness of the dangers pursuing him, more imperious than entreating, prepared if necessary to be ruthless; and the aging priest (we learn later that he already has a grown son), baffled by this unexpected irruption into the sanctuary, perhaps a little slow and formal, hardly able to glimpse the terrible destiny that is about to overtake him.

A general biblical principle for differentiating character in dialogue is at work through all of this. Where literary convention requires writers to make all their characters follow in their speech the decorum of normative literary Hebrew, allowing only the most fragmentary and oblique indications of a personal language, of individual tics and linguistic peculiarities, differentiation is brought out chiefly through contrast. The technique of contrastive dialogue is all the more feasible because the fixed practice of biblical narrative, with only a few rather marginal exceptions, limits scenes to two characters at a time—or sometimes, to the exchange between one character and a group speaking in a single voice as a collective interlocutor. The characterizing lineaments of David's use of language become more evident because they are juxtaposed with Ahimelech's rather different manner of speech, and vice versa.

Again and again the ancient Hebrew writers exploit the revelatory possibilities of this technique of contrastive dialogue. We may note a few familiar examples: Esau's inarticulate outbursts over against Jacob's calculated legalisms in the selling of the birthright (Gen. 25); Joseph's long-winded statement of morally aghast refusal over against the two-word sexual bluntness of Potiphar's wife (Gen. 39); Saul's choked cry after David's impassioned speech outside the cave at Ein Gedi (1 Sam. 24). As the last two instances may suggest, one of the most common devices of contrastive dialogue is to juxtapose some form of very brief statement with some form of verbosity. It will be seen that no particular thematic meaning is attached to either length or brevity: everything depends on the two characters in question, the way their statements are articulated, the situation in which they encounter each other. The brevity of the sexual proposition on the part of Potiphar's wife is a brilliant stylization— for as Thomas Mann was to observe at great length, she *must* have said more than that!—of the naked lust that impels her, and perhaps also of the peremptory tone she feels she can assume toward her Hebrew slave. The brevity of Saul's "Is it your voice, David, my son?" reflects a character overwhelmed with feeling, forced to pull up short in the midst of his mad pursuit and to return to the point of origin of his bond with David.

Let me mention briefly four other examples of the technique of contrastive dialogue in order to indicate its range of expressive possibilities. In 1 Kings 18, Elijah, who has been pursued by Ahab, is met on the road by Obadiah, Ahab's majordomo, who has secretly saved a hundred prophets of the Lord from Jezebel's wrath. Elijah bids Obadiah to tell the king that he is there. The majordomo reacts with a relatively lengthy speech (1 Kings 18:9–14) full of repetitions in which his words seem to stumble all over each other as he expresses his horror at the risk involved for him in announcing to the king the presence of his mortal enemy Elijah. Elijah's response to all this terrified verbal commotion is a succinct statement of inexorable purpose: "By the Lord of Hosts whom I have served, today I will appear before him (1 Kings 18:15). The contrastive form of the dialogue, which has a certain element of grim comedy, dramatizes the profound difference in character between the two speakers: the one, a God-fearing person who has taken certain chances because of his conscience but who is, after all, an ordinary man with understandable human fears and hesitations; the other, a fiercely uncompromising agent of God's purpose, impelled by the imperative sense of his own prophetic authority.

The dialogue in the story of Amnon and Tamar (2 Samuel 13) looks like a conscious allusion to the technique used in the episode of Joseph and Potiphar's wife. Amnon addresses to his half-sister exactly the same words with which Potiphar's wife accosts Joseph—"lie with me"—adding to them only one word, the thematically loaded "sister" (2 Sam. 13:11). She responds with an elaborate protestation, like Joseph before her; in Tamar's case, the relatively lengthy reply is a kind of panicked catalogue of reasons for Amnon to desist, a desperate attempt at persuasion. No further dialogue is assigned to Amnon; he now speaks only through action—the rape. Then, after he has taken her by force, he addresses to her just two final words: *qumi lekhi,* "Get out!" (2 Sam. 13:15).

Two opposite instances in which length and brevity are correlated with rhetorical calculation and directness respectively occur in the frame-story of Job (Job 1–2) and in the episode of the contradictory counsels given to Absalom (2 Samuel 17). God's first words in Job, addressed to the Adversary, are almost brusque—"Where are you coming from?" (Job 1:7)—and He employs devices of symmetrical repetition only when He is echoing verbatim the narrator's initial characterization of Job. The Adversary, on the other hand, in his relatively longer speeches, shows a fondness for verse-insets, clever citation of folk-sayings, argumentative positioning of syntactical members for the most persuasive effect. In short, as befits a prosecuting attorney, he is a master of conscious rhetoric, alongside of whom God seems plainspoken.

In the story of Absalom's rebellion, Ahitophel's militarily correct advice takes about forty words in the Hebrew. It consists mainly of a chain of jussive verbs—"let me pick men . . . let me set out . . . let me pursue David tonight" (2 Sam. 17:1)—which perfectly expresses both the content and the mood of Ahitophel's counsel. There is not a moment to lose, the only course is to hit David hard before he can regroup his forces, and the statement itself has no time for fancy rhetorical maneuvers. By contrast, Hushai's counsel is three and a half times as long, and makes itself felt at virtually every point as a brilliant rhetorical contrivance, abounding in persuasive similes (in biblical narrative it is almost always the characters, not the narrator, who introduce figurative language), some of which reverberate with earlier moments in the David story; and Absalom's response to the military possibilities that Hushai calls forth is nicely controlled from phrase to phrase by the speaker's subtle choice of specific terms.[3] This cunning rhetoric will destroy Absalom, so the contrastive dialogue to begin with juxtaposes a plainspoken Ahitophel, succinctly telling the truth, with a devious Hushai. But rhetoric is not necessarily evil in the Bible, and the contrastive technique takes a dialectical turn here, for Absalom is, after all, a usurper, and Hushai, bravely loyal to David, is using his ability to deceive through words in order to restore the rightful king to his throne.

From all I have said about the primacy of dialogue, several general rules suggest themselves for the alert reading of biblical narrative. In any given narrative event, and especially, at the beginning of any new story, the point at which dialogue first emerges will be worthy of special attention, and in most instances, the initial words spoken by a personage will be revelatory, perhaps more in manner than in matter, constituting an important moment in the exposition of character. The obverse of this

---

[3] The artfulness of Hushai's speech has been illuminated in an admirable analysis by Shimon Bar-Efrat, in *The Art of the Biblical Story*, pp. 32–43.

necessity to watch for the when and how of the beginning of dialogue is equally interesting: in a narrative tradition where dialogue is preponderant, it may often prove instructive to ask why the writer has decided to use narration instead of dialogue for a particular block of material or even for a particular brief moment in a scene. A quick review of the main functions served by narration in the Bible will give us a better sense of the special rhythm with which the Hebrew writers tell their tales: beginning with narration, they move into dialogue, drawing back momentarily or at length to narrate again, but always centering on the sharply salient verbal intercourse of the characters, who act upon one another, discover themselves, affirm or expose their relation to God, through the force of language.

Perhaps the most general use to which narration is put is to provide a chronicle—as a rule, a summarizing overview rather than a scenic representation—of public events. Extended sections of the Books of Kings, for example, are devoted to more or less uninterrupted narration because they are intended to chronicle wars and political intrigues, national cultic trespasses and their supposed historical consequences. The fictional imagination, which creates individualized personages grappling with one another and with circumstances to realize their destinies, is dilute in these passages.

More interesting are the occasions when a relatively brief segment of chronicle is made a significant compositional element in the historicized fiction. Chapters 10 and 11 of 2 Samuel provide an instructive instance of such contrastive composition. Chapter 10 is an account of Israel's war with the Ammonites and their Aramean allies. In the first half of the chapter, which begins with the diplomatic incident that triggered the hostilities and ends with Joab's exhortation to the Israelite troops before the first battle, narration is interspersed with dialogue. The second half of the chapter, which covers Joab's initial victory, his return to Jerusalem, the political-military maneuvers of the eastern alliance against Israel, and a successful Israelite expedition into the territory of its assembled enemies, is uninterrupted narration. The disproportion in this second half of the chapter between narrated time and narrating time is striking: the complicated actions of many months are reported in a few verses, allowing for no proper narrative events. A battle won, for example, is conveyed through the following generalized summary: "Joab and the troops with him went out to battle against the Arameans, who fled before him" (2 Sam. 10:13).

But what immediately follows this military chronicle in Chapter 10 is the story of David and Bathsheba in Chapter 11. That memorable tale, dense with moral and psychological meanings and possibilities of meaning, begins by informing us of the siege Joab has laid against the Ammonite capital of Rabbah. The opening verse of 2 Samuel 11—"And it happened at the turn of the year, the time when kings go out to do battle . . ."—is a brilliant transitional device. It firmly ties in the story of David as adulterer and murderer with the large national-historical perspective of the preceding chronicle. As the narrative viewpoint moves into a close-up on David, we are reminded (as several commentators on this chapter have aptly noted) that while the king of Israel is home enjoying his siesta and then represented peeping at a bathing beauty on a neighboring roof, the fighting men of Israel—who in the past, including the last campaign just reported in Chapter 10, were commanded personally by their monarch—are out on the dusty plains of Ammon, risking their lives to protect the national interest.

In the first few verses of Chapter 11, narration still predominates, though it is a narration more closely focused on particular actions: David pacing up and down on his roof-balcony, Bathsheba bathing on hers, David sending go-betweens first to find out about this lovely woman and then to bring her to his bed. At this point, in a characteristic biblical time-jump through summary from an action to its significant consequence, we move from David's lying with Bathsheba to her pregnancy. From this juncture—the end of verse 6, when Bathsheba sends the king a two-word message, "I'm pregnant"—to the conclusion of the story, narration-through-dialogue will predominate. This main part of the story is in fact one of the richest and most intricate examples in the Bible of how ambiguities are set up by what is said and left unsaid in dialogue, of how characters reveal themselves through what they repeat, report, or distort of the speech of others. The preceding chapter of summarizing narration may be in part a kind of textural contrast to all this, a change in narrative pace before this immensely complex rendering through direct discourse of a sequence of events from which will flow all the subsequent disasters that befall David's court. More significantly, however, the long view of the chronicle in Chapter 10 provides a context of meaning for the story that follows: the king's intimate moral biography, we are reminded from the outset, cannot be devoid of political and historical ramifications.

The considerations that determine the use of narration on a smaller scale, in the midst of a presentation of narrative events dominated by dialogue, are more varied. It would be tedious to attempt an exhaustive catalogue of these considerations, but it may help us to understand the dynamics of biblical narrative more clearly if we note that there are three general kinds of function served by the narration that is woven through or around dialogue. These are: the conveying of actions essential to the unfolding of the plot (other sorts of action are hardly ever reported) which could not be easily or adequately indicated in dialogue; the communication of data ancillary to the plot, often not strictly part of it because actions are not involved (data, in other words, essentially expository in nature); the verbatim mirroring, confirming, subverting, or focusing in narration of statements made in direct discourse by the characters (what I have referred to as dialogue-bound narration). Some brief examples will show how these different possibilities actually work in the text. I shall begin with dialogue-bound narration because we have already had occasion to observe one instance of it in the episode at the Nob sanctuary.

When there is no divergence between a statement as it occurs in narration and as it recurs in dialogue, or vice versa, the repetition generally has the effect of giving a weight of emphasis to the specific terms which the speaker chooses for his speech. When Asahel, Joab's younger brother whose fleetness will bring about his ruin, goes after the experienced warrior Abner on the battlefield (2 Sam. 2:19–21), the narrator reports, "He swerved neither to the right nor to the left in his pursuit of Abner." A moment later, the fleeing Abner recognizes Asahel and calls out, "Swerve to the right or to the left and seize one of the young men for yourself." Now, the fact of pursuit is what I have called an action essential to the plot and probably could not have been conveyed in dialogue without some awkwardness. The entire clause, however, about swerving neither right nor left is not, by the standard of biblical narrative economy, strictly necessary; and I would contend that it is there because it is bound to the bit of dialogue that immediately follows. That is, the verbal anticipation in narration of Abner's statement makes us feel the full dramatic urgency of his plea to the rash Asahel in the specific terms he has chosen for it. Here you are—his weighted words imply—in inexorable pursuit; you will have abundant opportunity for glory if you will just turn to one side or the other; but if you insist on following this terrible beeline after me, it will lead you only to death. The common idiom of swerving neither right nor left is thus converted through the repetition into a concrete image of the geometry of survival.

Even more frequently, dialogue-bound narration sets up a small but significant dissonance between the objective report and the terms in which the character restates the facts. When Naboth is stoned to death through Jezebel's instigation (1 Kings 21:13–15), the essential narrative facts are reiterated in the following sequence: First, the narrator reports, "They took him outside the town and stoned him and he died." In the next verse, the royal retainers succinctly transmit this as a message to Jezebel,

"Naboth has been stoned and is dead." Jezebel triumphantly announces the news to Ahab, prefacing it by telling him that he can at last hasten to take possession of the coveted vineyard, but in her version the formula is changed into "Naboth is not alive but dead." The little tautology may be to reassure her hesitant husband that Naboth is in fact now out of the way or perhaps to postpone for a moment the blunt monosyllable "dead" (met). What Jezebel of course omits strategically from her report is the ugly fact of the manner of death—by stoning as the verdict of a trial she has trumped up against Naboth. The dialogue-bound anticipation, then, helps to underline a note of characterization.[4]

There is another category of dialogue-bound narration that does not involve verbatim mirroring of dialogue: it is the report of the fact that speech has occurred. The simplest and most ubiquitous instance of this category is the formulaic phrases that introduce the direct discourse of each speaker in a dialogue—"and he said," "and he answered and said"—although, even with so mechanical a convention, a forewarned reader might consider whether the formulas shift at all in accordance with the kind of statement or response that the speaker goes on to make.

Summary of speech rather than actual quotation of it is fairly common, even if quotation, as we have seen, is the more general rule. Again, I think it is often useful to ask why at a particular narrative juncture the writer has chosen to diverge from the norm of dialogue and to summarize instead. The reasons for such divergence, depending on the narrative moment, would range from a felt need for rapid movement at a particular point in the narration, a desire to avoid excessive repetition (a writer who has contrived to have something repeated three times may want to resist the fourth time), some consideration of concealment or decorousness, or a devaluation of what is said.

Thus, as soon as the young shepherd David arrives in the Israelite camp with supplementary rations from home for his big brothers (1 Sam. 17:23), the narrator tells us, with no direct discourse preceding this statement, *"He was speaking with them* when, look, the champion came out, Goliath the Philistine of Gath by name, *and spoke the same words as before,* and David heard him." There are two reports of unquoted speech here, one at the beginning and the other at the end of the verse. In the first instance, the writer is clearly not concerned with any incidental chitchat between David and his brothers during their reunion. A moment later, when David inveighs against this insulting Philistine, we shall be given the actual dialogue between David and his oldest brother Eliab (verses 28–29) be-

---

4 More elaborate instances of such uses of divergent repetition will be considered in chapter 5.

cause it will vividly dramatize the impatience of the grown man with the impertinent kid brother, and that opposition is thematically relevant to the whole episode of David's unforeseen debut. In David's initial meeting with his brothers, however, only the mere fact of speaking is important for the story, not what is said. Goliath's previously cited words of provocation, on the other hand, are alluded to and not quoted here probably because the author felt that once was quite enough to assault our (Israelite) ears with such blasphemous abuse; and in any case, for the moment it is necessary to keep the narrative focus firmly on David among the Israelite soldiers, advancing toward that moment when he will make his unheard-of proposal to go out and fight the enormous Philistine himself.

Finally, the complement to such reports of the fact of speech or summaries of the content of speech is, rather less frequently, the narrator's informing us that a character has refrained from speech where we might have expected some utterance. The more common biblical practice, as we shall have occasion to see elsewhere, is simply to cut off one speaker in a dialogue without comment, leaving us to ponder the reasons for the interrupted exchange. When someone's silence is actually isolated for narration, we may infer that the refusal or avoidance of speech is itself a significant link in the concatenation of the plot. After Abner, the commander-in-chief of the house of Saul, has angrily rebuked Ish-bosheth, Saul's heir, the narrator takes pains to inform us, "And he could no longer answer a word to Abner because of his fear of him" (2 Sam. 3:11). This silence with its explanation is politically portentous, for it demonstrates the unfitness of the pusillanimous Ish-bosheth to reign, which will give Abner cause to turn from him to David, and so it is deemed worthy of narration. Still more strikingly, the silence of both David and Absalom after Amnon's rape of Tamar is singled out for narrative report (2 Sam. 13:21–22). For the king, the failure to speak is a sign of domestic and political impotence, leading directly to the calamities that will assail his household and his reign from this point onward. For Absalom, the refusal to say anything—to the perpetrator of the sexual crime, the narrator specifies—is ominous in an opposite way because it clearly betokens a grim resolution to act in due time, and will ultimately issue in murder and rebellion.

Of the two other general categories of reasons for narration in the Bible, the report of essential narrative data is self-evident. There are virtually no "free motifs"[5] in biblical narrative. The ancient Hebrew writer

[5] The distinction between free motifs and bound motifs—that is, details which cannot be deleted without essentially altering the plot—was first proposed by Boris Tomashevsky, "Thematics," *Russian Formalist Criticism,* ed. L. T. Lemon and M. J. Reis (Lincoln, Neb., 1965), pp. 66–95.

will never tell us, say, that a character lazily stretched both arms, simply out of an author's sheer mimetic pleasure in rendering a familiar human gesture; but he does report that the dying Jacob crossed his hands when he reached out to bless Joseph's two sons, because that is a gesture fraught with significance in effecting a transfer of privilege (the blessing of the right hand) from the elder to the younger son. Whatever is reported, then, can be assumed to be essential to the story, but sometimes special clues are provided in the tempo with which actions are conveyed. Verbs tend to dominate this biblical narration of the essential, and at intervals we encounter sudden dense concentrations or unbroken chains of verbs, usually attached to a single subject, which indicate some particular intensity, rapidity, or single-minded purposefulness of activity (Rebekah making the preparations for the deception of Isaac, David finishing off Goliath in battle).

The remaining general function of narration is for conveying what I have proposed we think of as expository information. The paradigmatic biblical story—compare, for example, the beginning of Ruth, the beginning of Job, the beginning of Samuel, the beginning of the Saul narrative in 1 Samuel 9, the beginning of the parable of the poor man's ewe in 2 Samuel 12—starts with a few brief statements that name the principal character or characters, locate them geographically, identify significant family relationships, and in some instances provide a succinct moral, social, or physical characterization of the protagonist. It should be noted that this initial exposition is as a rule devoid of verbs except for the verb "to be," which, as I have observed, often does not even appear textually. The opening exposition, then, is pretemporal, statically enumerating data that are not bound to a specific moment in time: they are facts that stand before the time of the story proper.

In many versions, these pretemporal verses are followed by a transitional segment in which true verbs are introduced; but, according to the indication of the adverbial phrases accompanying them (otherwise biblical verb tenses are ambiguous), these verbs must be construed as either iterative or habitual. This means that after an actionless beginning, events begin to happen, but only repeatedly, as a background of customarily patterned behavior to the real plot. Finally, the narration moves into the report of actions occurring in sequence at specific points in time (what Gérard Genette calls the "singulative" as against the iterative sense)[6] and from that point, of course, it generally moves on to dialogue.

Smaller pieces of exposition are withheld to be revealed at some appro-

[6] *Figures III* (Paris, 1972), p. 146.

priate moment in the midst of the tale. Rachel's beauty is not mentioned when she first appears but only just before we are told of Jacob's love for her. Such explicit reports of attitude—which usually occur in the simple form of x loved y, hated, feared, revered, had compassion for y, or in nonrelational statements like x was distressed, x rejoiced—I would regard as essentially expository assertions. That is, they do not convey to us actions but inner conditions that color the actions, affect them, explain them. In a novel, to be sure, one might well object to such a distinction, for what characters feel is often chiefly what happens—witness Virginia Woolf or the late Henry James—but I think the distinction holds by and large for biblical narrative, with its steady adherence to acts performed and words pronounced.

An analogous use of physical detail for exposition in the midst of narration occurs in the second of the two distinct versions of David's debut (1 Sam. 17:42), where David's ruddiness (or red hair, it is not certain which the word means) and his good looks are not mentioned until the moment Goliath lays eyes on him in the middle of the battlefield. At such a moment, of course, those facts of appearance can be made to leap out at the Philistine, as an added insult before the unexpected injury. A mere boy, and an egregiously redheaded, pretty boy at that (this is precisely the order of the original syntax, arranged to mimic Goliath's perceptions), has been sent to do battle with the mightiest Philistine warrior. Full-scale descriptions almost never occur, Goliath himself being one of the few marginal exceptions. In his case, we get four verses (1 Sam. 17:4–7) at the beginning of the episode cataloguing his armor, his weapons, and the exact measure and weight of the man and his implements. The thematic purpose of this exceptional attention to physical detail is obvious: Goliath moves into the action as a man of iron and bronze, an almost grotesquely quantitative embodiment of a hero, and this hulking monument to an obtusely mechanical conception of what constitutes power is marked to be felled by a clever shepherd boy with his slingshot.

To pull together this overview of the various modes of narrative presentation in the Bible, let us follow the nicely controlled sequence and interplay of exposition, narration proper, and dialogue at the beginning of one complex story: the birth of Samuel (1 Samuel 1).[7]

[7] My understanding of the finely regulated exposition in this chapter owes much to an astute seminar paper on the Hannah story by my student Chana Kronfeld. Ms. Kronfeld also considers in detail the function of type-scene here, though with a different emphasis from the one I shall propose.

1. Once there was a certain man from Ramathaim-Zofim in the hill country of Ephraim, named Elkanah son of Yeruham son of Elihu son of Tohu son of Zuf the Ephraimite. 2. He had two wives, one named Hannah and the other named Peninah. And Peninah had children but Hannah had no children.

The story opens with a clear-cut version of pretemporal exposition, identifying the protagonist, her husband, her co-wife, their hometown, and the genealogical line of the husband. The only verb here is "to be," the concept of "to have" in the Hebrew being expressed by the idiom, "to be unto. . . ." For a moment, it may appear as though Elkanah will be the protagonist—the patriarchal convention of biblical literature requires that the opening formula be "there was a man," not a woman, and that the male be the point of reference for defining relations. But the story of Hannah about to be told is, if anything, a matriarchal story, and that particular direction is signaled as early as verse 2, which invokes the background of an eminently matriarchal biblical type-scene: the annunciation of the birth of the hero to the barren wife (whose predicament may be highlighted, as in the case of Sarah and Hagar, Rachel and Leah, or here, by juxtaposition with a less-loved but fertile co-wife). The pretemporal exposition thus succinctly completed, the narration continues (verse 3) with a transitional statement in the iterative tense: "This man used to go up from his town every year to worship and to sacrifice to the Lord of Hosts at Shiloh, and Hophni and Phineas, the two sons of Eli, were priests of the Lord there." With this indication of habitual activity, which also introduces the two corrupt priests who will be challenged by the future Samuel, it would seem that the exposition is over and that the main plot will now be taken up, for the next verses begin with what looks like the notation of a specific moment in time:

4. One such day, Elkanah offered a sacrifice, and to Peninah his wife, to all her sons and daughters, he gave portions. 5. But to Hannah he gave [a special portion], for he loved Hannah, though God had closed her womb. 6. And her rival would vex her bitterly, taunting her that the Lord had closed her womb. 7. And thus would it happen from one year to the next, when she came up to the house of the Lord, thus would the other vex her and she would cry and would not eat. 8. And Elkanah her husband would say to her, "Hannah, why do you cry, and why do you not eat, and why are you distressed? Am I not better to you than ten sons?"

The "one such day"—the same formula, for example, introduces the scene in the celestial court in the Job frame-story—makes us think that the story proper has begun, but verse 7 clearly announces that the little drama of the sacrificial portions and the confrontation of co-wives was habitually enacted, from one year to the next. This places the action reported in these verses in what one might call a pseudo-singulative tense. Momentarily, that is, we might have assumed that the barren Hannah's ordeal by taunting took place just once, but then it becomes evident, alas, that she has to suffer this torment year after year. Perhaps the presentation in summary of the clash of the co-wives, so eminently the stuff of dialogue, is dictated by its status as a recurrent event. In any case, Elkanah's touching effort to console his beloved wife, though also a periodically repeated action, is given the emphasis of direct quotation as a climactic conclusion of the exposition—perhaps as a way of fully dramatizing Elkanah's tender devotion to Hannah before he must be moved off the scene to make way for Eli the priest, according to the requirements of the convention of dialogue that allows the interchange of only two characters at a time. It should be noted that Hannah is not assigned any response to this iterative plea of her husband's. Throughout the exposition she remains a silent, suffering figure, addressed for evil and good by Peninah and Elkanah respectively; when she herself finally speaks, it will be first to God, a formal mark of her dignity and her destiny. With no further setting of the concrete scene, the narrative now moves on to the main action:

9. Hannah arose after the eating[8] and drinking at Shiloh, with Eli the priest sitting on the seat by the doorpost of the house of the Lord. 10. Sorely embittered, she prayed to the Lord, weeping all the while. 11. And she made a vow and said, "Lord of Hosts, if You will truly look upon the affliction of Your maidservant and remember me and not forget your maidservant and give your maidservant male seed, I shall give him to the Lord all the days of his life, and no razor will touch his head." 12. And as she went on praying to the Lord, Eli was watching her mouth. 13. Hannah was speaking in her heart, only her lips moving, her voice inaudible, and Eli thought she was drunk. 14. Eli said to her, "How long will you be drunk? Put away your wine!" 15. And Hannah answered and said, "No, my lord, I am a miserable woman. Neither wine nor liquor have I drunk; I am pouring

[8] I vocalize "eating" differently than does the Masoretic text, which seems to make Hannah the subject, something contradicted by the indication that she is breaking a fast in verse 18.

out my heart to the Lord. 16. Do not take your maidservant for a woman of no account; it is only out of my great distress and vexation that I have been speaking all along." 17. And Eli answered and said, "Go in peace, and may the God of Israel grant the request you asked of Him." 18. And she said, "May your handmaiden find favor in your eyes." And the woman went on her way and ate, and was no longer downcast. 19. They rose early the next morning, did obeisance to the Lord, and returned to their home in Ramah. And Elkanah knew Hannah his wife and the Lord remembered her.

The eating and drinking after the annual or seasonal sacrifice, a joyous occasion in which, as we have seen, the anguished Hannah was repeatedly unwilling to join, serve as a cross-stitch binding the exposition to the main narrative. Or to invoke another simile of connection, the sacrificial feast works like a *faux raccord* between two scenes in a film: first we see the yearly feast and a weeping Hannah's refusal of food in a habitual time-scheme as part of Elkanah's iterative dialogue; then, one such feast has just been completed by the family, and a tearful, fasting Hannah is now seen alone at a particular moment in time—the moment she will make her entrance into history—praying to the Lord. The writer takes only two verses, one to locate Hannah and Eli temporally and spatially, the other to characterize her as embittered and still weeping, before he plunges into Hannah's direct discourse, in which her character and destiny will be most vividly revealed. Her story begins, then, with one-sided dialogue (there are of course many biblical instances in which there is two-sided dialogue between a human being and God) which is overseen rather than overheard by a second character. Hannah's prayer is meant to seem direct and artless. Poetic symmetries of statement are avoided; she strings out a series of overlapping verbs—see, remember, don't forget, give—that provide an anxious, cumulative statement of her urgent plea. The only evident "device" in the language of the prayer is the almost naive reversed *do ut des* formulation: "if You . . . *give* your maidservant male seed, I shall *give* him to the Lord." The meaning of this vow is then made explicit by the use of the formulaic expression for Nazirites, "no razor will touch his head." All in all, it is just the sort of prayer that a simple, sincere country wife, desperate in her barrenness, would utter.

The ensuing dialogue between Hannah and Eli exploits the principle of character differentiation through contrast that we have observed in other passages. After Hannah's naive speech, Eli expresses his mistaken rebuke in verse-like parallelism which in its formality resembles the beginning of a prophetic denunciation: "How long will you be drunk? / Put away your wine!" (This is, we might note, the second priest we have encountered who launches a dialogue with an obtuse statement couched in metrically regular form.) Hannah's response is respectful, as befits a simple Ephraimite woman addressing a priest, while her speech extends the syntactic pattern of stringing together brief direct statements that we observed in her prayer. Eli is immediately persuaded by the straightforwardness of her confession, and in a much gentler tone he prays that God grant her wish (it is also possible to construe his words grammatically as a *prediction* that God will grant her wish). Hannah concludes the dialogue with a reverential formula, "May your handmaiden find favor in your eyes" (the new Jewish Publication Society translation renders this less literally as: "You are most kind to your handmaid."). What follows, according to the urgent purposefulness of biblical narrative tempo, is: eating (a token of Hannah's inward reconciliation), departure, sexual intercourse, conception (God's "remembering" Hannah), and, in the subsequent verse, the birth of Samuel. The rising and the return to the place of origin formally mark the end of the narrative segment.

This entire interweaving of exposition, narration proper, and dialogue is executed within a frame of expectations set up by the annunciation type-scene, and the role of that particular convention ought to be mentioned in order to round out our sense of the artistry of the episode. The very use of the convention, of course, points to a weighty role in history for the child who is to be born, since only for such portentous figures is this sort of divine intervention in the natural order of conception required. (The story of the child born to the Shunamite woman in 2 Kings 4 is the sole exception; there the annunciation type-scene clearly occurs but the child remains anonymous and without a momentous future.) The initial elements of the type-scene, as we have noted, follow the fixed pattern: the strife between wives, the husband's special affection for the barren wife. Now, the crucial central motif in the annunciation type-scene is the barren wife's being vouchsafed an oracle, a prophecy from a man of God, or a promise from an angel, that she will be granted a son, sometimes with an explicit indication of the son's destiny, often with the invocation of the formula, "At this season next year, you will be embracing a son."

What is interesting about Hannah's annunciation, when it is compared with other occurrences of this particular type-scene, is the odd obliquity of the promise. We hear the words of Hannah's prayer but no immediate response from God. The barren mother's bitterness is given unusual prominence in this version—perhaps, one might conjecture, because it is a thematically apt introduction to the birth of a lonely leader whose ultimate authority the people will finally circumvent to establish the monarchy against which he warns.

The particular form taken here by the annunciation is virtually ironic. Eli the priest, who at first grossly misconstrued what Hannah was doing, prays for or perhaps promises the fulfillment of her prayer, and whatever his purpose, it appears to be sufficient to make Hannah feel reconciled with her present condition. If his statement is meant as a consoling prediction, he is a singularly ignorant conduit of divine intentions, for Hannah has not even told him what it was she was praying for, only that she was pleading to God in great anguish. The effect of all this is to subvert the priest's role as intercessor. The generalized petition/prediction he pronounces to her is really superfluous, for it is her specifically worded heartfelt supplication for a son that God answers through the fact of conception. Compared to the angels and men of God who deliver the good news in other annunciation type-scenes, the priest here plays a peripheral and perhaps slightly foolish role. This oblique undermining of Eli's authority is of course essentially relevant to the story of Samuel: the house of Eli will be cut off, his iniquitous sons will be replaced in the sanctuary by Samuel himself, and it will be Samuel, not his master Eli, who will hear the voice of God distinctly addressing him in the sanctuary. The idea of revelation, in other words, is paramount to the story of Samuel, whose authority will derive neither from cultic function, like the priests before him, nor from military power, like the judges before him and the kings after him, but from prophetic experience, from an immediate, morally directive call from God. For this exemplary figure of prophetic leadership, Hannah's silent, private prayer and the obtuseness of the well-meaning priest who superfluously offers himself as intercessor between her and God provide just the right kind of annunciation.

The key to these concerted means for the rendering of a narrative event in the Bible is the writer's desire to give each fictional situation, with minimal authorial intrusion, a marked thematic direction as well as moral-psychological depth. On the restricted scale of their highly laconic narratives, the ancient Hebrew authors contrived to achieve something resembling Flaubert's aspiration in his seminal art-novel to "achieve dramatic effect simply by the interweaving of dialogue and by contrasts of character."[9] In Flaubert's case, the ideal of authorial impassivity, the desire to be everywhere present but always invisible in the work, stems from a dream of godlike omnipotence; from a horror of being personally contaminated by the distasteful human reality of the represented world;

[9] Letter to Louise Colet, October 12, 1853.

and from the need to escape the effusiveness that had vitiated so much European literature of the previous half-century. In biblical narrative, impassivity would seem by contrast to flow from an intuitive sense of the theologically appropriate means for the representation of human lives under the overarching dominion of an ultimately unknowable but ethical God.

Every human agent must be allowed the freedom to struggle with his destiny through his own words and acts. Formally, this means that the writer must permit each character to manifest or reveal himself or herself chiefly through dialogue but of course also significantly through action, without the imposition of an obtrusive apparatus of authorial interpretation and judgment. The Hebrew narrator does not openly meddle with the personages he presents, just as God creates in each human personality a fierce tangle of intentions, emotions, and calculations caught in a translucent net of language, which is left for the individual himself to sort out in the evanescence of a single lifetime.

The intersection of characters through their own words matters before all else in this narrative definition of the human predicament, but such intersection does not take place in a trackless void. We have observed how a stylizing convention like the type-scene can offer thematic clues to the road that will be taken in the larger progress of the narrative and its implicit values. Still more specific thematic indicators are provided by the fine tracery of repetitive devices that marks almost every biblical tale, and this whole process of subtle elaboration through seeming reiteration now deserves closer attention.

5

The Techniques of

Repetition

ONE OF the most imposing barriers that stands between the modern reader and the imaginative subtlety of biblical narrative is the extraordinary prominence of verbatim repetition in the Bible. Accustomed as we are to modes of narration in which elements of repetition are made to seem far less obtrusive, this habit of constantly restating material is bound to give us trouble, especially in a narrative that otherwise adheres so evidently to the strictest economy of means. Repetition is, I would guess, the feature of biblical narrative that looks most "primitive" to the casual modern eye, reflecting, we may imagine, a mentality alien to our own and a radically different approach to ordering experience from the ones familiar to us.

In the more leisurely, simpler life-rhythms of the ancient Near East, so it would seem, every instruction, every prediction, every reported action had to be repeated word for word in an inexorable literalism as it was obeyed, fulfilled, or reported to another party. Perhaps, some have impressionistically conjectured, there is an "Oriental" sense of the intrinsic pleasingness of repetition in the underlying aesthetic of the Bible. The extreme instance would be the description in Numbers 7:12–83 of the gifts brought to the sanctuary by the princes of the twelve tribes. Each tribe offers an identical set of gifts, but these have to be enumerated twelve times in an identical sequence of verses, only the names of the princes and tribes being changed. It seems safe to assume some sort of cultic-historical function for this particular group of repetitions—one can imagine the members of each tribe waiting to hear the individual items on their own ancestors' archetypal offering to the Lord—though the entire passage surely presupposes a certain delight on the part of the writer and his audience in the very mechanism of patient repetition.

Thinking in somewhat more concrete historical terms, various commentators have attributed the repetitive features of biblical narrative to its oral origins, to the background of folklore from which it draws, and to the composite nature of the text that has been transmitted to us. The last of these three explanations is the least interesting and finally accounts for the smallest number of cases. There are occasional verses repeated out of scribal error, but under scrutiny most instances of repetition prove to be quite purposeful, and this would include the repetition not only of relatively brief statements but, as I shall try to show in chapter 7, of whole episodes presumably compiled from parallel traditions.

The notion of folklore covers a little more ground, though I think it is rarely the sufficient explanation for the occurrence of repetition that its more programmatic advocates imagine it to be. One of the infrequent cases in which repetition would appear to serve a primarily folkloric function is the presence of two competing etiological tales, both of which seem to have demanded representation in the text as explanations of the same fact. Thus, to account for a current folk-saying *(mashal)*, "Is Saul, too, among the prophets?," two different stories are reported of his meeting a company of prophets and joining them in manic ecstasy. Samuel presides, in rather different ways, over both encounters, but the first (1 Samuel 10) occurs immediately after Saul's anointment and is part of the process of his initiation as king, stressing the descent of God's spirit on him and his becoming "another man," while the second encounter (1 Samuel 19) deflects him from his pursuit of David and stresses the fact of his rolling naked in his prophetic frenzy. One can, of course, argue for a certain purposeful pattern even in such a repetition: the same divine power that makes Saul different from himself and enables him for the kingship later strips and reduces him as the divine election shifts from Saul to David. There is, however, at least a suspicion of narrative improbability in this identical bizarre action recurring in such different contexts, and one may reasonably conclude that the pressure of competing etiologies for the enigmatic folk-saying determined the repetition more than any artful treatment of character and theme.[1]

[1] The possibility of artistic purpose even in such duplications will be considered in chapter 7.

In many instances, the background of folklore is perceptible less in the specific material repeated than in the form the repetition assumes, the structure of the tale. Again and again one finds biblical stories cast in the familiar folktale form of incident, repetition, second repetition with variation or reversal (a form we all know from fairytales like "Goldilocks and the Three Bears" or "Rumpelstiltskin"). At times this pattern is followed with schematic simplicity, and in such cases folkloric practice may well be an adequate explanation of the repetitions. Thus, in 2 Kings 1, King Ahaziah sends a captain with his company three times to Elijah. The first two times, in identical verses, fire descends from the heavens and consumes the whole military contingent. The third time, the exact repetition is interrupted just as Elijah is about to perform his incendiary trick once more, when the third captain pleads for mercy and Elijah is prompted by an angel to grant the plea. The repetitions here may have a certain cumulative force but it is hard to see how the rigid pattern of the folktale has been in any significant way transformed or subtilized. Elsewhere, as we shall have occasion to observe, the one-two-three-change structure of folktale repetition is reshaped with conscious artistry.

Finally, the oral context of biblical narrative has been invoked as a general explanation of its repetitive mode of exposition. One does not necessarily have to assume, as some scholars have plausibly proposed, that the biblical narratives derive from long-standing oral traditions; for in any case it is altogether likely that they were written chiefly for oral presentation. As several indications in the Bible itself suggest, the narratives would typically have been read out from a scroll to some sort of assembled audience (many of whom would presumably not have been literate) rather than passed around to be read in our sense. The unrolling scroll, then, was in one respect like the unrolling spool of a film projector, for time and the sequence of events presented in it could not ordinarily be halted or altered, and the only convenient way of fixing a particular action or statement for special inspection was by repeating it.

The necessities of oral delivery can be imagined in still simpler terms. If you were a Judean herdsman standing in the outer circle of listeners while the story of the Ten Plagues was being read, you might miss a few phrases when God instructs Moses about turning the Nile into blood (Exod. 7:17–18), but you could easily pick up what you had lost when the instructions were almost immediately repeated verbatim as narrated action (Exod. 7:20–21). If you were close enough to the reader to catch every word, you could still enjoy the satisfaction of hearing each individual term of God's grim prediction, first stated in the prophetic future, then restated as accomplished fact, with an occasional elegant variation of the verbatim repetition through the substitution of a synonym (in verse 18 the Egyptians are unable to drink the water, *nil'u lishtot;* in verse 21, they cannot drink, *lo'-yakhlu lishtot*). Here, as elsewhere, the solution to what one infers were the physical difficulties of delivering the story orally jibes perfectly with the vision of history that informs the story; for biblical narrative, from the beginning of Genesis to the end of Chronicles, is an account of how divine word—and in more ambiguous ways, often human word as well—becomes historical fact. The constantly reiterated pattern, then, of command or prophecy closely followed by its verbatim fulfillment confirms an underlying view of historical causality; it translates into a central narrative device the unswerving authority of a monotheistic God manifesting Himself in language.

These large implications of repetition in biblical narrative will bear further reflection, but first the complexity and variety of this seemingly mechanical device have to be grasped in detail. Writers in all times and places have made artistic occasions out of the formal limitations of their medium and of their inherited conventions, and this is demonstrably true of the biblical authors. If the requirements of oral delivery and a time-honored tradition of storytelling may have prescribed a mode of narration in which frequent verbatim repetition was expected, the authors of the biblical narratives astutely discovered how the slightest strategic variations in the pattern of repetitions could serve the purposes of commentary, analysis, foreshadowing, thematic assertion, with a wonderful combination of subtle understatement and dramatic force.

Up to this point, it may seem as though I have been assuming an absolute distinctiveness in the Bible's use of repetition. This could hardly be the case, since at least some parts of a whole spectrum of repetitive devices are bound to be present wherever there is pattern in narration, from Homer to Günter Grass. Certain characteristic biblical uses of repetition closely resemble the kinds of repetition that are familiar artistic devices in short stories and novels, dramatic and epic poems, written elsewhere and later. *King Lear* can serve as an efficient analogue because it is a work that makes spectacularly brilliant use of a wide range of repetitive devices, and these have been conveniently classified by Bruce F. Kawin in *Telling It Again and Again,*[2] a study of the narrative uses of repetition. The most obvious and general kind of repetition in *Lear* is situational rather than literal, particularly embodied in the multiple parallels of the double plot. The Bible does not employ symmetrical double plots but it constantly insists on parallels of situation and reiterations of motif that provide moral and psychological commentary on each other

---

[2] *Telling It Again and Again: Repetition in Literature and Film* (Ithaca, 1972).

(like the chain of sibling struggles, the displacement of the elder by the younger, in Genesis). Since the use of such parallels and recurrent motifs is ubiquitous in narrative literature, there is no special need here to elucidate its presence in the Bible, though it is an aspect of the biblical tale that always needs careful scrutiny.

At the other end of the spectrum of repetition in *Lear* is the reiteration of the same word in unbroken sequence (like the mad Lear's "kill, kill, kill, kill . . ." or Lear's "never, never, never, never, never" over the body of Cordelia)—what Kawin aptly describes as "a syntax of pure emphasis." This extreme possibility of repetition, where the device has a totally dramatic justification as the expression of a kind of mental stammer, is bound to be relatively rare, especially in nondramatic literature, but it does occur occasionally in the Bible, most memorably when David is informed of Absalom's death (2 Samuel 19). The poet-king, who elsewhere responds to the report of deaths with eloquent elegies, here simply sobs, "Absalom, Absalom, my son, my son," repeating "my son" eight times in two verses (2 Sam. 19:1,5).

More pervasively, one discovers in *Lear,* as in so many plays and novels, a repetition of certain key-words (like the verb "crack") that become thematic ideas through their recurrence at different junctures, carrying, as Kawin puts it, "the meanings they have acquired in earlier contexts with them into their present and future contexts, immensely complicating and interrelating the concerns and actions of the play."

This kind of word-motif, as a good many commentators have recognized, is one of the most common features of the narrative art of the Bible. But in biblical prose, the reiteration of key-words has been formalized into a prominent convention which is made to play a much more central role in the development of thematic argument than does the repetition of such key-words in other narrative traditions. Hebrew writers may have been led to evolve this convention by the very structure of the language, which with its system of triliteral roots makes the etymological nucleus of both verbs and nouns, however conjugated and declined, constantly transparent, and probably also by the idiomatic patterns of Hebrew, which tolerate a much higher degree of repetition than is common in Western languages. Martin Buber and Franz Rosenzweig, in the explanatory prefaces to their German translation of the Bible done nearly half a century ago, were the first to recognize that this kind of purposeful repetition of words constitutes a distinctive convention of biblical prose, which they called *Leitwortstil* (literally, "leading-word style"), coining *Leitwort* on the model of *Leitmotiv.* Buber's description of the phenomenon remains definitive:

A *Leitwort* is a word or a word-root that recurs significantly in a text, in a continuum of texts, or in a configuration of texts: by following these repetitions, one is able to decipher or grasp a meaning of the text, or at any rate, the meaning will be revealed more strikingly. The repetition, as we have said, need not be merely of the word itself but also of the word-root; in fact, the very difference of words can often intensify the dynamic action of the repetition. I call it "dynamic" because between combinations of sounds related to one another in this manner a kind of movement takes place: if one imagines the entire text deployed before him, one can sense waves moving back and forth between the words. The measured repetition that matches the inner rhythm of the text, or rather, that wells up from it, is one of the most powerful means for conveying meaning without expressing it.[3]

The operation of the *Leitwort,* of course, will not be so evident in translation as in the original: Buber and Rosenzweig went to extreme lengths in their German version to preserve all *Leitwörter;* unfortunately, most modern English translations go to the opposite extreme, constantly translating the same word with different English equivalents for the sake of fluency and supposed precision. Nevertheless, the repetition of key-words is so prominent in many biblical narratives that one can still follow it fairly well in translation, especially if one uses the King James Version (and in my own *ad hoc* translations throughout this study I have tried within reasonable limits to remain faithful to these patterns of repetition).

Let me for the moment cite just one relatively simple example where a repeated word in a single episode serves as the chief means of thematic exposition within the limited unit. The confrontation between Samuel and Saul over the king's failure to destroy all of the Amalekites and all of their possessions (1 Samuel 15) is woven out of a series of variations on the key terms *listen, voice, word.* Samuel begins by enjoining Saul to listen to the voice of God; when the king returns victorious from battle, the prophet is dismayed by the voice (or sound, *qol*) of sheep and the voice of cattle that he hears. Thundering denunciation in verse, he tells Saul that what the Lord wants is "Listening to the voice of God, / For to listen is better than sacrifice. / To hearken, than the fat of rams" (1 Sam. 15:22); and a contrite Saul apologizes that he has transgressed the word of the Lord and instead listened to the voice of the people (*vox populi* being here the thematic opposite of *vox dei*). In the next chapter, moreover, as the writer moves from the rejection of Saul to the election

[3] *Werker,* vol. 2, *Schriften zur Bibel* (Munich, 1964), p. 1131 (my translation). In Hebrew, *Darko shel miqra'* (Jerusalem, 1964), p. 284.

of David, he deftly changes his key-word from *listen* to *see:* after the king's failure to listen, we have the prophet's learning to see the one truly fit to be king.[4]

Word-motifs are more typically used, however, in larger narrative units, to sustain a thematic development and to establish instructive connections between seemingly disparate episodes. Michael Fishbane has convincingly argued that the entire cycle of tales about Jacob is structured through the reiteration of *Leitwörter* and themes as a series of "symmetrical framings" which "reflect a considered technique of composition." The two most decisive words for the organization of this material in Genesis are *blessing* and *birthright* (in Hebrew a pun, *berakhah* and *bekhorah*). These keywords, supported by a whole set of subsidiary word-motifs, mark the connections between thematically parallel narrative units, creating "a formal structure of inclusions and order which stand in ironic contrast to the machinations of the content."[5] Although other extended narratives may not exhibit the symmetry of structure Fishbane finds in the Jacob cycle, this significant recurrence of a few key-words over long stretches of text is equally evident elsewhere—perhaps most strikingly in the Joseph story, where the *Leitwörter* are *recognize, man, master, slave,* and *house.*

This sort of literary mechanism, at once a unifying device and a focus of development in the narrative, will be recognizable to anyone familiar with, say, Shakespeare's elaboration of the multiple implications of the word *time* in *1 Henry IV,* or with Fielding's multifariously ironic treatment of *prudence* in *Tom Jones,* or, in a more musically formal compositional deployment, Joyce's conjuring with *yes* in Molly Bloom's soliloquy.

The characteristic biblical strategy, clearest in the convention of *Leitwortstil,* is to call explicit attention to the verbal repetition; but there are also numerous instances in which repetition becomes a Jamesian "figure in the carpet," half-hidden, subliminally insistent, in the manner most congenial to modern literary sensibilities. Samson, for example, is quietly but effectively associated with a verbal and imagistic motif of fire (Judges 14–16). The various cords that fail to bind him are likened to flax dissolving in fire when he snaps them with his strength (Judg. 15:14). The thirty Philistine men threaten his first wife with death by fire if she does not obtain for them the answer to Samson's riddle (Judg. 14:15). When Samson is discarded as a husband by the action of his first father-in-law, he responds by tying torches to the tails of foxes and setting the Philistine fields on fire (Judg. 15:4–5). The immediate reaction of the Philistines is to make a roaring bonfire out of the household of Sam-

---

[4] For a discussion of this aspect of 1 Samuel 16, see chapter 7, pp. 149–150.

[5] *Text and Texture* (New York, 1979), pp. 40–62.

son's recent wife, with her and her father in the midst of the flames (Judg. 15:6). By the time we get to the captive Samson bringing down the temple of Dagon on himself and several thousand of his enemies, though there is no actual fire in this climactic scene, fire has become a metonymic image of Samson himself: a blind, uncontrolled force, leaving a terrible swath of destruction behind it, finally consuming itself together with whatever stands in its way.

What we find, then, in biblical narrative is an elaborately integrated system of repetitions, some dependent on the actual recurrence of individual phonemes, words, or short phrases, others linked instead to the actions, images, and ideas that are part of the world of the narrative we "reconstruct" as readers but that are not necessarily woven into the verbal texture of the narrative. The two kinds of repetition, of course, are somewhat different in their effect, but they are often used together by the Hebrew writers to reinforce each other and to produce a concerted whole. Let me propose a scale of repetitive structuring and focusing devices in biblical narrative running from the smallest and most unitary elements to the largest and most composite ones:

1. *Leitwort.* Through abundant repetition, the semantic range of the word-root is explored, different forms of the root are deployed, branching off at times into phonetic relatives (that is, word-play), synonymity, and antonymity; by virtue of its verbal status, the *Leitwort* refers immediately to meaning and thus to theme as well. (For example, *go* and *return* in the Book of Ruth; the verb *to see* with its poetic synonyms in the Balaam story.)

2. *Motif.* A concrete image, sensory quality, action, or object recurs through a particular narrative; it may be intermittently associated with a *Leitwort;* it has no meaning in itself without the defining context of the narrative; it may be incipiently symbolic or instead primarily a means of giving formal coherence to a narrative. (For example, fire in the Samson story; stones and the colors white and red in the Jacob story; water in the Moses cycle; dreams, prisons and pits, silver in the Joseph story.)

3. *Theme.* An idea which is part of the value-system of the narrative—it may be moral, moral-psychological, legal, political, historiosophical, theological—is made evident in some recurring pattern. It is often associated with one or more *Leitwörter* but it is not co-extensive with them; it may also be associated with a motif. (For example, the reversal of primogeniture in Genesis; obedience versus rebellion in the Wilderness stories; knowledge in the Joseph story; exile and promised land; the rejection and election of the monarch in Samuel and Kings.)

4. *Sequence of actions.* This pattern appears most commonly and most

clearly in the folktale form of three consecutive repetitions, or three plus one, with some intensification or increment from one occurrence to the next, usually concluding either in a climax or a reversal. (For example, the three captains and their companies threatened with fiery destruction in 2 Kings 1; the three catastrophes that destroy Job's possessions, followed by a fourth in which his children are killed; Balaam's failure to direct the ass three times.)

5. *Type-scene.* This is an episode occurring at a portentous moment in the career of the hero which is composed of a fixed sequence of motifs. It is often associated with certain recurrent themes; it is not bound to specific *Leitwörter,* though occasionally a recurrent term or phrase may help mark the presence of a particular type-scene. (For example, the annunciation of the birth of the hero, the betrothal by the well, the trial in the wilderness.)

It will be noted that the two ends of this schema of structuring devices, the *Leitwort* and the type-scene, reflect distinctively biblical literary conventions (though of course one can find approximate analogues in other narrative traditions), while the three middle terms, motif, theme,[6] and sequence of actions, are abundantly present in the broadest spectrum of narrative works. The uses of repetition, then, which we have been reviewing are to an appreciable degree shared by the Bible with other kinds of narrative literature. What most distinguishes repetition in biblical narrative is the explicitness and formality with which it is generally employed, qualities that, to return to our initial difficulty, support an unusual proportion of verbatim restatement. In order to appreciate the artfulness of this kind of repetition, a modern reader has to cultivate the complementary opposite of the habits of perception he most frequently puts to use in his reading. That is, in narratives where there is a great density of specified fictional data and some commitment to making the mimetic elements of style and structure more prominent than the poetic ones, repetition tends to be at least partly camouflaged, and we are expected to *detect* it, to pick it out as a subtle thread of recurrence in a variegated pattern, a flash of suggestive likeness in seeming differences. (The obvious exception to this tendency in Western literature would be extreme fictional experiments in stylization, like those of Gertrude Stein or Alain Robbe-Grillet, where formal repetition is made an obtrusive structural principle.)

---

[6] There is, alas, a welter of confusion in the way these two terms have been used by different literary theorists and critics. In the meanings I propose, I think I am staying reasonably close to ordinary language usage by insisting that motif is concrete while theme implies value and therefore some operation of abstraction. Because of the understandable association between motif and *Leitmotiv,* it seems to me sensible to link motif with purposeful recurrence and not use it, as some theorists have, to designate any isolable element in a story.

When, on the other hand, you are confronted with an extremely spare narrative, marked by formal symmetries, which exhibits a high degree of literal repetition, what you have to look for more frequently is the small but revealing differences in the seeming similarities, the nodes of emergent new meanings in the pattern of regular expectations created by explicit repetition.

Perhaps the conceptual matrix for this way of using repetition is to be sought in biblical poetry, which, as in most cultures, antedates prose as a vehicle of literary expression. Such connections are bound to be conjectural, but what I have in mind is essentially this: the parallelism of biblical verse constituted a structure in which, through the approximately synonymous hemistichs, there was constant repetition that was never really repetition. This is true not just inadvertently because there are no true synonyms, so that every restatement is a new statement, but because the conscious or intuitive art of poetic parallelism was to advance the poetic argument in seeming to repeat it—intensifying, specifying, complementing, qualifying, contrasting, expanding the semantic material of each initial hemistich in its apparent repetition. Biblical prose, of course, operates stylistically in exactly the opposite way, word-for-word restatement rather than inventive synonymity being the norm for repetition; but in both cases, I would suggest, the ideal reader (originally, listener) is expected to attend closely to the constantly emerging differences in a medium that seems predicated on constant recurrence.

Such attention is particularly crucial to the understanding of a major narrative convention of the Bible to which I should now like to turn. So far, in dealing with *Leitwort*, motif, theme, and sequence of actions, we have been concerned with the sort of repetition that is essentially *reiterative:* some developing aspect of the story is highlighted through repetition in the linear deployment of the narrative. But there is a different kind of biblical repetition, which is phrasal rather than verbal or a matter of motif, theme, and action. Here entire statements are repeated, either by different characters, by the narrator, or by the narrator and one or more of the characters in concert, with small but important changes introduced in what usually looks at first glance like verbatim repetition. Many of the psychological, moral, and dramatic complications of biblical narrative are produced through this technique.

How it actually works will become clear through some examples. Broadly, when repetitions with significant variations occur in biblical narrative, the changes introduced can point to an intensification, climactic development, acceleration, of the actions and attitudes initially represented, or, on the other hand, to some unexpected, perhaps unsettling, new revelation of character or plot. The former category is the simpler of the two, related as it is to the device of incremental repetition we might expect in an ancient narrative, and one illustration will suffice.

In 1 Kings 1, after Adonijah has laid claim to the throne, Nathan the prophet gives the following advice to Bathsheba: "Go to King David and say to him—My lord king, did you not swear to your handmaid in these words: 'Solomon your son will reign after me and he will sit on my throne?' Then why has Adonijah become king?" (1 Kings 1:13). Nathan goes on to assure Bathsheba that he will make his entrance while she is still speaking to David and will fill in (that is literally the verb he uses) whatever she has left unsaid. Now, one of the intriguing aspects of this whole story—for the omissions of biblical narrative are as cunning as its repetitions—is that we have no way of knowing whether David in fact made such a pledge in favor of Solomon or whether it is a pious (?) fraud that Nathan and Bathsheba are foisting on the old and failing king, who hardly seems to know at this point what is happening around him.

Bathsheba carries out her instructions, addressing these words to David:

17. My lord, you swore by the Lord your God to your handmaid, "Solomon your son will reign after me and he will sit on my throne." 18. But now Adonijah has become king, without, my lord king, your knowing. 19. He has slaughtered an abundance of oxen, fatlings, and sheep, inviting all the sons of the king and Ebiathar the priest and Joab the general of the army, but Solomon your servant he did not invite. 20. You, my lord king, the eyes of all Israel are upon you to tell them who will sit on the throne of my lord king after him. 21. For when my lord king lies with his forefathers, I and my son Solomon will be held guilty.

It is a brilliant speech, in which Bathsheba repeats the lines Nathan has given her but also expands them with the most persuasive inventiveness. The two-word indication, *malakh 'Adoniyahu*, Adonijah has become king, in verse 11, blossoms out into her review of the usurper's invitation list for his feast, her description of all Israel waiting breathlessly for the king's pronouncement, and her pathetic evocation of the fate that will soon attend her and her son if David fails to act. Even in what she repeats verbatim from Nathan's instructions, she introduces one small but revealing addition: she claims that David swore to her about Solomon's succession "by the Lord [his] God," which would indicate a higher order of binding solemnity to the vow. Perhaps Nathan as a man of God was nervous about taking His name in vain (especially, of course, if the whole idea of the pledge was a hoax) and so omitted that phrase from his instructions. David, carrying this particular incremental repetition a half-step further, will announce to Bathsheba (after he has been persuaded by her and Nathan that he did make such a vow), "As I swore to you by the Lord God of Israel, 'Solomon your son will reign after me . . .' " (1 Kings 1:30), giving that solemn vow the concluding flourish of an official proclamation.

Nathan, faithful to the scenario he has sketched out, enters just at the point when Bathsheba has conjured up her prospective plight after David's demise. Shrewdly, since he could not be presumed to know of a pledge given by David directly to Bathsheba, he takes the precise verbal formulas of the supposed vow (which he has in fact just dictated to Bathsheba) and turns them into a barbed question about Adonijah: "My lord king, did you say, 'Adonijah will reign after me and he will sit on my throne'?" (1 Kings 1:24). Then, without waiting for an answer, he plunges into an account of the usurper's politically designing feast in which, following the pattern of incremental repetition, some pointed details appear that were not present in Bathsheba's version:

> 25. For today he went down to slaughter an abundance of oxen, fatlings, and sheep, inviting all the sons of the king and the generals of the army and Ebiathar the priest, and there they are eating and drinking in his presence, and they have proclaimed, "Long live King Adonijah." 26. But me, me your servant, and Zadok the priest and Benaiah the son of Jehoiada and Solomon your servant, he did not invite.

The differences between Nathan's version and Bathsheba's version are wonderfully in character for both. Bathsheba's presentation reveals the distressed mother and suppliant wife emphasizing the injustice done to her son, the imminent danger threatening mother and son, the absolute dependence of the nation on the powerful word of the king. Nathan, by what he adds, sharpens the more general political aspects of the threat from Adonijah. In his repetition of the shared script, it is not just Joab the commander but the whole military elite that has been suborned by the pretender, and he has a fuller list of David's faithful who have been set aside by Adonijah, beginning emphatically with "me your servant" (Bathsheba prudently left Nathan out of her account) and closing the series with a symmetrical counterpart, "Solomon your servant." Most crucially, Nathan adds a little vignette of Adonijah's company eating and drinking and shouting "Long live King Adonijah," a scene certainly calculated to rouse the ire of the still reigning king. In tactful contrast to the usurper's followers, Bathsheba at the end of this meeting will say to the aged monarch, "May my lord King David live forever." The effect of this whole process of repeating and adding is to overwhelm David with a crescendo of arguments. Incremental repetition, which in its more schematic usages simply provides a progressive intensification or elaboration of an initial statement, here has the fullest dramatic and psychological justification. It conveys, without the need for explicit commentary, aspects of the distinctive character of each of the personages involved in the scene, and it becomes as well a convincingly effective means of bringing about a change in the course of events—for here as elsewhere in the Bible, language manifestly makes things happen.[7]

When, as in 1 Kings 1, the intent of varied repetition is a progressive effect, noticeably large elements of new material may be added to the repeated statements. More typically, I think, when some sort of reversal of an initial impression is intended, the modification of perception is achieved through the substitution, suppression, or addition of a single phrase, or through a strategic change in the order of repeated items. A simple example of omission used in this way would be 1 Kings 12, where Rehoboam's young friends advise him to answer a popular demand for lower taxes with the following words: "My little finger is thicker than my father's loins. If my father loaded you with a heavy yoke, I will add to your yoke. My father scourged you with whips, and I will scourge you with scorpions" (1 Kings 12:10–11). Rehoboam duly and disastrously follows this hard line, repeating his advisors' words verbatim to the people, but he revealingly omits the hyperbolic comparison between his little finger and his father's loins (1 Kings 12:14), wisely deciding not to compound his budgetary harshness by making extravagant public claims about his own stature vis-à-vis that of the deceased Solomon.

Variation in repetition is sometimes used to adumbrate not a feature of character but a development of plot. The effect this produces is thoroughly characteristic of the Bible's narrative art. In the kind of foreshadowing we are more accustomed to, an eventual dénouement is anticipated by some momentary insistence of action, image, or narrator's assertion. Julien Sorel near the beginning of *The Red and the Black* enters a church where he finds a scrap of printed paper reporting the execution of one Louis Jenrel, the anagram of his own name, and as he leaves, the sunlight coming through the red curtains makes the holy water look like blood—

[7] It is characteristic of conventional Bible scholarship that an excellent historical-philological commentary on Kings, that of John Gray (Philadelphia, 1963), should note the frequent repetitions here, cite as a parallel the Ras Shamra myths, and then say nothing more than, "Such repetition is of course a feature of popular narrative and is found in ballad literature."

a tremolo note typical of the convention of foreshadowing but, fortunately, not of Stendhal's novels. In the Bible, on the other hand, terse understatement remains the norm, and future turns of events are adumbrated by the slight, disturbing dissonance produced when in a pattern of repetition some ambiguous phrase is substituted for a more reassuring one. What is conveyed to the reader is a subliminal intimation of things to come rather than some emphatic though obscure warning.

When, for example, Manoah's wife (Judges 13) is told by the angel that she will conceive and bear a son, she repeats almost all the terms of the divine promise word for word to her husband, but she significantly changes the final phrase of the annunciation. The angel had said, "The lad will be a Nazarene to God from the womb, and he will begin to save Israel from the Philistines" (Judg. 13:5). In her repetition, the future mother of Samson concludes, "The lad will be a Nazarene to God from the womb to the day of his death" (Judg. 13:7). It is surely a little unsettling that the promise which ended with the liberation—though, pointedly, only the *beginning* of liberation—of Israel from its Philistine oppressors now concludes with no mention of "salvation" but instead with the word "death." From the womb to the day of death is, of course, a proverbial and neutral way of saying "all his life." In context, however, the woman's silence on the explicit promise of political salvation and the counterpoising of the three-word phrase, ʿad-yom moto, to the day of his death, against the echo of the whole clause on the lad's future career as a liberator, turn the substituted phrase into an implicit commentary on the prophecy and restore to that final "death" a hint of its independent negative force. The absence of salvation in the wife's version would seem to be underscored when Manoah subsequently questions the angel about "what will be the regimen for the lad and his deeds." The angel, after all, has already given the answer to both parts of the question in his words to Manoah's wife, but the crucial information about the child's future deeds was deleted from her report to Manoah. In sum, the dissonance of a single phrase subtly sets the scene for a powerful but spiritually dubious savior of Israel who will end up sowing as much destruction as salvation.

Let me offer one more example of varied repetition as a foreshadowing device because, occurring at a moment of much greater narrative suspense, it illustrates how the folktale pattern of a whole series of exact repetitions concluded by a reversal can be employed with considerable artistic sophistication. In 2 Samuel 3, Abner, Saul's commander-in-chief, decides to end the long civil war with the house of David and comes to David's capital at Hebron to confer with the warrior-king. After a feast and an

amicable discussion in which Abner pledges to win over all his people
to the signing of a treaty and the recognition of David as king,

21. David sent Abner off and he went in peace [*vayelekh beshalom*]. 22.
And here were David's retainers and Joab coming back from a sortie
bringing much booty with them, and Abner was not with David in
Hebron, for he had sent him off and he went in peace. 23. As Joab
and the troops with him returned, Joab was told the following: "Abner
son of Ner came to the king, and he sent him off and he went in
peace." 24. Joab came to the king and said: "What have you done?
Here, Abner came to you, why did you send him off and he went
indeed?" [*vayelekh halokh*].

After three occurrences in rapid succession of a departure in peace, Joab's
substitution of an intensifying infinitive, to go, *halokh*, for *beshalom*, in
peace, falls like the clatter of a dagger after the ringing of bells. Joab
says "he went indeed" instead of "he went in peace" partly because he
is seething with anger at the thought that David actually let Abner go
off when he had him in his hands, partly because his own steely intention
is to make sure that this going off will not be in peace. Joab quickly
proceeds to berate David for giving aid and comfort to the enemy who
could have come only to spy, then he rushes off messengers to call Abner
back to Hebron. When the adversary commander returns, Joab, this tough-
est of ancient Near Eastern mafiosi, draws Abner over to the city gate
and stabs him to death, thus avenging his brother Asahel killed in battle
by Abner. By the time we arrive at the rapid dénouement of the episode,
we may even wonder retrospectively whether the breaking of the series
of repetitions with the infinitive of the verb "to go" was not merely to
intensify the meaning of the verb but to call attention to its possible
application by Abner in another sense—as a euphemism for death. (For
some indication that this secondary meaning was current in biblical usage,
see Job 27:21 and Jeremiah 22:10.) In any case, it should be clear that
in order to grasp the full freight of the character's intention and the
subtlety of narrative structure in such a story, one must be alert even
to the shift of a single word in what may first seem a strictly formulaic
pattern.

Now, one might object that what I have been proposing as a sophisticated convention of purposeful minute variation of verbatim repetition
is in fact an accidental product of ancient texts which sometimes repeated
things word for word, sometimes only approximately word for word.
This is in essence the objection raised by an Israeli Bible scholar, Yair

Hoffman, to a view of repetition as a deliberate technique close to the one I have outlined here put forth in an article by Meir Sternberg.[8] Hoffman, because he can find instances in the Bible of divergence from verbatim repetition in which no literary "meaning" can be convincingly inferred, concludes that there is no way of empirically proving there was such a convention, and that all such readings can be dismissed as the exercise of fanciful ingenuity. What this argument fails to recognize, of course, is that very few literary conventions are treated by writers as invariable and hence obligatory without exception. This might be true of the requirement that a sonnet have fourteen lines (though fifteen-line sonnets have actually been written); but a far more typical convention would be, say, the introduction of a fictional personage in a nineteenth-century novel through a formal "character"—a thumbnail sketch of physical and moral traits. One may find all sorts of divergences from this model in the novels of the age, but it is common enough—it is used, let me guess, in perhaps 70 percent of the cases where a new character is introduced—to be a clearly recognizable convention, and against the background of that convention we can better see how individual writers exercise their craft. It is by no means necessary to insist, then, that every biblical instance of a small variation in repeated phrases should yield a significance, for I think such significances can be persuasively shown to be present in enough cases—here 70 percent would be a rather conservative estimate—to justify the inference that this was in fact an artful convention used by writers and recognized by their readers.

Hoffman makes the interesting suggestion that the oscillation between verbatim strictness and looseness in the biblical use of repetition is a function of historical circumstances. That is, strict formulaic repetition was the literary norm in Mesopotamia to the east and in Ugarit to the north of biblical Israel, while Egyptian literature to the south was governed by no such practice. Similarly, the earlier biblical narratives include much more verbatim repetition, remaining closer to their archaic Near Eastern literary antecedents, while the later—that is, post-exilic—narratives move away from the norm of repetition in consonance with the changing literary procedures of the Near East in later antiquity. Hoffman thus proposes that the variations between strict and loose repetition are a consequence

---

[8] Hoffman, "Between Conventionality and Strategy: On Repetition in Biblical Narrative" (Hebrew), *Ha-Sifrut* 28 (April 1979), pp. 89–99. Sternberg's article is "The Structure of Repetition in Biblical Narrative" (Hebrew), *Ha-Sifrut* 25 (October 1977), pp. 110–150. I might add that Sternberg and I developed similar understandings of the biblical convention of repetition quite independently, an early version of the present chapter having been published as an article in 1976. We both even arrived separately at closely parallel readings of the use of minutely varied repetition in Genesis 39, a convergence of perceptions which suggests that we are in fact contemplating the same literary object.

of the transition of biblical narrative from one geographical pole to another and from one historical era to another.

Historical inquiry might perhaps be able to confirm this intriguing hypothesis (though the role of Egypt in the scheme is a bit problematic), but that, of course, would in no way refute the existence of this kind of phrasal repetition as an artful convention. The conventions of any literary corpus will naturally reflect the contexts of literary history in which the corpus was shaped. The golden age of narrative creation in biblical literature, when the principal narratives of the Pentateuch and the Former Prophets were produced, was roughly from the tenth through the seventh centuries B.C.E. It is quite conceivable that the Hebrew writers of this period felt a certain fluidity in the norm of repetition they had inherited because they were caught in a broad cultural movement of change, shifting, as it were, from early to late Near Eastern antiquity and from the Semitic north and east to the Egyptian (and later Hellenistic) south. If this was in fact the case, the essential point is that they made out of the ambiguities of their literary-historical situation, as writers generally will, an occasion for distinctive artistry, creating a convention of verbatim repetition with strategic variations that was extraordinary for its suppleness and its subtlety. Indeed, the complex achievement of this great age of Hebrew narrative may in part be attributed to the resources of this convention, which the later, post-exilic Hebrew writers had abandoned, or no longer knew how to use.

Let me try, by way of conclusion, to make the nature of that achievement clearer through two more elaborate illustrations in which a carefully orchestrated ensemble of repetitive devices provides the complex structure for an entire story. The two examples are complementary opposites in the spectrum of repetitive narration, one building on repeated key-words and actions, with only certain thematic phrases and a bit of dialogue restated verbatim, the other an intricate tapestry of literally repeated, intertwined, and ingeniously reordered statements. The first example illustrates the reiterative devices of repetition; the second example, while putting reiterative devices to excellent use, is chiefly an instance of phrasal repetition, where we are invited to attend to emerging differences in seeming restatements.

My first example, the story of Balaam, the gentile prophet (Numbers 22:2–24:25), is unfortunately too long to comment on here verse by verse, but I shall try to show how it works through a summary analysis. The second example, the attempted seduction of Joseph by Potiphar's wife (Genesis 39), is more compact and by virtue of the way it uses repetition will require closer attention to details of the text.

The very first word in the Hebrew of the Balaam story is the verb *to see* (Num. 22:2), which appropriately becomes, with some synonyms, the main *Leitwort* in this tale about the nature of prophecy or vision. First Balak, king of Moab, sees what Israel has done to the Amorites; later Balaam, in a climactic series of visions, will see Israel sprawling out below him in a vast spatial perspective ("I see them from the cliff-tops, / Espy them from the heights" [Num. 23:9]) which, in the last of his prophecies, becomes a temporal perspective of foreseeing ("I see it but it is not yet, / I behold it but it won't be soon" [Num. 24:17]). Balaam prefaces his last two prophecies with a formulaic affirmation of his prowess as a professional clairvoyant or ecstatic seer: "Word of Balaam son of Beor, / Word of the man with open eyes, / Word of him who hears God's speech, / Who beholds divine visions, / Prostrate with eyes unveiled" (Num. 24:3–4). All this accomplished hullabaloo of visionary practice stands in ironic contrast, of course, to the spectacle of Balaam persistently blind to the presence of an angel his ass can plainly see, until God chooses to "unveil his eyes" (Num. 22:31).

This steady insistence on God as the exclusive source of vision is complemented by reiterated phrase-motifs bearing on the disposition of blessings and curses. Balak sends for Balaam to put a hex on Israel because in his pagan naivete he believes, as he says to Balaam, that "What you bless is blessed / And what you curse is cursed" (Num. 22:6). God Himself is quick to set matters straight in a night-vision to Balaam in which He uses the same two verb-stems (Num. 22:12): "You shall not curse the people because it is blessed." A whole series of changes is rung on the curse-blessing opposition, both in Balaam's visionary verse and in the exasperated dialogues between him and Balak. The appropriate thematic conclusion is explicitly made by Balaam in the preamble to his first prophecy (Num. 23:7–8): "From Aram Balak has brought me, / Moab's king from the eastern mountains: / Come curse me Jacob, / Come, pronounce Israel's doom. / How can I curse what God has not cursed, / How can I doom what the Lord has not doomed?" These verses interestingly illustrate how the prosodic repetitions of poetic parallelism can be effectively interwoven with the thematic repetition of phrases in the prose. It is important that Balaam is a poet as well as a seer, for the story is ultimately concerned with whether language confers or confirms blessings and curses, and with the source of the power of language.

It is particularly the structure of parallel actions in the Balaam story that demonstrates how, in contrast to the complaints of Voltaire and others, the Bible's polemic monotheism can produce high comedy. Balaam goes riding off on his ass to answer Balak's invitation. In the familiar folktale pattern, there are three occurrences of the same incident, the ass shying away from the sword-brandishing angel Balaam cannot see, each time with a more discomfiting effect on her rider: first he is carried into a field, then he is squeezed against a fence, and finally the ass simply lies down under him. When he begins to beat her furiously for the third time, the Lord "opens up her mouth" (elsewhere Balaam repeatedly insists that he can speak only "what the Lord puts in my mouth"), and she complains "What have I done to you that you should have beaten me these three times?" (Num. 22:28). The author, one notes, makes a point of calling our attention to the three times, for the number will be important in the second half of the story. Balaam in his wrath hardly seems to notice the miraculous gift of speech but responds as though he were accustomed to having daily domestic wrangles with his asses (Num. 22:29): "You have humiliated me! If I had a sword in my hand, I would kill you." (The Midrash *BeMidbar Rabbah*, 20:21, shrewdly notes the irony of Balaam's wanting a sword to kill an ass when he has set out to destroy a whole nation with his words alone.) Meanwhile, of course, the unseen angel has been standing by, sword in hand. Only when God chooses finally to reveal to Balaam the armed angel standing in the way does the irate seer repent for ill-treating the innocent creature.

It seems fairly clear that the ass in this episode plays the role of Balaam—beholding divine visions with eyes unveiled—to Balaam's Balak. The parallel between the two halves of the story is emphasized by the fact that in Balaam's prophecies there are again three symmetrically arranged occurrences of the same incident, each time with greater discomfort to Balak. In Balaam's prophetic imagery, first Israel is spread out like dust, then crouched like a lion, and finally rises like a star, so that the Moabite king, waiting for a first-class imprecation, is progressively reduced to impotent fury, quite in the manner of Balaam's blind rage against the wayward ass.

Now, a sequence of repeated actions in such a folktale pattern is of course a mechanical thing, and part of the genius of the biblical author here is to realize, three millennia before Bergson's formulation of the principle, that the mechanical in human affairs is a primary source of comedy. Balak's and Balaam's repetitions are much more elaborate than those of Balaam with the ass: each of the three times, Balaam instructs Balak to build seven altars and to sacrifice on them seven oxen and seven sheep, as the distraught king trundles him around from one lofty lookout point to the next; each time, the painstaking preparations result only in heightened frustration for Balak. Paganism, with its notion that divine powers can be manipulated by a caste of professionals through a set of carefully prescribed procedures, is trapped in the reflexes of a mechanistic world-view while from the biblical perspective reality is in fact controlled by the will of an omnipotent God beyond all human manipulation. The contrast between these two conflicting conceptions of reality is brilliantly brought forth in the story's artful pattern of repetitions. In each repeated instance, the Moabite king and his hired prophet go through identical preparations, and each time Balaam speaks in soaring verse—the words God has put in his mouth—which constitutes a crescendo repetition of powerful vision in counterpoint to the mechanical repetition of their futile human actions. The harmony of theological argument and narrative art in the whole story is beautifully complete.

The narrator in Numbers 22–24 deploys repetitive patterns in broad, bold strokes. The narrator of Genesis 39 indicates them in a series of finer, more minutely interrelated movements:

1. Joseph was brought down to Egypt, and a certain Egyptian, Potiphar, a courtier of Pharaoh and his chief steward, purchased him from the Ishmaelites who had brought him down there. 2. The Lord was with Joseph, and he was a successful man [*'ish matzliaḥ*], and he stayed in the house of his Egyptian master. 3. His master saw that the Lord was with him, making all that he did succeed [*matzliaḥ*]. 4. So Joseph pleased him and served him, and he put him in charge of his household, placing in his hands all that he had. 5. And from the moment he put him in charge of his household, over all he had, God blessed the house of the Egyptian for Joseph's sake, and the Lord's blessing was on all he had, in house and field. 6. All that he had he left in Joseph's hands, and, with him there, he gave no thought to anything except the food that he ate. And Joseph was handsome in figure and handsome in features.

These six verses are the introductory frame for Joseph's encounter with his master's wife, setting the scene for it not only in regard to narrative data but also in the announcing of formal themes. The reiterated verbal motifs function like the statement of musical themes at the beginning of the first movement of a classical symphony. Joseph is successful (*matzliaḥ* as an intransitive) and God makes him succeed (*matzliaḥ* as a causative verb). God repeatedly "is with" Joseph, a condition that clearly relates to success as cause to effect and that, spreading from the man to whatever he touches, manifests itself as *blessing*. The word "all" (*kol*) is insisted upon five times, clearly exceeding the norm of biblical repetition and thus calling attention to itself as a thematic assertion: the scope of blessing or success this man realizes is virtually unlimited; everything prospers, everything is entrusted to him. On a miniature scale, we have a confirmation of his own grandiose dreams and an adumbration of his future glory as vizier of Egypt. The seemingly incongruous last clause of the frame, which appears in the Hebrew parataxis as an equal member of the sequence of parallel statements that it concludes, is a signal of warning in the midst of blessing that Joseph may suffer from one endowment too many. We are now prepared for the entrance of Potiphar's wife:

7. After a time, his master's wife cast her eyes upon Joseph and said, "Lie with me." 8. He refused. "Look," he said to his master's wife, "with me here my master has given no thought to anything in this house, and all that he has, he has given into my hands. 9. He is not greater in this house than I am, he has withheld nothing from me except you, for you are his wife, and so how could I do this wicked thing and sin before God?" 10. And though she coaxed Joseph day after day, he would not agree to lie with her, to be with her. 11. One such day, when he came into the house to do his work, and none of the household staff was in the house, 12. she caught hold of him by his robe saying, "Lie with me." He left his robe in her hand and fled, and escaped outside. 13. When she saw that he had left his robe in her hand and had fled outside, 14. she called out to the household staff and said to them: "Look, he has brought us a Hebrew fellow to dally with us [or, to mock us]. He came to lie with me, but I screamed [literally, called out] in a loud voice. 15. And when he heard me raise my voice and scream, he left his robe by me and fled outside." 16. She kept his robe by her until his master came home. 17. Then she spoke to him with these same words: "The Hebrew slave came to me, the one you brought us, to dally with me. 18. But when I raised my voice and screamed, he left his robe by me and fled outside." 19. When his master heard the words his wife had spoken to him, "Such and such your slave did to me," he was furious. 20. So Joseph's master took him and put him in the jailhouse, where the king's prisoners were confined, and Joseph stayed there in the jailhouse.

The first appearance of dialogue in the entire story is the naked directness, without preliminaries or explanations, of the wife's sexual proposition, presented almost as though these two words (in the Hebrew) were all she ever spoke to Joseph, day after day (verse 10), until finally the plain meaning of the words is translated into the physical act of grabbing the man (verse 12). By contrast, Joseph's refusal (verses 8–9) is a voluble outpouring of language, full of repetitions which are both dramatically appropriate—as a loyal servant, he is emphatically protesting the moral scandal of the deed proposed—and thematically pointed. The key-word *all* is picked up from the frame and used to stress the comprehensiveness of the responsibility that has been entrusted to Joseph. Another thematic word associated with Joseph's trust, *house,* which also appears five times in the frame-verses, is used twice by him here, and figures prominently through the rest of his story. When the master comes home in verse 16, he literally "returns to his house," and it is of course the usurpation of the master's role and his house which the wife implicitly encourages in propositioning Joseph. Reinforcing this theme through still another strategy of verbal reiteration, the writer takes advantage of every occasion to refer to the Egyptian candidate for cuckoldry as "his [Joseph's] master" and to the concupiscent lady as "his [Potiphar's] wife."

It is in the account of the attempted sexual assault, however, that the verbatim repetition of whole phrases and clauses becomes crucial to the story. When Joseph flees (verse 12), "he left his robe in her hand," an exact echo, ironically wrenched from a context of trust to one of conjugal betrayal, of verse 6: "All that he had he left in Joseph's hands" (in the Hebrew, *yad,* hand, is singular in all its occurrences in the chapter). Verse 13 literally repeats the entire last sentence of verse 12 (omitting only one reinforcing verb) for two reasons: the repetition arrests for our attention the critical evidential fact of the robe in her hand, which is *followed* (verse 14) by her "calling out"; and it provides a fine moment of suspended narrative progress, while we wait to hear what move she can possibly devise to get out of this compromising situation. Her story to the household servants cleverly enlists their sympathies against the foreigner who constitutes a sexual threat and an insult to them all (he has been brought "to dally with/mock us" in the pun of *letzaheq banu*) and is meant to stir them against the husband who has introduced this dangerous alien presence in their midst. Because she uses precisely the same series of phrases in her speech (verses 14–15) that had been used twice just before by the narrator (verses 12–13) but reverses their order, so that her calling out *precedes* Joseph's flight, the blatancy of her lie is forcefully conveyed without commentary. That blatancy is even more sharply focused through the change of a single word in one phrase she repeats from the preceding narration. As we noted, the act of leaving something in someone's hand is given particular emphasis because it echoes verbatim the leaving, giving, entrusting in Joseph's hands stressed in the frame-verses. In the version of Potiphar's wife, the incriminating *beyadah*, "in her hand," of verses 12 and 13, is quietly transformed in verse 15 into *ʾetzli*, "by me," so that Joseph will appear to have disrobed quite voluntarily as a preliminary to rape. Joseph, of course, is again linked with the misleading evidence of a garment, as he was when his brothers brought the blood-soaked tunic to his father. The wife carefully places the robe "by her" (verse 16) as an arranged prop for the story she will now repeat to her husband when he returns. (The Midrash *Bereshit Rabbah* 87:10 makes the brilliant if somewhat fanciful observation on the narrative specification of this laying-by of the garment that she spent the time kissing and caressing it.)

When she finally speaks to her husband, her virtual repetition is once more a studied rearrangement of phrases. In addressing the servants, she had begun with the contemptuous reference to her husband's bringing a Hebrew fellow to dally with them. Now, she starts (verse 17) with the shock of "The Hebrew slave came to me," which, by itself, could easily be taken to mean, in good biblical idiom, "has had sexual intercourse with me." Then she qualifies, "the one you brought us, to dally with me." This lady who before had exhibited a speech-repertoire of two carnal words here shows herself a subtle mistress of syntactic equivocation. In her words to the servants, the husband had unambiguously brought the Hebrew "to dally with us." When she repeats the whole short clause in direct address to her husband, she places it so that it could be read in two ways: "the slave came to me—the one you brought us—to dally with me"; or, "the slave came to me, the one you brought us to dally with me." (The Hebrew text, of course, offers no clarifying punctuation.) The second reading obviously would be a sharp rebuke to the husband, suggesting that he had perversely invited trouble by introducing such a sexual menace into the household, but the wife is cunning enough to word the accusation in such a way that he will be left the choice of taking it as a direct rebuke or as only an implicit and mild one. One should also note that in her words to the other servants Joseph was called a "fellow" (or simply, "man"), while in restating this to her husband, she is careful to identify the Hebrew as "slave," thus provoking the wrath of a master who should feel that a trust has been violated and that the most lowly has presumed to assault the most high.[9]

[9] I am grateful to Meir Sternberg for the perception, in his article on the structure of repetition, of this small but crucial shift from "fellow" to "slave." On the same verse, he makes an observation similar to mine on the shrewd exploitation of syntactic ambiguity. "The Structure of Repetition in Biblical Narrative," p. 142.

Otherwise, in her version to the husband she once more repeats the lying rearrangement of the sequence of phrases, the crucial substitution of "by me" for "in my hand," and the-lady-doth-protest-too-much insistence of her own raising of the voice and screaming. Amusingly, the screaming now no longer appears as an independent clause—"I screamed in a loud voice"—but becomes an assumed action reduced to a subordinate clause—"When I raised my voice and screamed [as of course I would do, being a virtuous woman]." The definition of character and relationship through repetition in dialogue is dazzlingly effective. The husband witlessly responds just as she has coolly calculated, Joseph is thrown into prison, and we are given three frame-verses which close off the story, carefully balancing the frame-verses at the beginning:

21. The Lord was with Joseph. He extended kindness to him and disposed the chief jailor in his favor. 22. The chief jailor placed in Joseph's hands all the prisoners who were in the jailhouse, and all that was done there was his doing. 23. The chief jailor gave no heed to anything that was in his hands, because the Lord was with him, and whatever he did the Lord made succeed.

These final verses are a triumph of formal composition. Though Joseph has been cast into another kind of pit, the grand recapitulation of verbal motifs makes it clear that the rhythm of blessing which is his destiny is once more asserting itself. "He stayed in the jailhouse" (end of verse 20) just as "he stayed in the house of his Egyptian master" (end of verse 2) before. (I have translated *beyt-sohar* as "jailhouse," despite the Wild West connotations, in order to retain the way the Hebrew continues the motif of the house and the blessing conferred on it by Joseph's presence through to the conclusion of the story.) Once again, God "is with" Joseph, so that he finds favor—or here, in a slight variation of the idiom, is literally "given" favor—in the eyes of his Egyptian master. Once again, "all" is entrusted to him, placed "in his hands" (a final corrective reversal of the garment left "in the hand" of the female assailant). In verse 6, Potiphar "gave no thought to anything" because of the confidence he placed in Joseph; here, the chief jailor "gave no heed to anything" for exactly the same reason. This essential pattern of total trust will receive its ultimate confirmation when Pharaoh places the administration of the entire country in the hands of Joseph. The formula of the Lord's being with Joseph that introduced the whole account of his activities in Egypt (verse 2) now recurs near the end of the concluding verse of the episode,

111

and the very last word of the story is, most appropriately, *matzliaḥ*, "causes to succeed."

All these varied instances of artful repetition reflect in different ways an underlying assumption of biblical narrative. Language in the biblical stories is never conceived as a transparent envelope of the narrated events or an aesthetic embellishment of them but as an integral and dynamic component—an insistent dimension—of what is being narrated. With language God creates the world; through language He reveals His design in history to men. There is a supreme confidence in an ultimate coherence of meaning through language that informs the biblical vision. When the action and speech of men and women, always seen in some fateful course of convergence with or divergence from divine instruction, are reported to us in biblical narrative, repetition continually sets their lives into an intricate patterning of words. Again and again, we become aware of the power of words to make things happen. God or one of His intermediaries or a purely human authority speaks: man may repeat and fulfill the words of revelation, repeat and delete, repeat and transform; but always there is the original urgent message to contend with, a message which in the potency of its concrete verbal formulation does not allow itself to be forgotten or ignored. On the human plane, a master speaks (for spiritual and social hierarchy is implicit in this patterning), his servant is called upon to repeat through enactment; and, most frequent of all, an action is reported by the narrator, then its protagonist recounts the action in virtually the same terms, the discrepancy between "virtually" and "exactly" providing the finely calibrated measure of the character's problematic subjective viewpoint. As human actors reshape recurrence in language along the biases of their own intentions or misconceptions, we see how language can be an instrument of masking or deception as well as of revelation; yet even in such deflected form we witness language repeatedly evincing the power to translate itself into history, a history whose very substance seems sometimes men and their actions, sometimes the language they use.

Beyond this constant interplay through repetition between speech and narration, biblical personages and events are caught in a finer web of reiteration in the design of thematic words and phrases constantly recurring. No act or gesture is incidental and the sequence of events is never fortuitous. Joseph may move swiftly from slave-caravan to manor-house to prison to palace: through it all, the strong punctuation of verbal motifs repeatedly signals to us the direction in which he is headed, the purpose of his arduous path. The human figures in the large biblical landscape act as free agents out of the impulses of a memorable and often fiercely assertive individuality, but the actions they perform all ultimately fall into the symmetries and recurrences of God's comprehensive design. Finally, it is the inescapable tension between human freedom and divine historical plan that is brought forth so luminously through the pervasive repetitions of the Bible's narrative art.

6

Characterization and the

Art of Reticence

Howdoes the Bible manage to evoke such a sense of depth and complexity in its representation of character with what would seem to be such sparse, even rudimentary means? Biblical narrative offers us, after all, nothing in the way of minute analysis of motive or detailed rendering of mental processes; whatever indications we may be vouchsafed of feeling, attitude, or intention are rather minimal; and we are given only the barest hints about the physical appearance, the tics and gestures, the dress and implements of the characters, the material milieu in which they enact their destinies. In short, all the indicators of nuanced individuality to which the Western literary tradition has accustomed us—preeminently in the novel, but ultimately going back to the Greek epics and romances—would appear to be absent from the Bible. In what way, then, is one to explain how, from these laconic texts, figures like Rebekah, Jacob, Joseph, Judah, Tamar, Moses, Saul, David, and Ruth emerge, characters who, beyond any archetypal role they may play as bearers of a divine mandate, have been etched as indelibly vivid individuals in the imagination of a hundred generations?

It is true enough to say, as Erich Auerbach and others have done, that the sparely sketched foreground of biblical narrative somehow implies a large background dense with possibilities of interpretation, but the critical issue here is the specific means through which that "somehow" is achieved. Though biblical narrative is often silent where later modes of fiction will choose to be loquacious, it is selectively silent in a purposeful way: about different personages, or about the same personages at different junctures of the narration, or about different aspects of their thought, feeling, behavior. I would suggest, in fact, that the biblical writers, while seeming to preserve a continuity with the relatively simple treatment of character of their Mesopotamian and Syro-Palestinian literary predecessors, actually worked out a set of new and surprisingly supple techniques for the imaginative representation of human individuality.

Since art does not develop in a vacuum, these literary techniques must be associated with the conception of human nature implicit in biblical monotheism: every person is created by an all-seeing God but abandoned to his own unfathomable freedom, made in God's likeness as a matter of cosmogonic principle but almost never as a matter of accomplished ethical fact; and each individual instance of this bundle of paradoxes, encompassing the zenith and the nadir of the created world, requires a special cunning attentiveness in literary representation. The purposeful selectivity of means, the repeatedly contrastive or comparative technical strategies used in the rendering of biblical characters, are in a sense dictated by the biblical view of man.

All this will become clearer through illustration. I would like to focus on a series of related passages from the story of David, the most complex and elaborately presented of biblical characters. A consideration of the entire literary portrait of David would take far too much space, but in order to see how the Bible's artful selectivity produces both sharply defined surfaces and a sense of ambiguous depths in character, it will suffice to follow David's unfolding relationship with his wife Michal, which also involves his relation to Saul, to his subsequent wives, and to his men. Michal is introduced into the narrative shortly after David, a young man from the provincial town of Bethlehem, has made his debut as a military hero and won the adulation of the people (1 Samuel 18). We have just been informed, in a pointed pun, that the spirit of the Lord, now with David, has "turned away" from Saul and that the troubled king has "turned David away" from his presence by sending him into battle as a front-line commander. What follows is worth quoting at length because, as the initial presentation of David and Michal's relationship, it offers a small spectrum of nicely differentiated means of characterization:

14. David succeeded in all his ways, and the Lord was with him. 15. Saul saw that he succeeded remarkably and was afraid of him. 16.

But all Israel and Judah loved David for he led them in battle. 17. Saul said to David, "Here is my oldest daughter, Merab; her shall I give you as a wife. But you must be a good warrior for me and fight the Lord's battles." And Saul was thinking, "Let not my hand strike him down, let it be the hand of the Philistines." 18. David said to Saul, "Who am I, and what is my life, my father's family in Israel, that I should become the son-in-law of the king?" 19. But at the time Merab the daughter of Saul should have been given to David, she was given as a wife to Adriel the Meholathite. 20. And Michal the daughter of Saul loved David; this was told to Saul and he was pleased. 21. And Saul thought, "I shall give her to him and she can be a snare to him, so that the hand of the Philistines can strike him down." And Saul said to David, "[Through the second one] you can now become my son-in-law." 22. Saul instructed his retainers, "Speak to David privately in these words—'The king desires you, all his subjects love you, and so now become the king's son-in-law.'" 23. Saul's retainers repeated these words to David, and David said, "Is it a little thing in your eyes to become the king's son-in-law, and I am a pauper, a man of little consequence?" 24. Saul's retainers told him, "These were the words David spoke." 25. Saul said, "This is what you should say to David—'The king desires no bride price but a hundred Philistine foreskins to take vengeance against the enemies of the king.'" And Saul intended to bring David down by the hand of the Philistines. 26. His retainers repeated these words to David, and David was pleased by the thing, to become the king's son-in-law. [Before the time had expired,] 27. David arose and went off, he and his men with him, and killed two hundred Philistines. David brought back their foreskins [and counted them out] for the king in order to become his son-in-law, and Saul gave him Michal his daughter as a wife. 28. Saul realized that the Lord was with David, while Michal the daughter of Saul loved him. 29. Saul feared David all the more, and Saul was David's constant enemy. 30. The Philistine chieftains came out to do battle, but whenever they came out, David succeeded beyond all Saul's retainers, and his name became very great.

Now, in reliable third-person narrations, such as in the Bible, there is a scale of means, in ascending order of explicitness and certainty, for conveying information about the motives, the attitudes, the moral nature of characters. Character can be revealed through the report of actions; through appearance, gestures, posture, costume; through one character's comments on another; through direct speech by the character; through inward speech, either summarized or quoted as interior monologue; or through statements by the narrator about the attitudes and intentions of the personages, which may come either as flat assertions or motivated explanations.

The lower end of this scale—character revealed through actions or appearance—leaves us substantially in the realm of inference. The middle categories, involving direct speech either by a character himself or by others about him, lead us from inference to the weighing of claims. Although a character's own statements might seem a straightforward enough revelation of who he is and what he makes of things, in fact the biblical writers are quite as aware as any James or Proust that speech may reflect the occasion more than the speaker, may be more a drawn shutter than an open window. With the report of inward speech, we enter the realm of relative certainty about character: there is certainty, in any case, about the character's conscious intentions, though we may still feel free to question the motive behind the intention. Finally, at the top of the ascending scale, we have the reliable narrator's explicit statement of what the characters feel, intend, desire; here we are accorded certainty, though biblical narrative, as the passage before us demonstrates, may choose for its own good purposes either to explain the ascription of attitude or to state it baldly and thus leave its cause as an enigma for us to ponder.

With all this in mind, if we return to our passage from 1 Samuel 18, we can readily see how the writer, far from being committed to a monolithic or "primitive" method of characterization, shrewdly varies his means of presentation from one personage to the next. Like many biblical episodes, the passage has a formal frame: David is said to be eminently successful, which is both proof and consequence of God's being with him, and immensely popular because of his success, both at the beginning of the episode and at the end; and if, as I would assume, this passage was written later than Genesis 39, the story of Joseph, another precocious high achiever in trouble, it probably alludes to that chapter from Genesis, which is similarly framed by verses at the beginning and end that stress the hero's success, God's being with him, and his popularity. In any case, the frame-verses here tell us something about David's divine election to the newly created throne of Israel, but nothing about his moral character, and one of the most probing general perceptions of the biblical writers is that there is often a tension, sometimes perhaps even an absolute contradiction, between election and moral character. But it is important for the writer to leave this tension under a shadow of ambiguity in order to suggest a complex sense of David the private person and public man. David, then, remains a complete opacity in this episode, while Saul is a total transparency and Michal a sliver of transparency surrounded by darkness.

The means of presenting Saul are drawn from the top of our ascending scale of certainties. The narrator tells us exactly what Saul feels toward David—fear—and why he feels it—David's astonishing military success (in this instance, the parataxis of "Saul saw . . . and was afraid" is a clear causal indication). We are given Saul's decorous public speech to David (verse 17), but his words are immediately commented on and exposed by a revelation of his inward speech in which he plots David's death. (In the Hebrew, these transitions from outward to inward speech are effected more elegantly and more pointedly because the same verb, ʾamr, is used to introduce both actual speech and thought or intention.) The next discussion of betrothal between Saul and David (verse 21) neatly reverses this order: first we get the interior monologue of the plotting king, then his decorous statement to the intended victim of his scheme. By the time we are given Saul's words to be conveyed by his henchmen, who are probably not conscious accomplices, to David, we know exactly what is behind those words.

As elsewhere in the Bible, attention is directed toward the use of language as a medium of manipulation. To make sure that we do not forget even momentarily just what Saul is up to, the narrator intervenes in his own voice in the second half of verse 25, after Saul's stipulation of bride-price, to tell us what the king's real intention is. The transparency of presentation might even be intended to imply a transparency in Saul's efforts as a Machiavellian schemer: he is a simple character, inclined to clumsy lunges rather than deft thrusts, and perhaps for that reason not *political* enough to retain the throne. Does David himself see through the king's scheme and decide to play along because he is confident he can overcome all dangers and bring back the gory bride-price? This is one of several key determinations concerning the characters about which the text leads us to speculate without providing sufficient information to draw any certain conclusions.

Michal leaps out of the void as a name, a significant relation (Saul's daughter), and an emotion (her love for David). This love, twice stated here, is bound to have special salience because it is the only instance in all biblical narrative in which we are explicitly told that a woman loves a man. But unlike Saul's fear, Michal's love is stated entirely without motivated explanation; this does not mean, of course, that it is inexplicable, only that the writer wants us to conjecture about it. The people love David because of his brilliance on the battlefield; Michal might love him for the same reason, or for qualities not yet intimated, or because of aspects of her own character about which we will begin to guess only later.

The means used to represent David, meanwhile, are deliberately limited to the lower and middle range of our ascending scale of certainties. We know in a general way about his actions in battle, we know what others feel about him, but there is no ascription of feeling, as in the case of Michal, no revelation of interior speech and intention, as with Saul. What we are given is David's speech, first to Saul, later to Saul's intermediaries. These are strictly public occasions, and the words David chooses for them are properly diplomatic. Indeed, one of the most striking aspects of the entire David story is that until his career reaches its crucial breaking point with his murder-by-proxy of Uriah after his adultery with Bathsheba, almost all his speeches are in public situations and can be read as politically motivated. It is only after the death of the child born of his union with Bathsheba that the personal voice of a shaken David begins to emerge.[1]

What does David feel, what is he really thinking, when he responds to Saul or to Saul's spokesmen? Does he genuinely feel humble as a poor Ephraimite farm boy suddenly taken up by the court? Is he merely following the expected effusive formulas of court language in these gestures of self-effacement before the king? Or, guessing the king's intention but confident he has a stronger hand to play than Saul realizes, is he through his protestations of unworthiness being careful not to appear too eager to marry into the royal family because of what such a desire might suggest about his political ambitions? The narrator leaves these various "readings" of David hovering by presenting his public utterance without comment, and in this way is able to suggest the fluctuating or multiple nature of motives in this prime biblical instance of man as a political animal. One or all of these considerations might explain David's words; precisely by not specifying, the narrator allows each its claim.

The subsequent episodes of the David–Michal story consistently maintain this studied effect of opacity in the presentation of the warrior-king, and may be touched on more briefly. In the next chapter (1 Samuel 19), Saul sends his henchmen to David and Michal's house in order to ambush David when he comes out in the morning. In some unspecified way, the alert Michal learns of the plot and warns David in these urgent,

---

[1] Scholarly opinion still tends to assume, on rather tenuous stylistic and form-critical grounds, that there is a separate "succession narrative" which begins in 2 Samuel 9, but the evidence for a unified imaginative conception of the whole David story seems to me persuasive.

compact words: "If you don't escape tonight, tomorrow you're a dead man" (1 Sam. 19:11). This is immediately followed neither by a verbal response from David nor by any indication of what he feels, but only by Michal's brisk action and David's emphatic compliance: "Michal lowered David through the window and he went off and fled and escaped" (1 Sam. 19:12). These three verbs for the one in Michal's breathless instructions underline David's singleminded attention to the crucial business of saving himself.

Michal, meanwhile, is wily enough to cover David's escape by improvising a dummy in bed out of the household idols *(terafim)* covered with a cloth and a goat's-hair bolster for a head. This is obviously an allusion to Rachel, who, in fleeing with Jacob from her father (Genesis 31), steals Laban's *terafim* and hides them under the camel-pillow when he comes to search her tent. Perhaps the allusion is meant to foreshadow a fatality shared by Michal with Rachel, who becomes the object of Jacob's unwitting curse because of the theft (Gen. 31:32); what is certain is that the allusion reinforces our sense of Michal as a woman who has renounced allegiance to her father in her devotion to her husband. For when Saul, finding that David has slipped out of his hands, castigates his daughter for her treachery, Michal coolly turns around her own words to David and her actions of the previous night and pretends that David threatened her, saying, "Help me get away or I'll kill you" (1 Sam. 19:17).

It is noteworthy that the only words purportedly spoken by David to Michal are merely her invention to protect herself. So far, their relationship has been literally and figuratively a one-sided dialogue. First we were told twice that she loved him while all that could be safely inferred about his attitude toward her was that the marriage was politically useful. Now she vigorously demonstrates her love, and the practical intelligence behind it, by her words and actions at a moment of crisis, while the text, faithful to its principle of blocking access to the private David, envelops him in silence, representing him only as a man in mortal danger who goes off, flees, and escapes.

David, after putting Saul's homicidal intentions to the test one last time with the help of his friend Jonathan, heads for the badlands, accompanied by a band of tough fighting men disaffected from Saul. Michal now disappears from the scene. Bare mention of her occurs only at the end of 1 Samuel 25, in connection with David's taking another two wives. The happily widowed Abigail, another of those extraordinarily enterprising and practical biblical women, has just been seen taking off after David in a chain of verbs: "Abigail hurried and got up and rode on her donkey, her five maids in attendance, and went after David's messengers and became his wife" (1 Sam. 25:42). This is followed by an observation about David's matrimonial activity (probably to be construed as a pluperfect), which leads the narrator at last to inform us what has happened to Michal while David has been on the lam: "David had taken Ahinoam of Jezreel, and so both of them became his wives, while Saul had given his daughter Michal, the wife of David, to Palti the son of Laish from Gallim" (1 Sam. 25:43). Michal, last observed as a forceful initiator of action, now stands in contrast to the energetically active Abigail as an object acted upon, passed by her father from one man to another. The dubious legality of Saul's action is perhaps intimated by the use of the epithet "wife of David"; the motive, of course, for marrying off his daughter to someone else is political, in order to demonstrate, however clumsily, that David has no bond of kinship with the royal family and hence no claim to the throne. What Michal feels about this transaction, or about the absent David and his new wives of whom she may have heard, we are not told. The text is similarly silent about Palti's feelings—indeed, about his very identity—though he will later have his brief moment of memorable revelation.

The strategy of setting up a screen around David's intimate responses is deployed with almost teasing provocation a few chapters later (1 Samuel 30) when Abigail and Ahinoam, together with the wives and children of all David's men, are taken off as captives in an Amalekite raid on his headquarters at Ziklag. Returning from a sortie, David and his men find their town burned and their wives and children gone. David's reaction is reported with the most artful ambiguity: "David and the people with him cried out and wept until they had no more strength to weep. David's two wives had been taken captive, Ahinoam the Jezreelite and Abigail, wife of Nabal the Carmelite. And David was greatly distressed, for the people wanted to stone him, for all the people were embittered over their sons and daughters" (1 Sam. 30:4–6).

First there is the public expression of grief, the long fit of weeping, in which David naturally participates. Then we are informed that his two wives are among the captives, and in the paratactic flow of the verses, with no sentence divisions in the original text, it is easy enough to read this as cause and effect: "David's wives had been taken . . . and David was greatly distressed." The idiom I have translated as "distressed" *(vatetzer le)* can refer either to a feeling of distress or to the objective condition of being in straits, in physical danger, and the next clause, "for the people wanted to stone him," pirouettes on the ambiguity and turns around to the second meaning. Where we thought we had a spontaneous expression of David's grief over the loss of his wives, we are again confronted with

David the political leader in a tight corner, struggling to save both himself and the situation—which he promptly does by a devastating counterattack on the Amalekites in which the captives are rescued. It is not that we are led to infer any clear absence of personal feeling in David, but that again the private person has been displaced through the strategy of presentation by the public man, and the intimate David remains opaque.

Michal returns to the story as the result of a series of decisive political developments (2 Samuel 3). Saul has died, and after a bitter civil war, Abner, his commander-in-chief, is prepared to sue for peace with David, who makes it a precondition to negotiations that he be given back his wife Michal, "whom I betrothed with a hundred Philistine foreskins" (2 Sam. 3:14). This bloody reminder is meant to stress the legitimacy of David's right to Michal, for whom he has paid the full bride-price stipulated by her father, and that emphasis suggests it is not any personal bond but political calculation—Michal's utility as a means of reinforcing David's claim to the allegiance of Saul's subjects—which makes him insist on her return.

His demand is promptly met by Saul's son (2 Sam. 3:15–16): "Ish-Bosheth sent and had her taken from a man, Paltiel the son of Laish. Her man went with her, walking after and weeping, as far as Bahurim. Abner then said to him, 'Go back!' and he went back." The remarkable suggestiveness of the Bible's artistic economy could scarcely be better illustrated. This is all we ever know of Palti the son of Laish. He appears from the darkness to weep for his wife and to follow her, until he is driven back forever into the darkness by a man of power with whom he cannot hope to contend. He is called twice in close sequence Michal's man or husband (ʾish), a title to which at least his feelings give him legitimate claim, and which echoes ironically against David's use in the preceding verse of ʾishti, my wife or woman, to describe a relationship with Michal that is legal and political but perhaps not at all emotional on his side. The contrast between David, again speaking carefully weighed public words, and Palti, expressing private grief through publicly visible action, is pointed. As for Michal, who has been living for years as Palti's wife, we have no way of knowing whether she feels gratitude, love, pity, or contempt for her powerless second husband, though we may begin to guess that the feelings she now entertains toward David himself will be less than kindly.

The actual reunion between David and Michal is entirely suppressed, for the writer wants to leave us wondering a little longer while he attends to climactic political events (the murder of Abner, the end of the civil war, the conquest of Jerusalem), and thus to reserve the revelation of what their mutual attitudes now are for a final confrontation between them. The writer's artful sureness of selectivity in the means he adopts to present character is evident in the striking fact that, until the final meeting between Michal and David, at no point is there any dialogue between them—an avoidance of verbal exchange particularly noticeable in the Bible, where such a large part of the burden of narration is taken up by dialogue. When that exchange finally comes, it is an explosion.

David, having captured from the Jebusites the mountain stronghold that will be the capital of the dynasty he is founding, settles his family and entourage there and then personally leads the Ark of the Lord in a festive procession up to Jerusalem (2 Samuel 6). Michal enters this picture as an unhappy spectator (2 Sam. 6:16): "As the Ark of the Lord came into the City of David, Michal the daughter of Saul looked out the window and saw King David leaping and cavorting before the Lord, and she despised him in her heart." With a fine sense of the tactics of exposition, the narrator tells us exactly what Michal is feeling but not why. The hiatus in explanation, which will in part be filled by the ensuing dialogue, again opens the gates to multiple interpretation. The scorn for David welling up in Michal's heart is thus plausibly attributable in some degree to all of the following: the undignified public spectacle which David just now is making of himself; Michal's jealousy over the moment of glory David is enjoying while she sits alone, a neglected co-wife, back at the provisional palace; Michal's resentment over David's indifference to her all these years, over the other wives he has taken, over being torn away from the devoted Palti; David's dynastic ambitions—now clearly revealed in his establishing the Ark in the "City of David"— which will irrevocably displace the house of Saul. The distance between the spouses is nicely indicated here by the epithets chosen for each: she is the "daughter of Saul," and she sees him as the king. Michal's subsequent words to David seize on the immediate occasion, the leaping and cavorting, as the particular reason for her anger, but the biblical writer knows as well as any psychologically minded modern that one's emotional reaction to an immediate stimulus can have a complicated prehistory; and by suppressing any causal explanation in his initial statement of Michal's scorn, he beautifully suggests the "overdetermined" nature of her contemptuous ire, how it bears the weight of everything that has not been said but obliquely intimated about the relation between Michal and David.

There follow three verses which, leaving Michal in her fury at the window, describe in detail David's performance of his ceremonial functions as he offers sundry sacrifices, blesses the people, distributes delicacies. Then David returns to his house to bless—or perhaps the verb here means simply to greet—his own family:

20b. And Michal the daughter of Saul came out to meet David, and she said, "How honored today is the king of Israel, exposing himself before the eyes of his subjects' slavegirls as some worthless fellow might indeed expose himself!" 21. David said to Michal, "Before the Lord who chose me over your father and all his house to appoint me ruler of the Lord's people Israel, I will play before the Lord! 22. And I will dishonor myself even more than this and be base in my own eyes, and with the slavegirls you spoke of, with them will I be honored." 23. And Michal the daughter of Saul had no child till her dying day.

Michal, who at last must have her say with David, does not wait until he has actually entered the house but goes out to meet him (perhaps, one might speculate, with the added idea of having her words ring in the ears of his retinue outside). The exchange of whipsaw sarcasms between the two reflects the high-tension fusion of the personal and the political in their relationship. When Michal addresses David in the third person as king of Israel, it is not in deference to royalty but in insolent anger at this impossible man who does not know how to behave like a king. She makes David an exhibitionist in the technical, sexual sense ("as some worthless fellow might indeed expose himself": apparently his skirts were flying high as he cavorted before the Ark), stressing that the hungry eyes of the slavegirls have taken it all in—an emphasis which leads one to suspect there is a good deal of sexual jealousy behind what is ostensibly an objection to his lack of regal dignity. David responds to the daughter of Saul with a sonorous invocation of the Lord who has chosen him for the throne instead of Saul and his heirs. As divinely elected king, David is to be the judge of what is a decorous celebration before the Lord: he seizes Michal's sarcastic "honored," turns it into a defiant "I will dishonor myself" (the opposed Hebrew roots suggest etymologically "heavy" [kabbed], and "light" [qal]); then, hurling back to Michal the idea of how he has shown himself in the eyes of other women, insists that he will be honored by these lowly slavegirls for the behavior his wife thinks degrading. In all this, the writer is careful to conceal his own precise sympathies. He does not question the historically crucial fact of David's divine election, so prominently stressed by the king himself at the beginning of his speech; but theological rights do not necessarily justify domestic wrongs, and the anointed monarch of Israel may still be a harsh and unfeeling husband to the woman who has loved him and saved his life.

There is a strategically placed gap between the end of verse 22 and the beginning of verse 23. Michal, hardly a woman to swallow insults in silence, is refused the privilege of a reply to David, nor is there any indication of her inward response to this verbal assault. The breaking off of the dialogue at this point is itself an implicit commentary. David has the last word because, after all, he has the power, as he has just taken pains to point out to Michal. The daughter of a rejected royal house and by now a consort of only marginal political utility to the popularly acclaimed king, and the least favored of three or more co-wives, Michal can do nothing, and perhaps has literally nothing more to say, about her rage against her husband. Verse 23, the last one in which Michal will be accorded any mention, is a kind of epilogue to the confrontation, fastened to it with the special kind of ambiguity to which biblical parataxis lends itself. (Modern translators generally destroy the fineness of the effect of rendering the initial "and" as "so.") The narrator states the objective fact of Michal's barrenness—in the ancient Near East, a woman's greatest misfortune—but carefully avoids any subordinate conjunction or syntactical signal that would indicate a clear causal connection between the fact stated and the dialogue that precedes it. A theologically minded reader, and certainly any advocate of the divine right of the Davidic dynasty, is invited to read this statement as a declaration that Michal was punished by God for her presumption in rebuking His anointed king over an act of royal and cultic ceremony. A reader attending more to the personal drama that has been enacted between Michal and David might justifiably conclude that after this furious exchange, David simply ceased to have conjugal relations with Michal and so condemned her to barrenness. Finally, the paratactic link between the two verses leaves the teasing possibility, however less likely than the other two readings, that we may presume too much altogether in seeing here any definite relation of cause and effect: we cannot be entirely certain that Michal's childlessness is not a bitter coincidence, the last painful twist of a wronged woman's fate.

I would suggest that causation in human affairs is itself brought into a paradoxical double focus by the narrative techniques of the Bible. The biblical writers obviously exhibit, on the one hand, a profound belief in a strong, clearly demarcated pattern of causation in history and individual lives, and many of the framing devices, the motif-structures, the symmetries and recurrences in their narratives reflect this belief. God directs, history complies; a person sins, a person suffers; Israel backslides, Israel falls. The very perception, on the other hand, of godlike depths, unsoundable capacities for good and evil, in human nature, also leads these writers to render their protagonists in ways that destabilize any monolithic system of causation, set off a fluid movement among different orders of causation, some of them complementary or mutually reinforcing, others even mutually contradictory. The mere possibility that there might be no clear causal connection between Michal's anger against David and her barrenness, though marginal, serves to unsettle the sense of straightforward, unilinear consequence to which lazy mental habits—ancient and modern—accustom us. The accidents befalling and the actions performed by man as a free agent created in God's image are more intricately layered, more deviously ramified, than many earlier and competing views of humanity might lead us to imagine, and the narrative technique of studied reticences which generate an interplay of significantly patterned ambiguities is a faithful translation into art of this view of man.

Every biblical narrator is of course omniscient, but in contrast, for example, to the narrator of the Homeric poems, who makes his characters beautifully perspicuous even (as in the *Iliad*) when he is dealing with the most darkly irrational impulses of the human heart, the ancient Hebrew narrator displays his omniscience with a drastic selectivity. He may on occasion choose to privilege us with the knowledge of what God thinks of a particular character or action—omniscient narration can go no higher—but as a rule, because of his understanding of the nature of his human subjects, he leads us through varying darknesses which are lit up by intense but narrow beams, phantasmal glimmerings, sudden strobic flashes. We are compelled to get at character and motive, as in Impressionist writers like Conrad and Ford Madox Ford, through a process of inference from fragmentary data, often with crucial pieces of narrative exposition strategically withheld, and this leads to multiple or sometimes even wavering perspectives on the characters. There is, in other words, an abiding mystery in character as the biblical writers conceive it, which they embody in their typical methods of presentation.

This underlying approach to character is perhaps most easily seen in the capacity for change exhibited by the biblical personages who are treated at any length. Cognate with the biblical understanding of individual character as something which develops in and is transformed by time—preeminently in the stories of Jacob and David—is a sense of character as a center of surprise. This unpredictable and changing nature of character is one reason why biblical personages cannot have fixed Homeric epithets (Jacob is not "wily Jacob," Moses is not "sagacious Moses") but only relational epithets determined by the strategic requirements of the imme-diate context: Michal, as the circumstances vary, is either "daughter of Saul" or "wife of David."[2]

Achilles in the *Iliad* undergoes violent fluctuations of mood and attitude, first sulking in his tent, then transformed into a blind force of destruction by the death in battle of his beloved companion Patroklos, then at the end brought back to his human senses by the pleas of the bereaved Priam; but there is a stable substratum of the man Achilles, and these are, after all, oscillations in feeling and action, not in character. David, on the other hand, in the many decades through which we follow his career, is first a provincial *ingénu* and public charmer, then a shrewd political manipulator and a tough guerrilla leader, later a helpless father floundering in the entanglements of his sons' intrigues and rebellion, a refugee suddenly and astoundingly abasing himself before the scathing curses of Shimei, then a doddering old man bamboozled or at least directed by Bathsheba and Nathan, and, in still another surprise on his very deathbed, an impla-cable seeker of vengeance against the same Shimei whom he had forgiven after the defeat of Absalom's insurrection.

As a final illustration of how the Bible's strategies of narrative exposition reflect a sense of the unknowable and the unforeseeable in human nature, I would like to contrast two scenes of mourning, one from Homer, the other from the David story. Priam's confrontation of Achilles in the last book of the *Iliad* to beg for the body of his son Hektor is surely one of the most poignant moments in ancient literature. "I have gone through what no other mortal on earth has gone through," Priam concludes his plea to Achilles, "I put my lips to the hands of the man who has killed my children." Here are the first few lines, in the translation by Richmond Lattimore, that describe the effect of Priam's bold entreaty:

So he spoke, and stirred in the other a passion of grieving
for his own father. He took the old man's hand and pushed him
gently away, and the two remembered, as Priam sat huddled
at the feet of Achilles and wept close for manslaughtering Hektor
and Achilles wept now for his own father, now again
for Patroklos. The sound of their mourning moved in the house.

The emotions of these two sadly remembering figures are as clearly exposed for us as their physical positions—old Priam huddled at the

[2] A similar observation on the lack of fixed epithets and its connection with a dynamic conception of character has been made by Shimon Bar-Efrat in *The Art of the Biblical Story* (Hebrew) (Jerusalem, 1979), pp. 110–111.

127

feet of the mighty young Achilles. In a moment Achilles will speak soft words of compassion to Priam. The transition from murderous rage to kindness is deeply moving yet not, in the biblical manner, surprising. Achilles' anger has estranged him from his own humanity, but, in the view of the Greek poet, there are universal emotions, universal facts of existence, shared by all men, and Priam's plea has reminded Achilles that, though they are separated by enmity and age, they share identically in this human heritage of relation and feeling. All men have fathers, all men love, all must grieve when they lose those they love. Part of the power of the scene comes from the fact that the connection between these two figures, weeping together as each separately recalls his own lost ones, is so lucidly revealed through the narrator's simultaneous overview of the external scene and the inner experience of both characters.

In 2 Samuel 12, when David's first son by Bathsheba is stricken with an incurable illness, the king entreats God for the sake of the baby, fasting and sleeping on the ground. He refuses all sustenance for seven days, and when on the seventh day the child dies, his servants are afraid to tell him, assuming that, if his behavior was so extreme while the child was still alive, he will go to even more extravagant lengths when he learns of the child's death.

> 19. David saw that his servants were whispering to each other and he realized the child was dead, and he said to his servants, "Is the child dead?" and they answered, "Yes." 20. David then got up from the ground, bathed and anointed himself, changed his robe, went into the House of the Lord, prostrated himself, went home, asked for food, which was set before him, and he ate. 21. His servants said to him, "What is this thing you have done? For the living child you fasted and wept, and when the child died, you got up and ate food!" 22. He answered, "When the child was still alive I fasted and wept, for I thought, 'Who knows, perhaps the Lord will take pity on me and the child will live.' 23. But now that he is dead, why should I fast? Can I bring him back again? I am going to him but he will not come back to me." 24. David consoled his wife Bathsheba. He came into her and lay with her, and she bore a son and named him Solomon, and the Lord loved him.

The paradox of David's behavior in his grief is mirrored in the strategies of narrative exposition adopted to present it. The whispered words of the servants (which were directly reported in verse 18) prepare us for a terrific outburst from the king. Instead, as soon as he hears the monosyllabic confirmation of his worst suspicions, "Yes" (in the Hebrew, *met*, "dead"), he rises, and we see him in a rapid sequence of acts, conveyed in a chain of nine uninterrupted verbs, which are left entirely enigmatic until his simple, starkly eloquent words of explanation to the baffled servants. All men may indeed grieve over the loss of their loved ones, but this universal fact does not produce a universal response because the expression of feeling, the very experience of the feeling, takes place through the whorled and deeply grained medium of each person's stubborn individuality. As readers, we are quite as surprised as the servants by David's actions, then his words, for there is very little in the narrative before this point that could have prepared us for this sudden, yet utterly convincing, revelation of the sorrowing David, so bleakly aware of his own inevitable mortality as he mourns his dead son.

The exchange between David and the servants is cut off after his answer, without any dramatic closure. Their reaction is no longer of any interest, and, in typical biblical fashion, as we leap forward to the conjugal consoling of Bathsheba and the birth of the divinely favored son that balances out the death of the first child, we are given no hints from the narrator for the imaginative reconstruction of David's recovery from this bereavement. The symmetrically marked pattern of divine punishment for the founder of the Israelite dynasty followed by divine compensation frames the whole episode; but David, as his speech to the servants vividly illustrates, is a sentient person, not just a pawn in God's grand historical design, and about many facets of this person—in contrast to the Homeric heroes—we are left to wonder. But this sober moment of strange mourning will continue to echo in our memory, for we shall soon enough be provided in the stories of Amnon and Tamar, and of Absalom, with still more troubling instances of the aging David's anguish as a father.

The Greek tendency to narrative specification, as I suggested earlier, seems to be one that modern literary practice has by and large adopted and developed. Precisely for that reason, we have to readjust our habits as readers in order to bring an adequate attentiveness to the rather different narrative maneuvers that are characteristic of the Hebrew Bible. But the underlying biblical conception of character as often unpredictable, in some ways impenetrable, constantly emerging from and slipping back into a penumbra of ambiguity, in fact has greater affinity with dominant modern notions than do the habits of conceiving character typical of the Greek epics. The monotheistic revolution in consciousness profoundly altered the ways in which man as well as God was imagined, and the effects of that revolution probably still determine certain aspects of our conceptual world more than we suspect. This altered consciousness was of course expressed ideologically in the legislative and prophetic impulses of the Bible, but in biblical narrative it was also realized through the bold and subtle articulation of an innovative literary form. The narrative art of the Bible, then, is more than an aesthetic enterprise, and learning to read its fine calibrations may bring us closer than the broad-gauge concepts of intellectual history and comparative religion to a structure of imagination in whose shadow we still stand.

7

Composite Artistry

ANY ATTEMPT to recover the literary art of the Bible is bound to encounter a variety of obstacles intervening between the would-be knower and the object of knowledge. We may, of course, have certain limited advantages as modern readers approaching this body of texts which hitherto has been treated mainly in theological, philological, and historical terms. That is, what we bring to the Bible as readers, say, of Boccaccio, Flaubert, Tolstoy, Conrad, and Kafka, may on occasion throw unexpected light on the ancient text because, given the finite repertory of fictional modes available at any time, there may be certain partial but substantial affinities between ancient and modern narrative practice. Yet it must also be recognized that there is but a step from such serendipity to the pitfall of gratuitously modernizing the ancient through the subtle pressure of interpretive ingenuity. More commonly, I should think, one discovers that the characteristic procedures of biblical narrative differ noticeably from those of later Western fiction but that the biblical conventions can be grasped by some process of cautious analogy with conventions more familiar to us, as is the case with the use of type-scenes and verbatim repetition in the biblical stories. There are, however, still other aspects of the Bible that would appear to baffle our efforts to make sense of it as literary form.

The chief of these problematic aspects is the often ambiguous status of those components of the biblical corpus commonly called "books," or, indeed, of many discrete narrative segments within the individual books. The usual object of literary investigation is a book, or, as many prefer to say now under the influence of recent French intellectual fashions, a text. But the biblical text often proves under scrutiny to be at once multiple and fragmentary. Quite frequently, we cannot be sure what the boundaries of a given text are, how it is continued in surrounding texts, why it may be ignored, echoed, cited, or even actually duplicated elsewhere in the biblical corpus. A still graver challenge to the integrity of many biblical texts which we might want to look at as literary wholes is the elaborately layered nature of the material articulated in ancient tradition. A century of analytic scholarship has made powerful arguments to the effect that where we might naively imagine that we are reading a text, what we actually have is a constant stitching together of earlier texts drawn from divergent literary and sometimes oral traditions, with minor or major interventions by later editors in the form of glosses, connecting passages, conflations of sources, and so forth. The most eminent instance of this composite character of the biblical text has been found by scholars in the first four books of the Pentateuch, which, on the evidence of style, consistency of narrative data, theological outlook, and historical assumptions, have been exhaustively analyzed as a splicing of three separate primary strands—the Yahwistic Document *(J)*, the Elohistic Document *(E)*, and the Priestly Document *(P)*. *J* might date back to the tenth century B.C.E.; *E* could be about a century later, *P* would appear to be the work of a tradition of priestly writers, not one author, that begins fairly early in the First Temple period and continues into the sixth and fifth centuries B.C.E. (Scholarly ingenuity being what it is, various sub-documents as well as intermediate stages between the original literary traditions and the final editing have been proposed, but the intricacies of the argument need not concern us here, only the basic proposition, which seems convincing enough, that the text as we have it was not the work of a single hand, or of a single moment in time.) Beyond the Pentateuch, the textual components of the narrative books of the Bible have not been blessed with the classroom clarity of these alphabetical markers, but under analysis a good many passages in the Former Prophets reveal composite elements analogous to, and perhaps sometimes even continuous with, what has been discovered in the Pentateuch.

All this would seem to be an embarrassment for the kind of literary analysis I have been advocating, for in discussing works of literature, one still likes to assume that there is something "esemplastic," as Coleridge put it, in the activity of the literary imagination, some deep intuition of art that finely interweaves, shaping a complex and meaningful whole which is more than the sum of its parts. What, then, are we to do with our literary notions of intricate design in reading these texts which the experts have invited us to view, at least in the more extreme instances, as a crazy quilt of ancient traditions?

At the outset of this inquiry, I suggested that the editorial combination of different literary sources might usefully be conceived as the final stage in the process of artistic creation which produced biblical narrative. The illustration I used, however—the interpolated story of Judah and Tamar in Genesis 38—does not touch the root of the problem, for even in the unitary texts of much later writers like Cervantes, Fielding, Diderot, and Dickens, one may find deliberate interpolations that have important thematic and structural functions, while the composite texts of the Bible sometimes confront us with discontinuities, duplications, and contradictions which cannot be so readily accommodated to our own assumptions about literary unity. What I should like to propose here is that the biblical writers and redactors—since the line between the two is not always clear, I prefer to stick to the more familiar and literary of the two terms—had certain notions of unity rather different from our own, and that the fullness of statement they aspired to achieve as writers in fact led them at times to violate what a later age and culture would be disposed to think of as canons of unity and logical coherence. The biblical text may not be the whole cloth imagined by pre-modern Judeo-Christian tradition, but the confused textual patchwork that scholarship has often found to displace such earlier views may prove upon further scrutiny to be purposeful pattern.

Admittedly, the effort to reconstruct a conception of structural unity divergent from our own and separated from us by three millennia can have no easy guarantee of success. There are passages of biblical narrative that seem to resist any harmonizing interpretation, leading one to conclude either that there were certain circumstances in the transmission and editing of ancient Hebrew texts which could on occasion lead to intrinsic incoherence, or that the biblical notion of what constituted a meaningful and unified narrative continuum might at times be unfathomable from the enormous distance of intellectual and historical evolution that stands between us and these creations of the early Iron Age. My own experience as a reader makes me suspect that such insoluble cruxes deriving from the composite nature of the text are a good deal rarer than scholars tend to assume, but in order to make the problem with which we are dealing perfectly clear, I should like to begin by describing just such a crux. From there I shall proceed to a borderline case, where there is a duplication of sources and a logical contradiction that may have some inferable justification in the writer's need to encompass his subject with satisfying fullness. Finally, I shall propose two extended illustrations of what I think can be convincingly construed as the use of composite materials to achieve a comprehensiveness of vision that is distinctively biblical.

Numbers 16 gives us a detailed account of the aborted rebellion in the wilderness by Korah and his followers against the authority of Moses. The story is forceful enough to have made Korah a kind of archetype of the willful rebel against legitimate rule, but careful scrutiny suggests that the reports of two different rebellions have been superimposed upon one another, leaving evident contradictions as to the identity of the rebels, the purpose of the rebellion, the place of confrontation with Moses, and the manner in which the rebels are destroyed.[1]

The story begins with a somewhat confusing introduction (Num. 16:1–2) of the conspirators which in its very syntactical flaccidity would appear to reflect the writer's difficulties in combining disparate materials: "Then Korah son of Izhar son of Kohath son of Levi betook himself, and Dathan and Abiram sons of Eliab and On son of Peleth, the Reubenites, to rise up against Moses, with two hundred and fifty Israelites, chieftains of the congregation, elect of the assembly, men of standing." Korah is a Levite, and, logically enough, his motive for rebellion is the desire to assume priestly prerogatives, as the next block of verses (Num. 16:3–11) makes quite clear. His rebellion is said to be directed not just against Moses but against Moses and Aaron, the High Priest (verse 3). Moses addresses "Korah and his congregation," specifically turning to them as "sons of Levi" (verse 8), with no allusion whatever to the Reubenites Dathan and Abiram, who would in any case have had no special interest in priestly privileges. The legitimacy of Korah's claim to officiate in the cult is to be tested by a cultic trial: he and his two hundred and fifty followers are challenged to offer incense to the Lord in firepans before the Tent of Assembly, and to suffer the consequences if God should reject their assumption of sacerdotal rights.

Dathan and Abiram, introduced as a dangling syntactical member without a predicate in the initial verse of the chapter, do not enter the story at all until verse 12. Verses 12 through 15 then set aside Korah and his followers to concentrate exclusively on Dathan and Abiram. Here it becomes evident that the Reubenite rebellion, unlike that of the Levites, is directed against Moses alone, not against Moses and Aaron, and what is at issue is political authority—appropriately enough, if one recalls that Reuben is the firstborn of Jacob. Verses 16 through 22 abandon Dathan and Abiram once more to report the preparatory stage of the trial of the firepans involving only the Korahites. Verses 23 through 34 narrate the destruction of Dathan and Abiram and their families, which takes place not at the Tent of Assembly but by the tents of the Reubenites,

---

[1] In what follows, my awareness of the textual problems of this chapter has been considerably sharpened through discussions with my colleague Jacob Milgrom, and through a fine essay by my student Nitza Ben-Dov.

Dathan and Abiram having defiantly refused Moses' summons to "come up" from their dwellings to parley with him. An editorial attempt to keep the two stories together is reflected in the strangely fused locution (verses 23 and 27), "the dwelling of Korah, Dathan and Abiram" (Korah, as a member of a different tribe, would hardly have shared tents with the two Reubenites). Dathan and Abiram perish by being swallowed up by the earth. The addition of Korah and his people to this catastrophe just before the end of verse 32 looks like an editorial afterthought that is inconsistent with the preceding account of Dathan and Abiram, *sans* Levites, standing at the entrance of their tents as the convulsion of the earth begins. Finally, the annihilation of the rebel Levites, firepans in hand, actually occurs at another location, the area in front of the Tent of Assembly, and the method of destruction is not engulfment but incineration, a fire shooting out from the Lord (verse 35, the last verse of the chapter).

The internal contradictions of Numbers 16 are grave enough to have caught the attention of pre-modern commentators. Thus the twelfth-century Abraham Ibn Ezra, one of the most acute and one of the most rationalistic of traditional Hebrew exegetes, succinctly defines the very problem we have been considering in his comment on the end of the chapter:

> Some say that Korah was among those swallowed up, and the proof is "The earth swallowed them up, and Korah" [Num. 26:10]. Others say he was incinerated, and their evidence is "And Korah, when the congregation perished, when the fire consumed" [the very next clauses of the same verse, Num. 26:10]. And our sages of blessed memory say that he was both incinerated and swallowed up. But in my opinion, only in the place of Dathan and Abiram did the earth split open, for Korah is not mentioned there; in fact, Korah was standing with the chieftains who were offering the incense.

The biblical account actually seems devised to confuse the two stories and the two modes of destruction, an intention revealed not only in some of the formal features of the story we have just reviewed but also in the retrospective comment of Numbers 26:10, where the syntactically ambiguous phrase "and Korah" hovers uneasily between seismic convulsion and divine fire. Ibn Ezra, who was a remarkably gifted Hebrew poet as well as an exegete, tries to rescue the narrative coherence of the story by proposing that in its dénouement it bifurcates into two locations, with different victims and different modes of destruction in each. But the writer's own editorial maneuvers indicate that he would prefer us to see the two rebellious parties and the two catastrophes as one, or at least as somehow blurred together.

Why he should have wanted to do this is bound to remain a matter of conjecture because it runs so drastically counter to later notions of how a story should be put together. I don't think the confusion can be facilely attributed to mere editorial sloppiness, for there is evidence of some careful aesthetic and thematic structuring in the story. The initial speech of the Korahite rebellion begins with the phrase, "It's too much for you"; Moses, toward the end of his rejoinder, invokes the antithesis, "Isn't it enough for you?" This formal symmetry is extended as the Reubenite speech of rebellion begins with the phrase, "Isn't it enough?" In the story of Dathan and Abiram, where the rebels want to rise to political domination, the recurrent thematic key-word is "to go up," completed ironically in the dénouement when they "go down" into the chasm of the underworld. Correspondingly, in the Korahite rebellion, where the aspiration is to priesthood, the *Leitwörter* are "to take" and "to come [or bring] close," terms of horizontal movement toward the center of the cult instead of vertical movement toward or away from dominion.[2]

All this leads one to suspect that the Hebrew writer may have known what he was doing but that we do not. Certainly our notions about the spatial integrity of the location of a narrated action, the identity of personages, the consistency of agency and motive in the development of plot, are all flagrantly violated. Given the subject of the story, perhaps there were compelling political reasons for fusing the two rebellions. Perhaps all these considerations of narrative coherence seemed less important to the writer than the need to assert thematically that the two separate events—the attempt to seize political power and the usurpation of sacerdotal function—comprised one archetypal rebellion against divine authority and so must be told as one tale. The rebels are destroyed when the earth opens up its mouth, as it did to take in the blood of the murdered Abel, and by divine fire, like the rain of fire that descended on Sodom and Gomorrah. The story may deliberately echo, then, both the first act of sibling violence that prefigures all later struggles for power, and the proverbial tale of a society destroyed because it was utterly pervaded by corruption. For us, the two agencies of destruction are mutually contradictory; for the ancient Hebrew, they conceivably may have been mutually reinforcing, as the two paradigmatic images of divine retribution, suggesting an ultimate identity of the political and religious realms under God's dominion. In any case, the perplexities raised by the intertwined stories of Korah and Dathan and Abiram illustrate that there are aspects of

[2] I am indebted to Nitza Ben-Dov for her perception of these *Leitwörter*.

the composite nature of biblical narrative texts that we cannot confidently encompass in our own explanatory systems.

Let us now consider a more compact example of composite narrative, where there is duplication together with seeming contradiction, but not the sort of bewildering entanglement of narrative strands we have seen in Numbers 16. At the end of the first visit of Joseph's brothers to Egypt (Genesis 42), Joseph—still of course perceived by them only as the alien Egyptian viceroy—gives secret instructions for the money they have paid for their grain to be slipped back into their sacks (Gen. 42:25). They have already been badly shaken, we should recall, by their temporary imprisonment on the charge of being spies, and by Joseph's holding Simeon as hostage and insisting that they bring Benjamin back with them to Egypt. These last two acts of the viceroy have led the brothers, by an obvious path of guilty associations, to recall their cruelty to the young Joseph and to wonder whether retribution for that crime has finally overtaken them. Now, at the first encampment on the way north to Canaan (Gen. 42:27–28), one of them opens his sack to feed his donkey, "and he saw his money, and there it was at the mouth of his bag." (Lest there be any doubt, we learn from the brothers' later report of this event to Joseph [Gen. 43:21] that all nine of them made this same discovery.) "And he said to his brothers, 'My money has been returned, and here it is in my bag.' Their hearts failed them, and trembling, they said to one another, 'What is this God has done to us?' "

As soon as this question is raised about the strange workings of destiny—for the force of the word for God in the original is not far from "fate"—the narrator hurries the brothers home to Canaan, where they relate to their father Jacob the troubles they have had with the Egyptian viceroy, concluding with an explanation of Simeon's absence and the Egyptian's demand that Benjamin be brought to him. Just at this point, the money hidden in the sacks makes an odd reappearance (Gen. 42:35–36): "As they were emptying their sacks, look, each man's money-bag was in his sack, and they saw their money-bags, they and their father, and they were afraid. Then Jacob their father said to them:

> "Me have you bereaved.
> Joseph is gone and Simeon is gone,
> and would you take Benjamin?
> Upon me are all these things."

According to our own understanding of narrative logic, it is obviously impossible that the brothers could discover the hidden money twice—

once at the encampment and once in Canaan in their father's presence—
and be surprised and frightened both times. (The biblical norms of narrative reliability will not really allow us to harmonize the second occurrence
with the first by construing "and they were frightened" in verse 35 as
a false show of fear staged to make an impression on Jacob.) Biblical
scholarship essentially explains this duplication as a clumsy piece of editing. There were, so the accepted hypothesis runs, two parallel accounts
of the Joseph story, E and J, which differed in some essential details. E,
which conveniently enough for the purposes of identification consistently
employs the term *saq* for "sack," is the main source used, and in that
version the money is discovered only when the brothers reach home,
the provender for the pack animals presumably having been carried in
separate packs, so that the sacks with the money would have been left
unopened on the way. In J, the term for pack is *ʾamtaḥat* (rendered here
as "bag"), and the *ʾamtaḥat*, unlike the *saq*, contains both provender and
silver. Scholars tend to assume that whoever was responsible for the
final formulation of our text, whether out of misguided loyalty to his
second source or out of simple poor judgment, included an excerpt from
J (verses 27–28, quoted above) in which, contradictorily, the money is
discovered at the encampment.

Precisely in this regard, I would like to raise a question of general
principle, for it may help us see the point of more elaborate instances
of manifest duplication in biblical narrative. The contradiction between
verses 27–28 and verse 35 is so evident that it seems naive on the part
of any modern reader to conclude that the ancient Hebrew writer was
so inept or unperceptive that the conflict between the two versions could
have somehow escaped him. Let me suggest that, quite to the contrary,
the Hebrew writer was perfectly aware of the contradiction but viewed
it as a superficial one. In linear logic, the same action could not have
occurred twice in two different ways; but in the narrative logic with
which the writer worked, it made sense to incorporate both versions
available to him because together they brought forth mutually complementary implications of the narrated event, thus enabling him to give a
complete imaginative account of it.

In the J version, where the brothers make the discovery when they
are all alone on the caravan track between Egypt and Canaan, their sheer
wonder over what has happened is stressed. It is true that they "tremble"
at the sight of the money, but the emphasis is on their sense of the
strange ways of destiny: "What is this God has done to us?" The J version
in this way is crucial for the writer because it ties in the discovery of
the money with the theme of Joseph's knowledge opposed to the brothers'

ignorance that is central to both meetings in Egypt and, indeed, to the entire story. When the brothers ask what is it *'Elohim*—God, fate, and even judge or master in biblical Hebrew—has done to them, we as readers perceive a dramatic irony continuous with the dramatic ironies of the previous scene in the viceregal palace: Joseph in fact is serving as the agent of destiny, as God's instrument, in the large plan of the story; and the very brothers who earlier were shocked at Joseph's dream of having the sun and moon and eleven stars bow down to him now unwittingly say "God" when we as readers know that they are referring to that which Joseph has wrought.

The *E* version of the same event, where the discovery occurs in the presence of Jacob, is much briefer, reporting the brothers' response to the presence of the money in their sacks with the single verb of fear, and with no dialogue to represent their amazed reflection on the ways of Providence. This version, let me suggest, indicates simple fear without wonder because it means to convey a direct connection between finding the money and the brothers' feelings of guilt over what they have done to Joseph. There is a whole network of motifs in this latter part of the Joseph story built on cunning repetitions and reversals of motifs that appear in the early part of the story. The brothers sold Joseph southward into slavery for twenty pieces of silver *(kesef)*; now they find at the end of their own northward journey from the place to which they sent him that the silver *(kesef)* they paid out has mysteriously reappeared in their saddle-packs, and this touches a raw nerve of guilt in them that had been laid bare earlier by Joseph's imprisonment of Simeon and his demand for Benjamin. One should note that the discovery of the money occurs in their recapitulation for Jacob of Joseph's speech to them (verses 33–34) at the exact point where, following the actual speech (verses 20–21), they "discovered" their guilt toward Joseph. In characteristic biblical fashion, the guilt is not spelled out by the narrator, only intimated in the verb of fearing, then picked up in dialogue as Jacob responds—and it is important to understand that it is a response—to the brothers. With them, he has seen the money. He also must have seen their fear. Then, as though giving voice to their unspoken guilt at the discovery of the money, he turns to them with an accusation: "Me have you bereaved. . . ." Like his speech in Genesis 37 after Joseph's bloodied tunic was brought to him, he expresses himself with the dramatic heightening of scannable verse (in my translation, I have indicated typographically the division into semantically parallel hemistichs), placing himself and his suffering ("Me have you bereaved. . . . Upon me are all these things") at the beginning and the end of the poem. Interestingly, when

Joseph disappeared, Jacob made no direct accusation against his sons; but here, as though the momentum of his rhetoric were carrying him to the brink of the literal truth, he charges them with having bereaved him of both Joseph and Simeon.

The Joseph story has both a moral-psychological axis and a theological-historical one. In regard to the latter category, what is important is the mysterious workings of God, Joseph's role as an agent of divine destiny, and the paramount theme of knowledge versus ignorance. In regard to the former category, what is crucial is the painful process by which the brothers come to accept responsibility for what they have done and are led to work out their guilt. (Jacob's lament here as a chronically bereaved father is followed immediately by an extravagant offer on the part of Reuben to assume total responsibility for Benjamin's safety, and then, a little later, by a more measured statement on the part of Judah, who initiated the selling of Joseph and who will be the eloquent, conscience-stricken spokesman for the brothers in their ultimate arraignment by Joseph.) I cannot pretend to certainty in what I have inferred about the biblical writer's sense of appropriate form, but it seems to me at least plausible that he was prepared to include the minor inconvenience of duplication and seeming contradiction in his narrative because that inclusion enabled him to keep both major axes of his story clearly in view at a decisive juncture in his plot. A writer in another tradition might have tried somehow to combine the different aspects of the story in a single narrative event; the biblical author, dealing as he often did in the editing and splicing and artful montage of antecedent literary materials, would appear to have reached for this effect of multifaceted truth by setting in sequence two different versions that brought into focus two different dimensions of his subject.

The analogy of film montage in fact suggests something of the dynamic interplay between two different presentations of a subject in narrative sequence which we find in the Bible. Sergei Eisenstein's classic description of the montage effect is worth recalling in just this regard: "The juxtaposition of two separate shots by splicing them together resembles not so much a simple sum of one shot plus one shot—as it does a *creation*. It resembles a creation—rather than a sum of its parts—from the circumstance that in every such juxtaposition *the result is qualitatively* distinguishable from each component element viewed separately. . . . Each particular montage piece exists no longer as something unrelated, but as a given *particular representation* of the general theme" (the emphases are Eisenstein's).[3]

---

[3] *The Film Sense*, trans. and ed. Jay Leyda (London, 1943), p. 17.

Just such a technique of placing two parallel accounts in dynamically complementary sequence is splendidly evident at the very beginning of the Hebrew Bible. There are, of course, two different creation stories. The first, generally attributed to *P,* begins with Genesis 1:1 and concludes with the report of the primeval sabbath (Gen. 2:1–3), probably followed, as most scholars now think, by a formal summary in the first half of Genesis 2:4: "Such is the story of heaven and earth when they were created." The second version of the creation story, taken from the *J* Document, would then begin with the subordinate clause in the second half of Genesis 2:4, "When the Lord God made earth and heaven . . . ," going on to the creation of man, the vegetable world, the animal kingdom, and woman, in that order, and after the completion of creation proper at the end of Chapter 2, moving directly into the story of the serpent and the banishment from Eden.

Now, it is obvious enough that the two accounts are complementary rather than overlapping, each giving a different *kind* of information about how the world came into being. The *P* writer (for convenience, I shall refer to him in the singular even if this source may have been the product of a "school") is concerned with the cosmic plan of creation and so begins appropriately with the primordial abyss whose surface is rippled by a wind from (or spirit of) God. The *J* writer is interested in man as a cultivator of his environment and as a moral agent, and so he begins with a comment on the original lack of vegetation and irrigation and ends with an elaborate report of the creation of woman. There are also, however, certain seeming contradictions between the two versions. According to *P,* the sequence of creation is vegetation, animal life, and finally humanity. Although the chronology of acts of creation is not so schematically clear in *J,* the sequence there, as we have already noted, would appear to be man, vegetation, animal life, woman. In any case, the most glaring contradiction between the two versions is the separation of the creation of woman from the creation of man in *J*'s account. *P* states simply, "Male and female He created them," suggesting that the two sexes came into the world simultaneously and equally. *J,* on the other hand, imagines woman as a kind of divine afterthought, made to fill a need of man, and made, besides, out of one of man's spare parts.

Why should the author of Genesis have felt obliged to use both these accounts, and why did he not at least modify his sources enough to harmonize the contradictions? The scholars—who of course refer to him as redactor, not author—generally explain that he viewed his inherited literary materials as canonical, which meant both that he had to incorporate them and that he could not alter them. What of early Hebrew writings may have seemed canonical in, say, the fifth century B.C.E., or what that may have meant at the time is a matter of pure conjecture; but the text we have of the creation story has a coherence as significant form which we can examine, and I would argue that there were compelling literary reasons for the Genesis author to take advantage of both documents at his disposal—perhaps also rejecting others about which we do not know—and to take advantage as well of the contradictions between his sources. These reasons should become apparent through some close attention to the stylistic and thematic differences between the two creation stories.

Although *P* begins, according to the general convention of opening formulas for ancient Near Eastern creation epics, with an introductory adverbial clause, "When God began to create heaven and earth," his prose is grandly paratactic, moving forward in a stately parade of parallel clauses linked by "and" (the particle *vav*). Or, to switch the metaphor of motion, the language and the represented details of *P*'s account are all beautifully choreographed. Everything is numerically ordered; creation proceeds through a rhythmic process of incremental repetition; each day begins with God's world-making utterance ("And God said . . .") and ends with the formal refrain, "It was evening and it was morning," preceded in five instances by still another refrain, "And God saw that it was good." *P*'s narrative emphasizes both orderly sequence and a kind of vertical perspective, from God above all things down to the world He is creating. God is the constant subject of verbs of generation and the source of lengthy creative commands reported as direct speech. (By contrast, in *J*'s version, there is a whole block of verses [Gen. 2:10–14] where God is entirely absent as subject; man, moreover, performs independent action and utters speech; and the only direct discourse in the whole chapter assigned to God is His command to Adam not to eat from the Tree of Knowledge and His brief statement about man's need for a helpmate.)

The orderliness of *P*'s vision is expressed in another kind of symmetry that is both stylistic and conceptual: creation, as he represents it, advances through a series of balanced pairings, which in most instances are binary oppositions. *J* also begins by mentioning the creation of earth and heaven (significantly, earth comes first for him), but he makes nothing of the opposition in the development of his story, while *P* actually builds his picture of creation by showing how God splits off the realm of earth from the realm of heaven, sets luminaries in the heavens to shine on the earth, creates the birds of the heavens above together with the swarming things of the seas below. Darkness and light, night and day, evening and morning, water and sky, water and dry land, sun and moon, grass and trees, bird and sea-creature, beast of the field and creeping thing of the earth, human male and female—each moment of creation is conceived as a balancing of opposites or a bifurcation producing difference in some particular category of existence. In the first half of Chapter 1 (verses 1–19), for the first four days of creation, before the appearance of animate creatures, the governing verb, after the reiterated verbs of God's speaking, is "to divide," suggesting that the writer was quite aware of defining creation as a series of bifurcations or splittings-off. God divides primordial light from primordial darkness, the upper waters from the lower, day from night, terrestrial light from terrestrial darkness. In the second half of the story, as we pass on to the creation of the animal realm, the verbs of division disappear, and with the fuller details pertaining to animals and man, the symmetry is a little looser, less formulaic. Nevertheless, bracketed pairs continue to inform the account of cosmogony, and there is also a noticeable tendency to recapitulate many of the previous terms of creation as the narrative proceeds. The conclusion in the first sabbath vividly illustrates the emphatic stylistic balance, the fondness for parallelisms and incremental repetitions, that mark *P*'s entire account (Gen. 2:2–3):

And God completed on the seventh day His work which He had made.
And he ceased on the seventh day from all His work which He had
    made.
And God blessed the seventh day and He hallowed it.
For on it He had ceased from all His work which God created to make.

We have here not only incremental repetition but, as I have tried to show through this rather literal translation, a tightly symmetrical envelope structure, the end returning to the beginning: the first line of the passage ends with God's making or doing, as does the last, while the end of the last line, by also introducing the seemingly redundant phrase "God created," takes us all the way back to the opening of the creation story, "When God began to create." In *P*'s magisterial formulation, everything is ordered, set in its appointed place, and contained within a symmetrical frame.

All this reflects, of course, not simply a bundle of stylistic predilections but a particular vision of God, man, and the world. Coherence is the keynote of creation. Things come into being in orderly progression, measured in a numerical sequence which is defined by the sacred number seven. Law, manifested in the symmetrical dividings that are the process of creation and in the divine speech that initiates each stage of creation, is the underlying characteristic of the world as God makes it. Man, entering the picture climactically just before it is declared complete on the seventh day, is assigned a clearly demarcated role of dominance in a grand hierarchy. In this version of cosmogony, God, as Einstein was to put it in his own argument against randomness, decidedly does not play dice with the universe, though from a moral or historical point of view that is exactly what He does in *J*'s story by creating man and woman with their dangerous freedom of choice while imposing upon them the responsibility of a solemn prohibition.

J's strikingly different sense of the movement of creation makes itself felt from the outset in his syntax and in the rhythms of his prose. Instead of stylistic balance and stately progression, he begins with a subordinate clause that leads us into a long and sinuous complex sentence which winds its way through details of landscape and meteorology to the making of man (Gen. 2:4b–47):

> At the time when the Lord God was making earth and heaven, no shrub of the field yet being on the earth and no grain of the field yet having sprouted, for the Lord God had not made rain fall on the earth and there was no man to work the soil, but a flow would well up from the earth to water the whole surface of the soil—then the Lord God fashioned man from clods of the soil and blew into his nostrils the breath of life, and man became a living being.

J needs this kind of ramified syntax, so unlike *P*'s, because he constantly sees his subject in a complex network of relations that are causal, temporal, mechanical, and, later in the chapter, moral and psychological as well. His prose imparts a sense of rapid and perhaps precarious forward movement very different from *P*'s measured parade from first day to seventh. It is a movement of restless human interaction with the environment, even in Eden: here man *works* the soil, which cannot realize its full inventory of nourishing plant life until that work has begun; in *P*'s version, man, more grandly and more generally, has dominion over the natural world. Man as *J* imagines him is more essentially bound to the natural world, formed out of a humble clod, his name, *ʾadam*, in a significant etymological pun, derived from *ʾadamah*, soil. He is one with the earth as he is not in *P*'s hierarchical sequence; but he is also apart from it by virtue of the very faculty of consciousness that enables him to give things their names, and by virtue of the free will through which he will cause himself to be banished from the Garden, henceforth to work the soil as an arduous punishment rather than as a natural function.

P is interested in the large plan of creation; *J* is more interested in the complicated and difficult facts of human life in civilization, for which he provides an initial explanation through the story of what happened in Eden. Man culminates the scheme of creation in *P*, but man is the narrative center of *J*'s story, which is quite another matter. *P*'s verbs for creation are "to make" (ʿasoh) and "to create" (baroʾ), while *J* has God "fashioning" (yatzor), a word that is used for potters and craftsmen, and also makes him the subject of concrete agricultural verbs, planting and watering and causing to grow.

J's concern with the mechanics of things is continuous with his vision of God, man, and history. The world is stuff to be worked and shaped through effort, for both man and God; language has its role in ordering things, but it is not, as in *P*, generative. If man's role as worker of the earth is stressed at both the beginning and the end of the Eden story, one might also infer that God's work with man does not cease with the fashioning into creaturehood of the original clod of earth. In this version of creation, there is moral tension between man and God—a notion not hinted at in *P*—and also, as God's solicitude for man's loneliness shows, there is divine concern for man. It is instructive that here no speech of God occurs until He addresses man and reflects on man's condition. The verb "to say," which in the first account of creation introduced each of the divine utterances through which the world was brought into being, here is used to designate *thought* or interior speech, the brief divine monologue in which God ponders man's solitude and resolves to alleviate it (Gen. 2:18): "And the Lord God said, 'It is not good for man to be alone. I shall make him an aid fit for him.'"

The differences between our two versions are so pronounced that by now some readers may be inclined to conclude that what I have proposed as a complementary relationship is in fact a contradictory one. If, however, we can escape the modern provincialism of assuming that ancient writers must be simple because they are ancient, it may be possible to see that the Genesis author chose to combine these two versions of creation precisely because he understood that his subject was essentially contradictory, essentially resistant to consistent linear formulation, and that this was his way of giving it the most adequate literary expression. Let me explain this first in the notorious contradiction about the creation of woman, and then go on to comment briefly on the larger cosmogonic issues.

It may make no logical sense to have Eve created after Adam and inferior to him when we have already been told that she was created at the same time and in the same manner as he, but it makes perfect sense as an account of the contradictory facts of woman's role in the post-edenic scheme of things. On the one hand, the writer is a member of a patriarchal society in which women have more limited legal privileges and institutional functions than do men, and where social convention clearly invites one to see woman as subsidiary to man, her proper place, in the Psalmist's words, as a "fruitful vine in the corner of your house." Given such social facts and such entrenched attitudes, the story of Eve's being made from an unneeded rib of Adam's is a proper account of origins. On the other hand, our writer—one does not readily think of him as a bachelor—surely had a fund of personal observation to draw on which could lead him to conclude that woman, contrary to institutional definitions, could be a daunting adversary or worthy partner, quite man's equal in a moral or psychological perspective, capable of exerting just as much power as he through her intelligent resourcefulness. If this seems a fanciful inference, one need only recall the resounding evidence of subsequent biblical narrative, which includes a remarkable gallery of women—Rebekah, Tamar, Deborah, Ruth—who are not content with a vegetative existence in the corner of the house but, when thwarted by the male world or when they find it lacking in moral insight or practical initiative, do not hesitate to take their destiny, or the nation's, into their own hands. In the light of this extra-institutional awareness of woman's standing, the proper account of origins is a simultaneous creation of both sexes, in which man and woman are different aspects of the same divine image. "In the image of God He created him. Male and female He created them" (Gen. 1:27). The decision to place in sequence two ostensibly contradictory accounts of the same event is an approximate narrative equivalent to the technique of post-Cubist painting which gives us, for example, juxtaposed or superimposed, a profile and a frontal perspective of the same face. The ordinary eye could never see these two at once, but it is the painter's prerogative to represent them as a simultaneous perception within the visual frame of his painting, whether merely to explore the formal relations between the two views or to provide an encompassing representation of his subject. Analogously, the Hebrew writer takes advantage of the composite nature of his art to give us a tension of views that will govern most of the biblical stories—first, woman as man's equal sharer in dominion, standing exactly in the same relation to God as he; then, woman as man's subservient helpmate, whose weakness and blandishments will bring such woe into the world.

A similar encompassing of divergent perspectives is achieved through the combined versions in the broader vision of creation, man, and God. God is both transcendent and immanent (to invoke a much later theological opposition), both magisterial in His omnipotence and actively, empathically involved with His creation. The world is orderly, coherent, beautifully patterned, and at the same time it is a shifting tangle of resources and topography, both a mainstay and a baffling challenge to man. Humankind is the divinely appointed master of creation, and an internally divided rebel against the divine scheme, destined to scrabble a painful living from the soil that has been blighted because of man. The creation story might have been more "consistent" had it begun with Genesis 2:4b, but it would have lost much of its complexity as a satisfying account of a bewilderingly complex reality that involves the elusive interaction of God, man, and the natural world. It is of course possible, as scholars have tended to assume, that this complexity is the purely accidental result of some editor's pious compulsion to include disparate sources, but that is at least an ungenerous assumption and, to my mind, an implausible one as well.

The effectiveness of composite narrative as a purposeful technique is even more vividly evident when the primary aim is the presentation of character. The most elaborate biblical instance is the introduction of David, which, as has been often noted, occurs in two consecutive and seemingly contradictory versions (1 Samuel 16 and 17). In the first account, the prophet Samuel is sent to Bethlehem to anoint one of the sons of Jesse as successor to Saul, whose violation of divine injunction has just disqualified him for the kingship that was conferred on him. Samuel, after mistaking the eldest of the brothers as the divinely elected one, is directed by God to anoint David, the youngest (a pattern of displacing the firstborn familiar from Genesis). Following the anointment, David is called to Saul's court to soothe the king's mad fits by playing the lyre, and he assumes the official position of armor-bearer to Saul. In the second account, David is still back on the farm while his older brothers (here three in number rather than seven) are serving in Saul's army against the Philistines. There is no mention here of any previous ceremony of anointing, no allusion to David's musical abilities or to a position as royal armor-bearer (indeed, a good deal is made of his total unfamiliarity with armor). In this version David, having arrived on the battlefield with provisions for his brothers, makes his debut by slaying the Philistine champion, Goliath, and he is so unfamiliar a face to both Saul and Abner, Saul's commander-in-chief, that, at the end of the chapter, they both confess they have no idea who he is or what family he comes from, and he has to identify himself to Saul.

Logically, of course, Saul would have had to meet David for the first time either as music therapist in his court or as giant-killer on the battlefield, but he could not have done both. Both stories are necessary, however, for the writer's binocular vision of David. In this case, the inference of a deliberate decision to use two versions seems especially compelling, for the author of the David story, unlike the author of Genesis, is not working with traditions sanctified by several centuries of national experience, but is rendering an account of a historical figure separated from him by perhaps only a few decades, if that. One must assume that he had considerably greater freedom as to what he "had" to include than did the Genesis author, and therefore that if he chose to combine two versions of David's debut, one theological in cast and the other folkloric, it was because both were necessary to his conception of David's character and historical role. Much the same point has been made by Kenneth R. R. Gros Louis in an intelligent essay on the larger David story: "But surely whoever put the narrative into this final form was aware of the inconsistency too; such inconsistency in close proximity in a narrative is more than an author's nodding; it is the equivalent of deep sleep." Gros Louis goes on to propose that the two introductions of David correspond to two different aspects of the future king which are reflected in his relationship with Saul and which will remain in tension throughout his story—the private person and the public figure. Saul, in his different roles as troubled individual and jealous monarch, responds in different ways to these two aspects of David. "Saul the man can love his comforter and recall the refreshment brought to him by his music; Saul the king cannot bear to hear the Israelite women singing, 'Saul has slain his thousands, and David his ten thousands.' "[4] I think Gros Louis is quite right about the presence of a complex interplay between the public and private aspects of David throughout this extraordinary narrative, but those categories need to be supplemented in several ways in order to get a full sense of the range of complementary viewpoints that are brought to bear in the two accounts of David's debut. It is important to observe differences not only in thematic emphasis and narrated facts but, as we have done with the creation story, in matters of style and narrative approach.

Symmetry, pattern, formally defined closure, and what Buber and Rosenzweig called *Leitwortstil,* a style governed by thematic key-words, are all far more prominent in the first version than in the second. Chapter 16 of 1 Samuel begins with a dialogue between Samuel and God, and the divine view from above controls everything that happens in this version of the debut. God oversees, God intervenes directly in the designation of His anointed. "Go, I shall send you to Jesse the Bethlehemite," He tells Samuel at the outset, "for I have chosen Me from his sons a king" (1 Sam. 16:1). The verb "chosen" (*ra'oh be . . .*) points neatly in two

---

[4] "The Difficulty of Ruling Well: King David of Israel" *Semeia* 8 (1977), pp. 15–33.

thematic directions. It is an antonym of "reject" (*ma²os be . . .*) and "to choose not" (*lo² bahor be . . .*), which function as *Leitwörter* referring both to the turning away of Saul and the choices *not* to be made among Jesse's sons. At the same time, the literal meaning of the idiom is "to see in," and the verb "to see" will be the other dominant thematic key-word of the story. If God has already made His choice of the new king, why does He not tell Samuel from the start which of Jesse's sons it will be? Clearly, so that a didactic ritual of true choice after false, true sight after false, can be enacted. In the "vertical" perspective of the story, the substantive exchanges are all between God and His prophet, while dialogue between Samuel and the town elders, Samuel and Jesse, is kept to a minimum. This is how the election itself is presented:

6. And when they arrived, he saw Eliab and thought, "Surely before the Lord His anointed now stands." 7. And God said to Samuel, "Look not at his appearance [*mar²eihu*, verbal stem *ra²oh*] nor at his tall stature, for I have rejected him. For not as man sees [does the Lord see].[5] For man sees with the eyes, and the Lord sees with the heart." 8. Then Jesse called to Abinadab and had him pass before Samuel, and he said, "This one, too, the Lord has not chosen." 9. Then Jesse had Shammah pass by, and he said, "This one, too, the Lord has not chosen." 10. Thus Jesse had his seven sons pass before Samuel, and Samuel said to Jesse, "The Lord has not chosen these." 11. Then Samuel said to Jesse, "Are there no more lads?" And he answered, "The youngest still remains, and, here, he is tending the flock." Samuel said to Jesse, "Send someone to bring him, for we shall not sit down to eat till he comes." 12. So he sent and had him brought, and he was ruddy with beautiful eyes as well and of goodly appearance [*ro²i*, verbal stem *ra²oh*]. And the Lord said, "Rise and anoint him, for he is the one."

The whole event is an exercise in seeing right, not only for Jesse and his sons and the implied audience of the story, but also for Samuel, who was earlier designated seer (*ro²eh*). Samuel had first chosen as king Saul, who stood head and shoulders above ordinary men; now he nearly makes the same mistake with Jesse's strapping firstborn, Eliab, and so God, reading his thoughts, must instruct him: "Look not at his appearance nor at his tall stature." From the initial dialogue between Samuel and the Lord to the final anointing of David and the descent upon him of the spirit of the Lord (1 Sam. 16:13), God's steady perception manifestly commands the scene, distinguishing, as human eyes could not, between

[5] The bracketed phrase reflects the reading of the Septuagint.

Eliab's prepossessing appearance, which betokens no worthiness to rule, and David's goodly appearance, which happens to be joined with an inner nature made to do great things. Human interactions here are held at a distance, stylized, to make the perfect clarity of divine perception thematically transparent. We move in formulaic repetition from the first son to the seventh, the *"et cetera* principle" being invoked after the third son so that the rapid movement to the revelatory point—the youngest son called in from the flock—is not bogged down.

The spirit that descends on David, seizes him, as it did the Judges before him, then becomes the thematic key-word of the second half of the chapter. The spirit of the Lord which grips David "had departed from Saul" (1 Sam. 16:14), and in its place the king is racked by "an evil spirit from the Lord." When his courtiers suggest lyre-playing as a remedy, Saul enjoins them, "Choose [*re'u*, verbal stem *ra'oh*] me a man skilled in playing" (1 Sam. 16:17), and one of them volunteers, "I have seen [*ra'iti*] a son of Jesse the Bethlehemite, skilled in music, a valiant fellow and a warrior, prudent in speech, a handsome man, and the Lord is with him" (1 Sam. 16:18). The reference to David's martial prowess looks suspiciously like an attempt to harmonize Chapter 16 and Chapter 17, perhaps even by a later editor, for there has been no suggestion up to this point that the young shepherd David had any military experience, and if he were already known as a formidable warrior, it would make no sense for Saul to give him the menial role of armor-bearer (1 Sam. 16:21). Otherwise, David's appearance in court, lyre in hand, is beautifully consistent with the preceding story of his anointment. Samuel had anointed him "in the midst of his brothers," that is, within the secrecy of the family circle, so it is of course not known in court that he has any pretensions to the throne. Because, however, the spirit of the Lord has descended on him, his personal allure, his gift for succeeding, have begun to make themselves felt, and people already sense, as with Joseph, that "the Lord is with him." Having been graced with the spirit, David is then seen exerting mastery, through song, over the realm of spirits, a point underscored by a pun in the last verse of the chapter (1 Sam. 16:23): "And whenever the [evil] spirit [*ruah*] of God was upon Saul, David would take up his lyre and play, and Saul would be eased [*ravah*] and feel well, and the evil spirit [*ruah*] would depart from him."

The second version of David's debut, almost three times the length of the first, is too long for us to consider in close detail. The relative length of the story, however, reflects a very different conception of how David's fitness for the throne is first revealed. This chapter is as close as the Hebrew Bible comes to an "epic" presentation of its materials.

Unlike the previous chapter, where the three points of geographical reference—Bethlehem, the court, and Samuel's home at Ramah—are simply
stated, Chapter 17 of 1 Samuel gives us an elaborate panorama of the
geographical deployment of the two armies, then a detailed description
of Goliath's armor and weapons. The second version is much more concerned with how David will operate on the spatial coordinates and with
the material instruments of the political and military realm, and so it
adopts a style that draws us at once into the thick of historical experience.
The motif of the unknown young man who astonishes his elders and
slays the dread giant is common to many folkloric traditions, but here
it is woven persuasively into the texture of historical fiction, given the
concreteness of vividly verisimilar dialogue (David's angry exchange with
his contemptuous big brother Eliab, his verbal parrying with Goliath)
quite unlike the stylized and formulaic dialogue of the preceding story.
God does not speak at all here and is not a direct presence in the action.
Rather, the human hero of the story invokes Him in hurling back the
enemy's challenge: "You come to me with sword and spear and javelin,
and I come to you with the name of the Lord of Hosts, the God of the
battle-ranks of Israel whom you have defied. On this day the Lord will
deliver you into my hands" (1 Sam. 17:45–46). David's conquest by slingshot is a literal enactment of the monotheistic principle of "not by the
sword does the Lord give victory" which he announces to Goliath.

It should be observed that in Chapter 16 David never speaks, and
does very little, being the subject of only two verbs, "to take up" and
"to play" at the end of the chapter. Here, on the other hand, he speaks
at great length, in fact shows himself a master of rhetoric (in keeping
with the epithet "prudent in speech" assigned to him in 1 Sam. 16:18);
and he is, of course, a bold, adept, and energetic performer of actions.
At the narrative climax of Chapter 17, verses 45–51, he is the subject
of fourteen different verbs—rushing, running, taking, hurling, hitting,
cutting, killing—in quick succession. In the first version, David's pastoral
occupation is a static though probably also symbolic fact, since "shepherd"
is a recurrent biblical epithet for leader. In the second version, David
cites his shepherd's experience as evidence of the practical training he
has undergone to fit him for dangerous combat: just as he has repeatedly
destroyed lion and bear at close quarters in protecting his flock, he will
fell the overweening Philistine. He does not mention the lethal skill with
the slingshot that he has also acquired in his work as a shepherd, but
he will soon demonstrate that on the battlefield.

What is gained for the general presentation of David by putting these
two versions together? It might be noted that there is an approximate

analogy to the interaction of the two sources for the creation story in Genesis (though I am by no means suggesting that one derives from *P* and the other from *J!*): a human-centered, richly detailed "horizontal" view following a more concise, more symmetrically stylized, "vertical" view which moves from God above to the world below. These two views correspond in part, but only in part, to the public and private David, the David Saul envies, then hates as his rival, and the one whom he loves as his comforter. David will be the brilliant warrior-king and (as Shimei of the house of Saul one day will call him) the "man of blood," and for this identity the Goliath story is the fitting introduction. But he is also to figure as the eloquent elegist, the composer of psalms, the sensitive and passionate man who loves Jonathan and weeps for his dead sons; and this side of him is properly introduced in the story of his debut as a court musician with the gift of driving out evil spirits through his song.

These two versions are not only functions of David's character but of what we are to make of his election as king. In the first account, his election is absolute, an unambiguously divine choice, perhaps made because of what God knows about David's special nature, but clearly bestowed upon him as a gift, or a fate, without the slightest initiative on his part. In the second account, David secures the first toehold in his climb from sheepfold to throne by his own bold action—and in so doing, as the dialogue at the end of the chapter between Saul and Abner, then Saul and David, intimates, he stirs the first feelings of unease in the reigning king that a dangerous rival may have come forth from Bethlehem. In the first version, David is not referred to as man or boy, except in the possibly interpolated epithet of the courtier, who calls him a "man of war," for he is essentially imagined as a comely receptacle for the divine spirit that enters into him. In the second version, Goliath the champion (literally, "the man of the spaces between the two armies") invites a "man" to come out against him and is enraged when he finds himself confronted with a mere "lad" (1 Sam. 17:42)—a lad who will of course brilliantly prove his manhood by toppling his enormous adversary. To be sure, even in the second version, David performs his heroic act with the explicit consciousness that he is serving the ends of the omnipotent God of Israel; but the joining of the two accounts leaves us swaying in the dynamic interplay between two theologies, two conceptions of kingship and history, two views of David the man. In one, the king is imagined as God's instrument, elected through God's own initiative, manifesting his authority by commanding the realm of spirits good and evil, a figure who brings healing and inspires love. In the other account, the king's election is, one might say, ratified rather than initiated by God; instead of the spirit descending, we have a young man ascending through his own resourcefulness, cool courage, and quick reflexes, and also through his rhetorical skill. All this will lead not directly to the throne but, as things usually happen in the mixed medium of history, to a captaincy; further military successes, a devoted following; the provocation of jealousy in the king, which brings about his banishment; a career of daring action, subterfuge, hardship, and danger; a bloody civil war; and only then the throne. Without both these versions of David's beginnings and his claim to legitimacy as monarch, the Hebrew writer would have conveyed less than what he conceived to be the full truth about his subject.

Poetry and fiction, as literary theorists from the Russian Formalists and the Anglo-American New Critics onward have often observed, involve a condensation of meanings, a kind of thickening of discourse, in which multiple and even mutually contradictory perceptions of the same object can be fused within a single linguistic structure. An exemplary text in just this regard to set alongside 1 Samuel 16 and 17 is Andrew Marvell's "An Horatian Ode Upon Cromwell's Return from Ireland." When the poem was written in 1650, Marvell was moving from his early sympathy for the royalist cause to a sincere advocacy of the new revolutionary regime, and the poem would seem to embody antithetical views of the formidable Cromwell, who had just subdued (and fearfully devastated) Ireland, antithetical views held together under high tension. Thus, Marvell writes that Cromwell

> Could by industrious Valour climbe
> To ruine the great Work of Time,
>   And cast the Kingdome old
>   Into another Mold.

As elsewhere in the poem, virtually every phrase is abundantly susceptible of opposite constructions: Cromwell may be the paragon of political greatness, the man with the courage and resoluteness to change the course of history; and he may be an awesome horseman of the apocalypse, ruthlessly laying waste all that time has patiently wrought. In the stylistic compression of the poem, he is both at once, or constantly threatens to be one when he seems to be the other.

In biblical narrative, this kind of purposeful ambiguity of a single statement may occur, as I have suggested in discussing characterization, in the selective reticences of the narrator's reports and in the sudden breaking off of dialogue as well. In regard to larger blocks of narrative material, the characteristic biblical method for incorporating multiple perspectives appears to have been not a fusion of views in a single utterance but a montage of viewpoints arranged in sequence. Such a formula, of course, cannot smooth away all the perplexities of scribal and editorial work with which the biblical text confronts us; but we are well advised to keep in mind as readers that these ancient writers, like later ones, wanted to fashion a literary form that might embrace the abiding complexity of their subjects. The monotheistic revolution of biblical Israel was a continuing and disquieting one. It left little margin for neat and confident views about God, the created world, history, and man as political animal or moral agent, for it repeatedly had to make sense of the intersection of incompatibles—the relative and the absolute, human imperfection and divine perfection, the brawling chaos of historical experience and God's promise to fulfill a design in history. The biblical outlook is informed, I think, by a sense of stubborn contradiction, of a profound and ineradicable untidiness in the nature of things, and it is toward the expression of such a sense of moral and historical reality that the composite artistry of the Bible is directed.

8

Narration and Knowledge

THE CONCEPTION of biblical narrative as prose fiction which I have been proposing entails an emphasis on deliberate artistry and even playfulness that may seem a little odd according to common notions, both popular and scholarly, of what the Bible is. Having considered some of the major aspects of the Bible's narrative art, I think it may be useful now to restate a basic question raised near the outset of this inquiry. The ancient Hebrew writers, or at least the ones whose work has been preserved because it was eventually canonized in the biblical corpus, were obviously motivated by a sense of high theological purpose. Habitants of a tiny and often imperfectly monotheistic island in a vast and alluring sea of paganism, they wrote with an intent, frequently urgent awareness of fulfilling or perpetuating through the act of writing a momentous revolution in consciousness. It is obvious enough why the Prophets should have used poetry, with its resonances, emphases, significant symmetries, and forceful imageries, to convey their vision, for prophetic poetry is a form of direct address which is heightened, made memorable and almost inexorable through the rhetorical resources of formal verse. By contrast, biblical narrative, if it is also to be construed as a kind of discourse on God's purposes in history and His requirements of humanity, is indirect discourse on those subjects (the one great exception being the Book of Deuteronomy, which is cast in direct discourse as Moses' valedictory address to the people of Israel). The degree of *mediation* involved in talking about what the Lord requires by making characters talk and by reporting their actions and entanglements opens up what may seem to the moralistic theist a Pandora's box. For would it not be frivolous on the part of an anonymous Hebrew writer charged with the task of formulating sacred traditions for posterity to indulge in the writerly pleasures of sound-play and word-play, of inventing vivid characters with their own quirks and speech habits, of limning with all the resources of stylistic ingenuity the comic frustration of a failed seduction, the slow diplomatic progress of bargaining over a burial site, the wrangling of brothers, the foolishness of kings?

It seems to me perfectly plausible to assume, as I suggested earlier, that the makers of biblical narrative gave themselves to these various pleasures of invention and expression because, whatever their sense of divinely warranted mission, they were, after all, writers, moved to work out their vision of human nature and history in a particular medium, prose fiction, over which they had technical mastery, and in the manipulation of which they found continual delight. I think such an inference is amply confirmed by the fine articulations of the actual texts the biblical writers produced, though it may require an act of mental reorientation to see a closer *generic* link—the consideration of genre here is crucial—between Genesis and *Tom Jones* than between Genesis and the *Summa Theologiae* or the cabbalistic *Book of Creation*. This notion, however, of the biblical writers' vocation for fiction needs to be amplified. If fiction is a form of play, it is also, even in ultimate instances of flaunted playfulness, like *Gargantua and Pantagruel*, *Tristram Shandy*, and *Ulysses*, a form of play that involves a particular mode of knowledge.

We learn through fiction because we encounter in it the translucent images the writer has cunningly projected out of an intuitively grasped fund of experience not dissimilar to our own, only shaped, defined, ordered, probed in ways we never manage in the muddled and diffuse transactions of our own lives. The figures of fiction need not be verisimilar in an obvious way to embody such truths, for exaggeration or stylization may be a means of exposing what is ordinarily hidden, and fantasy may faithfully represent an inner or suppressed reality: Uncle Toby and Mr. Micawber, Panurge and Gregor Samsa, are vehicles of fictional knowledge as much as Anna Karenina and Dorothea Brooke. What I should like to stress is that fiction is a mode of knowledge not only because it is a certain way of imagining characters and events in their shifting, elusive, revelatory interconnections but also because it possesses a certain repertoire of techniques for telling a story. The writer of fiction has the technical flexibility, for example, to invent for each character in dialogue a language that reflects, as recorded speech in ordinary discourse would not necessarily reflect, the absolute individuality of the character, his precise location at a given intersection with other characters in a particular chain of events.

The writer of fiction exercises an even more spectacular freedom in his ability to shuttle rapidly between laconic summary and leisurely scenic representation, between panoramic overview and visual close-up, in his capacity to penetrate the emotions of his characters, imitate or summarize their inner speech, analyze their motives, move from the narrative present to the near or distant past and back again, and by all these means to control what we learn and what we are left to ponder about the characters and the meaning of the story. (In nearly all these regards, a more formulaic mode of storytelling like the folktale or even some kinds of epic has a more limited range of possibilities.)

In chapter 2, I contended that the biblical authors were among the pioneers of prose fiction in the Western tradition. Let me now add the suggestion that they were impelled to the creation of this new supple narrative medium at least in part because of the kind of knowledge it could make possible. The narrators of the biblical stories are of course "omniscient," and that theological term transferred to narrative technique has special justification in their case, for the biblical narrator is presumed to know, quite literally, what God knows, as on occasion he may remind us by reporting God's assessments and intentions, or even what He says to Himself. The biblical Prophet speaks in God's name—"thus saith the Lord"—as a highly visible human instrument for God's message, which often seems to seize him against his will. The biblical narrator, quite unlike the Prophet, divests himself of a personal history and the marks of individual identity in order to assume for the scope of his narrative a godlike comprehensiveness of knowledge that can encompass even God Himself. It is a dizzying epistemological trick done with narrative mirrors: despite anthropomorphism, the whole spectrum of biblical thought pre-supposes an absolute cleavage between man and God; man cannot become God and God (in contrast to later Christian developments) does not become man; and yet the self-effacing figures who narrate the biblical tales, by a tacit convention in which no attention is paid to their limited human status, can adopt the all-knowing, unfailing perspective of God.

The biblical tale might usefully be regarded as a narrative experiment in the possibilities of moral, spiritual, and historical knowledge, under-taken through a process of studied contrasts between the variously limited knowledge of the human characters and the divine omniscience quietly but firmly represented by the narrator. From time to time, a human figure is granted special knowledge or foreknowledge, but only through God's discretionary help: Joseph can interpret dreams truly, as he repeatedly affirms, only because the interpretation of dreams is the Lord's. Various of the biblical protagonists are vouchsafed promises, enigmatic predictions, but the future, like the moral reality of their contemporaries, remains for the most part veiled from them, even from an Abraham or a Moses who has been privileged with the most direct personal revelation of God's presence and will. Dedication to a divinely certified career of visionary leadership is itself no escape from the limitations of human knowledge: Samuel the seer, as we had occasion to note, mistakes physical for regal stature in the case of both Saul and Eliab, and has to undergo an object lesson in the way God sees, which is not with the eyes but with the heart—the heart in biblical physiology being the seat of understanding rather than of feeling. Human reality, perhaps most memorably illustrated in the cycle of stories from Jacob's birth to his death in Egypt with Joseph at his bedside, is a labyrinth of antagonisms, reversals, deceptions, shady deals, outright lies, disguises, misleading appearances, and ambiguous portents. While the narrator sees the labyrinth deployed before him in its exact intricate design, the characters generally have only broken threads to grasp as they seek their way.

We are never in serious doubt that the biblical narrator knows all there is to know about the motives and feelings, the moral nature and spiritual condition of his characters, but, as we have seen on repeated occasions, he is highly selective about sharing this omniscience with his readers. Were he to invite our full participation in his comprehensive knowledge, in the manner of a discursive Victorian novelist, the effect would be to open our eyes and make us "become like God, knowing good and evil." His typically monotheistic decision is to lead us to know as flesh-and-blood knows: character is revealed primarily through speech, action, gesture, with all the ambiguities that entails; motive is frequently, though not invariably, left in a penumbra of doubt; often we are able to draw plausible inferences about the personages and their destinies, but much remains a matter of conjecture or even of teasing multiple possibilities.

All this, however, is not to suggest that the Hebrew Bible is informed by the epistemological skepticism of fictions like James's *The Turn of the Screw,* Kafka's *The Castle,* and Robbe-Grillet's *Jealousy.* There is a horizon of perfect knowledge in biblical narrative, but it is a horizon we are permitted to glimpse only in the most momentary and fragmentary ways. The narrator intimates a meaningful pattern in the events through a variety of technical procedures, most of them modes of indirection. In the purposeful reticence of this kind of narration, the characters retain their aura of enigma, their ultimate impenetrability at least to the human eyes with which perforce we view them. At the same time, however, the omniscient narrator conveys a sense that personages and events produce a certain stable significance, one which in part can be measured by the varying distances of the characters from divine knowledge, by the course through which some of them are made to pass from dangerous ignorance to necessary knowledge of self and other, and of God's ways.

The preeminent instance of biblical narrative as a fictional experiment in knowledge is the story of Joseph and his brothers, for in it the central actions turn on the axis of true knowledge versus false, from the seventeen-year-old Joseph's dreams of grandeur to his climactic confrontation with his brothers in Egypt twenty-two years later. This theme of knowledge is formally enunciated through the paired key-words, *haker,* "recognize," and *yado⁽a,* "know," that run through the story (the French *connaître* and *savoir* may indicate the distinction between the terms better than these English equivalents). Joseph is of course the magisterial knower in this story, but at the outset even he has a lot to learn—painfully, as moral learning often occurs. In his early dreams, he as yet knows not what he knows about his own destiny, and those dreams which will prove prophetic might well seem at first the reflex of a spoiled adolescent's grandiosity, quite of a piece with his nasty habit of tale-bearing against his brothers and with his insensitivity to their feelings, obviously encouraged by his father's flagrant indulgence. The heretofore shrewd Jacob on his part is just as blind—and will remain so two decades later—as his old father Isaac was before him. He witlessly provokes the jealousy of the ten sons he had by his unloved wife Leah and by the concubines; then he allows himself to be duped about the actual fate of Joseph at least in part because of his excessive love for the boy and because of his rather melodramatic propensity to play the role of sufferer. Finally, the ten brothers are ignorant of Joseph's real nature and destiny, of the consequences of their own behavior, of the ineluctable feelings of guilt they will suffer because of their crime, and, climactically, of Joseph's identity when he stands before them as viceroy of Egypt. Events, or rather events aided by Joseph's manipulation, force them to knowledge and self-knowledge, this arduous transition providing the final resolution of the whole story.

It may be instructive to look closely at this grand climax of the Joseph story, not only because it illustrates so vividly the connections between fiction and knowledge but also because, with the author's extraordinary technical virtuosity (which we observed before in our readings of Genesis 38 and 39), these episodes provide a splendid synthesis of the various artful procedures of biblical narrative that we have been considering. The entire conclusion, from Jacob's dispatch of the ten brothers to Egypt in order to buy food to their second return to Canaan, when they inform their father that the long-mourned Joseph is alive and ruler of Egypt, is one tightly interwoven whole, but it is unfortunately too long to examine here verse by verse. A close reading, however, of Genesis 42, which reports the brothers' first encounter with Joseph in Egypt together with their return to Jacob in Canaan, should give an adequate idea of the complex interplay of narrative means through which the writer richly renders theme, motive, and character. Since this chapter is not a relatively self-contained unit, like Genesis 38, but rather the first movement in the climax of the story, I shall then proceed to comment briefly on how what is artfully articulated here is continued, developed, and brought to a resolution in the next three chapters.

Jacob, we should recall, has been out of the picture entirely since the end of Genesis 37, when his sons brought him Joseph's blood-soaked tunic and he drew the expected catastrophic conclusions from it. At that juncture, the sons merely asked him to recognize the garment, while, in a paroxysm of grief, he did most of the talking. Now, twenty-two years later and after two consecutive years of severe famine, Jacob does all the talking:

> 1. Jacob saw that there were emergency provisions in Egypt, and Jacob said to his sons, "Why are you staring at each other?" 2. And he said, "Look, I have heard that there are emergency provisions in Egypt. Go down there and get us provisions from there so that we may live and not die." 3. Then Joseph's brothers ten went down to get provisions of grain from Egypt. 4. But Benjamin, Joseph's brother, Jacob did not send with his brothers, for he thought he might meet disaster. 5. Thus the sons of Israel came to get provisions among the others who had come, for the famine had reached the land of Canaan.

Jacob sees that there is grain to be bought in Egypt, while his sons for the moment seem to be looking only at each other, an apt introduction to the series of events in which they will be forced to confront one another over their past actions. What is even more prominent as an introductory note is the fact that this segment of the story starts with the brothers inactive, made the object of a rebuke. There is a hiatus of silence between verse 1 and verse 2, between "Jacob said" and his saying again, a silence which tends to confirm Jacob's charge that his sons are simply standing there staring at one another when urgent action has to be taken. (This is still another illustration of the rule of thumb that when biblical dialogue is entirely one-sided or when an expected response is cut off, we are invited to draw inferences about the characters and their relations. The present passage gives us an exact reversal of the roles played by

Jacob and his sons at the end of Genesis 34, the conclusion of the story of the rape of Dinah. There, when Jacob upbraids Simeon and Levi for massacring the male population of Shechem, they answer, "Shall our sister be treated like a whore?" [Gen. 34:31] and on these defiant words the story concludes, Jacob's final silence providing an index of his impotence in the face of his violent sons.) The brothers, then, follow their father's command, in virtual or actual silence, and the narrator is careful to inform us that they are ten when they go down to Egypt, for the exact number of the brothers, indicating who is present and who is absent, will be important in what ensues. Though the ten are quite naturally identified as "the sons of Israel" when they arrive in Egypt, emissaries of their patriarchal father, as they set out they are called "Joseph's brothers." They are headed, of course, for an ultimate test of the nature of their brotherhood with Joseph, a bond which they have denied by selling him into slavery and which they will now be forced to recognize in a new way. When Benjamin is designated "Joseph's brother," the phrase means something different genealogically and emotionally, for he is Joseph's full brother, the only other son of Rachel. There is, then, a delicate play of ambiguous implications in verses 3 and 4 as we move from "Joseph's brothers" to "Joseph's brother" and "his [Benjamin's] brothers," and this interplay brings into the foreground the whole vexed question of fraternity soon to be dramatically resolved. We are told nothing of the ten brothers' response to their father's withholding of Benjamin, a repetition of the privileged treatment he once gave Joseph. The dénouement will in fact hinge on their ability to accept with full filial empathy this special concern of their father's for his remaining son by Rachel.

At this point, the narrator, in the characteristic rush of biblical narrative to the essential moment, catapults the brothers from Canaan to Egypt and into the presence of Joseph. The central narrative event will now be rendered, as the Hebrew writers typically do, through dialogue, though each of the succinct interventions of the narrator is tactically effective and thematically revealing, beginning with the ostensibly superfluous observation about Joseph's status that opens this section. Here is the entire account of the brothers' first visit to Egypt, up to the point where Joseph will give the command for their money to be slipped back into their packs, an episode we have already considered in connection with the issue of composite narrative.

6. And Joseph was the vizier of the land, it was he who dispensed provisions to all the people of the land. And Joseph's brothers came

and bowed down to him, their faces to the ground. 7. Joseph saw his brothers and recognized them, and he played the stranger to them and spoke harshly to them, saying to them, "Where have you come from?" And they said, "From the land of Canaan, to procure food." 8. Joseph recognized his brothers but they did not recognize him. 9. And Joseph remembered the dreams he had dreamt about them, and he said to them, "You are spies! To see the land in its nakedness you have come." 10. And they said to him, "No, my lord, for your servants have come to procure food. 11. We are all the sons of one man. We are honest. Your servants would never be spies." 12. He said to them, "No! For the land in its nakedness you have come to see." 13. And they said, "We your servants were twelve brothers, the sons of one man in the land of Canaan, and look, the youngest is now with our father, and one is no more." 14. Joseph said to them, "That's just what I told you: you are spies. 15. Let this be your test—I swear by Pharaoh that you shall not leave this place unless your youngest brother comes here! 16. Send one of you to bring your brother, and as for the rest of you, you will remain under arrest, and your words will be tested as to whether there is truth in you, and if not, by Pharaoh, you must be spies!" 17. And he confined them in the guardhouse for three days. 18. On the third day Joseph said to them, "Do this and you shall live, for I am a God-fearing man. 19. If you are honest, let one of you brothers be detained in your place of arrest, and the rest of you go forth and bring back provisions to your starving households. 20. And your youngest brother you shall bring to me, so that your words may be confirmed and you need not die." And they did accordingly. 21. And they said to one another, "Why, we are guilty for our brother, whose sore distress we saw when he pleaded with us and we did not listen. That is why this distress has overtaken us." 22. Then Reuben answered them in these words: "Didn't I say to you, 'Do not sin against the boy,' and you would not listen? And now comes the reckoning for his blood." 23. And they did not know that Joseph understood [literally, "was listening"], for there was an interpreter between them. 24. He turned away from them and wept and returned to them and spoke to them. And he took Simeon from them and placed him in fetters before their eyes.

We hardly needed to be told that Joseph was viceroy of Egypt and chief provisioner (verse 6) because both his investment in high office and his economic policy were related in detail in the last part of the preceding chapter. The thematic utility, however, of repeating this information in summary form just as the brothers arrive is evident. Joseph's two dreams are here literally fulfilled, the dream of the sun and moon and stars bowing down to him linked more directly to his role as vizier, the dream of sheaves of grain bowing down to him pointing more particularly to his role as provisioner. The brothers then enact that long ago dreamt-of prostration, a gesture of absolute obeisance concretized by the addition of the emphatic phrase "their faces to the ground." They, of course, are unaware of what the narrator reminds us (flaunting his omniscience in order to underline their ignorance): that their essential identity here is as "Joseph's brothers" (verse 6), and that it is Joseph who is vizier and dispenser of provisions. Their ignorance here of Joseph's actual identity is an ironic complement to their earlier failure to recognize his true destiny. The opposition between Joseph's knowledge (which is also the narrator's) and the brothers' ignorance is focused through the insistence of a *Leitwort* that figured earlier in the story: he recognizes them, they recognize him not; and in a pun characteristic of *Leitwortstil*, he makes himself a stranger or seems a stranger to them, *vayitnaker*, a verb with the same root, *nkr*, as "recognize," *haker*.

Verse 9, in which Joseph remembers his early dreams, is one of those rare moments in the Bible when a narrator chooses not only to give us temporary access to the inward experience of a character but also to report the character's consciousness of his past. That unusual note is entirely apt here both because Joseph himself is struck by the way past dreams have turned into present fact, and because he will force his brothers into a confrontation with their own past. The two previous episodes of the Joseph story (Genesis 40 and 41) had been devoted to knowledge of the future—Joseph's interpretations of the dreams of his two fellow prisoners, then of Pharaoh's two dreams. Genesis 42, by contrast, is devoted to knowledge of the past, which, unlike knowledge of the future, is not a guide to policy but a way of coming to terms with one's moral history, a way of working toward psychological integration.

No causal connection is specified between the fact of Joseph's remembering his dreams and the accusation of espionage he immediately levels against his brothers, a characteristic biblical reticence that allows for overlapping possibilities of motive. The narrator presumably knows the connection or connections but prefers to leave us guessing. Does the recollection of the dreams, coupled with the sight of the prostrate brothers, trigger a whole train of memories in Joseph, from the brothers' scornful anger after his report of the dreams to his terror in the pit, not knowing whether the brothers had left him there to die? Does Joseph now feel anger and an impulse to punish his brothers, or is he chiefly triumphant,

moved to play the inquisitor in order to act out still further the terms
of his dreams, in which the brothers must repeatedly address him self-
effacingly as "my lord" and identify themselves as "your servants"? Is
he moved chiefly by mistrust, considering his brothers' past behavior?
Is the accusation of espionage merely the most convenient way he as
viceroy can threaten these foreigners, or does he sense some underlying
affinity between the deceptiveness of spying and the deceptiveness of
fraternal treachery? One is even led to wonder whether the reiterated
phrase, "the land in its nakedness" (literally, "the nakedness of the land")
might not have a special psychological resonance for Joseph in regard
to what he perceives to be his brothers' relation to him and to his father.
All the other biblical occurrences of the common idiom "to see the nakedness of" or "to uncover the nakedness of" are explicitly sexual, usually
referring to incest (it is precisely the phrase used for the act Ham perpetrates on his father Noah), and perhaps Joseph feels a kind of incestuous
violence in what the brothers have done to him and through him to
his father. Reuben, it may be relevant to recall, the firstborn of the ten,
actually lay with Bilhah, Jacob's concubine and Rachel's maid and conjugal
surrogate, not long after Rachel's death, when Joseph was still a boy.
Perhaps none of these inferences is absolutely inevitable, but all are distinctly possible, and the narrator's refusal to supply specific connections
between Joseph's remembering and his speaking conveys a rich sense
of how the present is overdetermined by the past; for in this characteristic
biblical perspective no simple linear statement of causation can adequately
represent the density and the multiplicity of any person's motives and
emotions. Joseph is not unknowable either to God or to the narrator
but he must remain in certain respects opaque because he is a human
being and we, the readers of the story, see him with human eyes.

The entire dialogue between Joseph and his brothers is remarkable
for the way that words, creating the fragile surface of speech, repeatedly
plumb depths of moral relation of which the brothers are almost totally
unaware and which even Joseph grasps only in part. Ostensibly a political
interrogation, it is really the first of three climactic dialogues between
Joseph and his brothers about their shared past and the nature of their
fraternal bond. The ten brothers, of course, are throughout the object
of dramatic irony, not knowing what both Joseph and we know, for
example, when they announce, "We are all the sons of one man" (verse
11). (The double edge of this statement was not lost on earlier commentators. Thus Rashi, the great medieval French Hebrew exegete, observes:
"They had a sudden flash of divine inspiration and included him with
themselves.") But this is dramatic irony which outdoes itself through a

series of psychologically fraught double meanings that trace the chief convolutions of their troubled fraternity. We are twelve, the brothers tell Joseph (for despite the more logical translation, "we were," the Hebrew of verse 13 invites construal as a present-tense statement). Only the two sons of Rachel are distinguished from the twelve: the youngest one is with his father and another, also unnamed, is no more. The ambiguity of this euphemism for death—it might also mean simply "is not" or "is absent"—aptly reflects the ambiguity of the brothers' intentions toward Joseph and the uncertainty of their knowledge about what has become of him. First they had thought of actually killing him, and Reuben, who tried to save him and found the pit empty, apparently still imagines (verse 22) that Joseph was killed. In any case, having sent Joseph southward to a distant slavemarket, the brothers might properly think him gone forever, as good as dead, or perhaps after all these years of grinding servitude, dead in fact.

Joseph's sharp response (verses 14–16) to this report of the brothers is an apparent *non sequitur* in the surface dialogue but faithfully follows the logic of the subsurface exchange on the nature of their fraternal connection. Why, after all, should the admission of the ten that they have two more brothers, one at home and one gone, be seized as proof—"That's just what I told you!"—that they are spies? One may guess that the brothers' veiled statement about Joseph's fate trips a trigger of anger in him, reminding him of their treachery and thus driving him to repeat the accusation of espionage. He then demands that Benjamin be brought to him, not only because he may be eager to see his full brother but also because, with the memory of the ten brothers' act of betrayal uppermost in his mind, he can hardly trust these sons of Leah and the concubines; he may well wonder what they might have done to the other of Rachel's two sons. The "test" Joseph proposes has only a specious logic in the interrogation of spies: he implies that if one part of their statement about their family condition can be shown to be false, then there is no truth in them and they must be spies. (This obviously could not work as a test of spies because the converse would not hold: they might be telling the truth about their brother at home and yet be in Egypt to gather intelligence for unspecified Canaanite powers.) But the test has a profound logical function in the oblique interrogation of brothers: if in fact they have left Benjamin unharmed all these years, the truth of their words will be confirmed, that, despite past divisiveness, "we are twelve . . . brothers, the sons of one man."

The narrator, as we have noted, began the episode by emphatically and symmetrically stating Joseph's knowledge and the brothers' ignorance.

Now, through all this dialogue, he studiously refrains from comment, allowing the dynamics of the relationship between Joseph and his brothers to be revealed solely through their words, and leaving us to wonder in particular about Joseph's precise motives. Whatever those may be, the alertness to analogy to which biblical narrative should have accustomed us ought to make us see that Joseph perpetrates on the brothers first a reversal, then a repetition, of what they did to him. They once cast him into a pit where he lay uncertain of his fate; now he throws all ten of them into the guardhouse where he lets them stew for three days; then, as they did before, he isolates one brother—"one" of you brothers like the "one" who is said to be no more—and deprives him of his freedom for a period that might prove indefinite. (When Jacob learns of Simeon's absence, he is quick to make this equation: "Me have you bereaved. / Joseph is gone and Simeon is gone" [Gen. 42:36].) We as readers knowingly perceive this analogy between Joseph's past plight and the present one of the brothers. They, on their part, express at least an intuitive understanding of that connection, for they see the workings of a principle of retaliation in which "distress" is inflicted for "distress." What this means is that in their dialogue with each other (verses 21–22), the submerged interrogation on brotherhood present in their interview with Joseph breaks through to the surface: arrested as spies, they are impelled to confess to each other their guilt in having done away with their brother. It is a fine stroke of delayed exposition that only now are we informed that when Joseph was seized by his brothers, he pleaded with them and they turned a deaf ear. Genesis 37, which reports the actual event of the kidnaping, is entirely silent on Joseph's words and feelings at that terrible moment; now the brothers' guilt is compounded by this new revelation of an imploring Joseph surrounded by impassive brothers.

But do the brothers imagine they are guilty of murder or kidnaping? Conventional biblical scholarship misses the point by supposing that the entire narrative is a somewhat confused splicing of two disparate versions of the Joseph story, E and J: in E, Reuben is Joseph's advocate and concludes he is dead after the Midianites (having found the boy in the pit quite by chance) take him away; in J, Judah saves Joseph's life by proposing to sell him into slavery, the slavetraders here being identified as Ishmaelites. Though not all the details of the two versions have been harmonized as modern conventions of consistency would require, it seems to me clear that the writer needs both for a variety of reasons, the most urgent one at the present juncture being a desire to intimate some moral equivalence between kidnaping and murder. In both versions, the brothers as a group first intended to kill Joseph. When Reuben discovers Joseph has vanished from the pit from which he had planned secretly to rescue the boy, the well-meaning firstborn is persuaded that his brother is dead. This overlap of the supposedly fatal disappearance of Joseph with the deliberate selling of Joseph suggests that selling him into slavery is a virtual murder and thus undermines Judah's claim that by selling the boy the brothers will avoid the horror of blood-guilt. Now, as the brothers finally face their culpability two decades after the criminal fact, it is the voice of Reuben that is heard, accusing them of fratricide, and no one tries to deny the accusation because for all they know that may be, at least in effect, the crime they have committed by selling him as a slave.

At precisely this point (verses 23–24) the narrator, who has absented himself ever since the first half of verse 9, except to convey tersely the information that Joseph placed his brothers under arrest (verse 17), steps forward to report something about Joseph which changes the whole emotional configuration we have been observing. First, there is another piece of delayed exposition which was cunningly withheld for the perfect moment. Up till now, we have not been encouraged to puzzle about the language in which Joseph and his brothers communicated. Perhaps we might even have supposed that this Egyptian political wizard would naturally exhibit a fluency in Canaanite dialects, only taking care regularly to swear by Pharaoh as a token of his thoroughly Egyptian identity. In any case, the mention of an interpreter at the beginning of his first dialogue with the brothers would have blunted the sense of immediate confrontation which, as we have seen, is so essential psychologically and thematically in the progress of that scene. Now, when we are told that all along they have been speaking with a translator as intermediary, we are brought up short. Suddenly we realize that there is an added, technical dimension to the opposition between Joseph's knowledge and the brothers' ignorance: throughout this meeting, unknown to them, he has "understood" them or "listened to" them, and at this point he has just heard them twice confess their own past failure to listen to or understand him. "He turned away from them and wept and returned to them and spoke to them. And he took Simeon from them and placed him in fetters before their eyes." Until this moment, we might have assumed a perfect continuity between Joseph's harsh speech and his feelings. Perhaps, we may faintly wonder, these tears are tears of self-pity or anger, and we are to assume that the harshness persists. But it seems far more likely that as Joseph hears his brothers' expression of remorse, the first strong impulse of reconciliation takes place in his own feelings, though he cannot yet trust them and so must go on with the test. Through the knowing eyes of the omniscient narrator, we see him weeping in private, then resuming his stern

Egyptian mask as he returns to address the brothers and to take his hostage from them.

Joseph's weeping, moreover, at the end of this first encounter between the brothers initiates a beautifully regulated crescendo pattern in the story. Twice more he will weep. The second time (Gen. 43:30–31), when he first sets eyes on his brother Benjamin, is in its stylistic formulation an elaborate expansion of the first report of weeping: "Joseph hurried off, for he was overcome with feeling for his brother and wanted to weep, and he went into a room and wept there. Then he washed his face and came out and got control of himself." Unlike the account in Chapter 42, the motive for the weeping here is clearly stated, and the specification of minute actions—wanting to weep, going into another room, weeping, washing his face, composing himself—is far beyond the Bible's laconic norm, thus focusing the event and producing an effect of dramatic retardation in the narrative tempo. Manifestly, we are moving toward a climax, and it occurs in the third act of Joseph's weeping (Gen. 45:1–2), as at last he makes himself known to his brothers. Here, we are told that "he could no longer control himself," and the previously hidden weeping is now done in the presence of his brothers, turning into a tremendous sobbing that even the Egyptians standing outside can hear. The rising pattern, then, of three repetitions, begun with the eavesdropping Joseph of Gen. 42:24, is not only a formal symmetry through which the writer gives shape and order to his tale, but also the tracing of an emotional process in the hero, from the moment when twenty-two years of anger begin to dissolve to the one when he can bring himself to say "I am Joseph, your brother."

After Joseph's weeping and the imprisonment of Simeon in Genesis 42, the story moves on to the restoration of the brothers' money and then their first discovery of it (Gen. 42:25–28), which, as we saw in the previous chapter, stresses a sense of strange destiny and once more opposes the ignorance of the brothers to Joseph's knowledge. Immediately after this opening of the bags at the encampment, the brothers are placed back in Canaan in the presence of their father, and just as we would expect of the Bible's convention of verbatim repetition, they report what has befallen them in Egypt by an almost exact restatement of extensive phrasal elements from their earlier dialogue with Joseph. Understandably, this recapitulation (Gen. 42:29–34) of the previous scene in Egypt abbreviates it, but apart from the deletions, which speed up the narrative tempo in a way appropriate for the report of what has already been told, small, subtle changes in the phrasing and word order of the original dialogue nicely reflect the fact that the brothers are now addressing their father.

Joseph here is twice referred to as "the man who is lord of the land," in still another unwitting confirmation, this time shared by father and sons, of the dream that the sun and moon and eleven stars would bow down to him. In the brother's version for Jacob's benefit, first they affirm to Joseph the fact of their honesty and that they would never be spies, then that they are the twelve sons of one man, whereas in actually speaking to Joseph they first announced that they were all the sons of one man, as though somehow that were a necessary preamble to their declaration of honesty. "We were twelve brothers," they restate for Jacob their earlier speech to Joseph, "the sons of our father. One is no more and the youngest now is with our father in the land of Canaan" (Gen. 42:32). Naturally enough, in speaking to Jacob they refer to him as "our father" and not as "one man in the land of Canaan." They also reverse the order of the information they gave to Joseph, placing the brother who is no more first and the brother who is at home second. Perhaps they mean to suggest to their father that they divulged this precious fact of Benjamin's existence only grudgingly, at the end of their speech to the Egyptian overlord. In any case, "one is no more" is the climactic statement for Joseph, while "the youngest is now with our father" is the crucial revelation for Jacob, and so in each case what touches most deeply the person addressed is reserved for the last. When Joseph told the brothers of his intention to take a hostage, he said that one of them would be "detained" (the Hebrew word, *ye'aser,* could also mean, quite plainly, "be fettered") in prison; in repeating Joseph's words to Jacob, the brothers diplomatically soften this to "Leave one of your brothers with me." (This apt substitution of a tactful euphemism for the concrete image of incarceration beautifully demonstrates how the minor variations in the Bible's verbatim repetition are part of a deliberate pattern, not a matter of casual synonymity.) Finally, Joseph had concluded the terms of the test by saying that Benjamin would have to be brought to him if the brothers were to escape death; the brothers, in their report to Jacob, are careful to edit out this threatening talk of death and to make the vizier's speech end on a positive note, present only by implication in the actual words he used to them: "Then I shall know that you are not spies but that you are honest. Your brother I shall give back to you, and you will be free to move about in the land" (Gen. 42:34).

This attempt to give a faithful but also tactful account of what happened in Egypt is immediately followed by the second discovery of the money in the saddle-packs, the one that emphasizes the brothers' fear and, by implication, their sense of guilt. As we observed in chapter 7, Jacob responds to this moment and to the entire report that has preceded it by accusing his sons of having bereaved him and by exhibiting his own suffering in formal rhetorical emphasis. At this point, his firstborn steps forth:

37. Reuben said to his father, "My two sons you may put to death if I do not bring him back to you. Place him in my trust and I will return him to you." 38. And he said, "My son shall not go down with you. For his brother is dead and he alone remains, and should disaster befall him on the way, you would bring down my white head in grief to the underworld."

This dialogue—the narrator once more effaces himself and refrains from all "editorial" comment—provides a wonderful definition of the clash of different obtusities that so often constitutes family life and that has already had catastrophic consequences in this founding family of Israel. Reuben, the man of impulse who once violated his father's concubine and who also made a blundering attempt to save Joseph from the other brothers, invites Jacob to kill his own two sons if anything should happen to Benjamin. His father has just bemoaned being twice bereaved, and now Reuben compounds matters by proposing that Jacob do away with two of his grandsons if Benjamin should be lost! (There seems to be a deliberate matching of two lives for two here, for in Gen. 46:9 we learn that Reuben actually had four sons.) Again one understands why Reuben the firstborn will be passed over, and why the line of kings will spring from Judah, Joseph's second advocate, who in the next chapter (Gen. 43:8–9) will make a more reasonable statement of readiness to stand bond for Benjamin.

Jacob does not even honor Reuben's rash if well-meaning offer with a reply, but instead pronounces his determination not to allow Benjamin to go to Egypt. Before, he had said euphemistically and a little ambiguously that Joseph was gone; now he flatly states that Joseph is dead. Astonishingly, he remains as oblivious to the feelings of his ten sons as he was during Joseph's childhood. "He alone remains," he tells them to their faces, omitting the necessary phrase "from his mother," as though only the sons of Rachel, and not they, were his sons. Twenty-two years before, he had announced that he would go down to the underworld mourning his son. Now he concludes this episode by once more envisaging the descent of his white head to the underworld in inconsolable sorrow. Jacob is ever the rhetorician of grief, fond of verbal symmetries in his plaints, and so his speech begins with the words *lo'yered*, "he shall not go down," and concludes with the "bringing down" *(vehoradtem)* of his old man's head to the underworld, thus forming a neat envelope structure. There may be an ironic play between Sheol, the underworld, and Egypt, that alien land to the south famous for its monumental cult of the dead. Benjamin, of course, will duly go down to Egypt, and as things turn out, Jacob will be brought down by his sons not to the underworld but to Egypt, where Joseph is alive and resplendent in his viceregal power.

Having closely followed through Genesis 42 the minute development of this thematic opposition between knowledge and ignorance—an ignorance on the part of Jacob and his sons not only of Joseph's actual fate but also of the underlying moral configuration of their family—we may now hurry on to the denouement, with just a few brief comments on the passages that lead up to it (Gen. 43:1–44:17). Before long Jacob is forced to abandon his resolution concerning Benjamin by the brute force of circumstances: the persistence and worsening of the famine. At first he asks his sons in a rather gingerly phrase to "go back and get us a bit of food" (Gen. 43:2), as though it were a matter of a trip to a nearby market. Judah, now emphatically assuming the role of spokesman, makes it inexorably clear that the provisions can be obtained only if Benjamin comes along. "For the man said to us," he quotes Joseph, " 'You shall not see my face unless your brother is with you' " (Gen. 43:5). In point of fact, these particular words do not appear in the dialogue between Joseph and his brothers, but of course Judah is trying to drive home the idea to his reluctant father that the man who holds the keys to the life-sustaining grain will remain totally inaccessible without Benjamin. Judah attributes one other utterance to Joseph that did not figure in the actual dialogue in Egypt: the question, "Is your father still alive?" The way the Bible uses verbatim repetition with additions makes it at least possible to imagine that Joseph really asked such a question but that it simply was not included in the reported dialogue, so it is not absolutely necessary to construe it as an invention of Judah's. In any case, the main reason for introducing that question here is proleptic, pointing forward to Joseph's anxious inquiry (Gen. 43:27) of the brothers as to whether their father is still alive, and to his more urgent question, "Is my father still alive?" (Gen. 45:3) once he reveals himself—that is, now that you know I am Joseph, you can tell me the real truth about our father. Jacob bemoans his sons' imprudence in having even mentioned Benjamin's existence to the Egyptian, but Judah, with perfect thematic appropriateness, points out that they were caught in a web of consequences of which before the fact they were quite ignorant: "Know? How could we know that he would say, 'Bring down your brother'?" (Gen. 43:7). And so Jacob consents, grimly, reluctantly, to let Benjamin go, his last words to his sons striking a note of paternal grievance in perfect keeping with his previous speeches: "And as for me, if I am to be bereaved, then let me be bereaved" (Gen. 43:14).

Before this, however, he has instructed the brothers to take with them to Egypt double the money that was placed in their bags as well as balm, honey, gum, ladanum, pistachio nuts, and almonds (Gen. 43:11–12). By giving these orders, he unwittingly carries forward the pattern of restitution that marks the entire conclusion of the story. Money—specifically, pieces of silver—passed from the hands of the Ishmaelite traders to the brothers in exchange for Joseph, who was carried down to Egypt. Then Joseph sent money hidden in the bags back northward to Canaan. Now Jacob orders double the money to be sent back to Egypt. (The money/ silver motif, as we shall soon see, will be given one more climactic twist.) The ironic connection with the Ishmaelite traders is ingeniously reinforced by the other half of Jacob's instructions: that caravan long ago was seen (Gen. 37:25) "carrying gum, balm, and ladanum to be taken to Egypt," and now the brothers will constitute another such caravan, bearing exactly the same goods together with a few extra items, not bringing Joseph as a slave but headed, unawares, to the discovery of his identity as supreme master.

In the characteristic rapidity with which biblical narrative elides unessential transitions, the brothers are then immediately placed in Joseph's presence ("They arose and went down to Egypt and stood before Joseph" [Gen. 43:15]). As soon as they arrive, they are brought in haste by Joseph's officials to the viceregal palace, which makes them fear they are about to be accused of having stolen the money they had found in their bags. On the threshold of the palace, they proclaim their innocence in this regard to Joseph's majordomo. He assures them that nothing is amiss and that their God and the God of their father must have restored the money to them. (In this way an association is once more confirmed between Joseph's machinations and the workings of Providence.) Joseph at last sees Benjamin, "his brother, his mother's son" (Gen. 43:29), and, as we have already observed, he is overwhelmed with emotion, going out to another room to weep. At the feast to which he invites the brothers, he sits them in the exact order of their birth, from eldest to youngest, which dumbfounds the brothers: the contrast between his knowledge and their ignorance is thus acted out in a kind of ritual performance.

The brothers then are sent off on the road to Canaan, Joseph once again instructing his majordomo to hide the money they have paid in their bags, but this time adding that his silver divining goblet is to be slipped into Benjamin's bag (Gen. 44:2). The majordomo, in accordance with Joseph's orders, then chases after the brothers and, quickly overtaking them, angrily accuses them of having stolen the precious goblet. They, of course, are aghast at this new charge, and feel sure enough of their innocence to tell him that if any one of them is found with the goblet, that person should be put to death. This grim detail invokes a parallel to a much earlier moment in their father's story when, pursued by a wrathful Laban in part because someone had stolen Laban's household gods, Jacob confidently invited his father-in-law to search his tent and pronounced that if anyone were found to have taken the household gods, that person should not live (Gen. 31:32). On that occasion, the stolen cult objects were not discovered, but the thief, Jacob's beloved wife Rachel, seems to have suffered the consequence of his sentence when she died giving birth to Benjamin. Now, the shadow of a similar doom is made to pass over that very son before the comic resolution of the plot. (The majordomo, it should be observed, immediately softens these fatal terms: "Only the one with whom it is found will be my slave, and the rest of you will go free" [Gen. 44:10].) The choice of a silver divining goblet for this false accusation of Benjamin is an ingenious fusion of the motif of silver—illicitly received, surreptitiously restored, and ultimately linked with the brothers' guilt toward Joseph—with the central theme of knowledge, for it is an instrument supposedly used by Joseph to foretell the future, as he has done more prominently with dreams. "What is this deed you have done?" he asks the brothers when they are brought back under arrest to the palace (Gen. 44:15), and the general terms in which he couches his accusation touch all the way back to their criminal act against him two decades past. "Didn't you know"—and of course there was all too much they did not know—"that a man like me would certainly practice divination [or, would certainly manage to divine it]?"

We are now at the final climactic turning of this extraordinary story. Judah comes forward to speak for all the brothers (Gen. 44:16): "What can we say to my lord, what can we speak, by what can we prove our innocence? God has found out the crime of your servants. Here we are, then, slaves to my lord, the rest of us no less than the one with whom the goblet was found." This is the final confirmation by the brothers themselves of Joseph's dreamt-of supremacy, their necessary subservience. It is also an open admission of guilt which at least psychologically must refer to the real crime, the selling of Joseph for silver, and not to the imputed crime of stealing the silver goblet. Judah may understandably feel that he and his brothers cannot prove their innocence in regard to the stolen goblet, but he could not seriously believe it is an act they have knowingly committed, and the crime that God Himself has at last found out is certainly the making away with Joseph. Judah's proposal that all eleven brothers become slaves is rejected by Joseph as unjust: the thief alone should be confined. Judah, confronted with the prospect of inadvertently losing Benjamin after they have caused Joseph to be lost, steps closer to Joseph and pronounces his great impassioned plea.

18. I beg of you, my lord, let your servant speak a word in my lord's ears, and be not angry with your servant, for you are Pharaoh's equal. 19. My lord asked his servants, "Do you have a father or brother?" 20. And we said to my lord, "We have an old father with a child of his old age, the youngest. His brother is dead and he alone remains from his mother, and his father loves him." 21. And you said to your servants, "Bring him down to me, that I may set my eyes on him." 22. And we said to my lord, "The lad cannot leave his father. If he were to leave him, his father would die." 23. And you said to your servants, "If your youngest brother does not come down with you, you shall not see my face again." 24. And so when we returned to your servant my father, we told him my lord's words, 25. and my father said, "Go back and get us a bit of food." 26. Then we said, "We cannot go down. Only if our youngest brother is with us can we go down, for we cannot see the man's face unless our youngest brother is with us." 27. Then your servant my father said to us, "You know that my wife bore me two sons. 28. One is gone from me, and I said, 'Surely he has been devoured,' nor have I seen him since. 29. If you take this one, too, from me and disaster befalls him, you will bring my white head down to the underworld in evil." 30. Now, if I come to your servant my father and the lad is not with us, for his very life is bound up with the lad's, 31. and when he sees that the lad is not, he will die, and your servants will bring down the white head of your servant our father in grief to the underworld. 32. For your servant has pledged himself for the boy to my father, saying, "If I do not bring him back, I shall stand guilty to my father forever." 33. And so, let your servant stay here instead of the lad as a slave to my lord, and let the lad return with his brothers. 34. For how could I return to my father if the lad is not with me? Let me not witness the evil fate that would overtake my father.

In the light of all that we have seen about the story of Joseph and his brothers, it should be clear that this remarkable speech is a point-for-point undoing, morally and psychologically, of the brothers' earlier violation of fraternal and filial bonds. A basic biblical perception about both human relations and relations between God and man is that love is unpredictable, arbitrary, at times perhaps seemingly unjust, and Judah now comes to an acceptance of that fact with all its consequences. His father, he states clearly to Joseph, has singled out Benjamin for a special love, as he singled out Rachel's other son before. It is a painful reality of favoritism with which Judah, in contrast to the earlier jealousy over Joseph, is here reconciled, out of filial duty and more, out of filial love. His entire speech is motivated by the deepest empathy for his father, by a real understanding of what it means for the old man's very life to be bound up with that of the lad. He can even bring himself to quote sympathetically (verse 27) Jacob's typically extravagant statement that his wife bore him two sons—as though Leah were not also his wife and the other ten were not also his sons. Twenty-two years earlier, Judah engineered the selling of Joseph into slavery; now he is prepared to offer himself as a slave so that the other son of Rachel can be set free. Twenty-two years earlier, he stood with his brothers and silently watched when the bloodied tunic they had brought to Jacob sent their father into a fit of anguish; now he is willing to do anything in order not to have to see his father suffer that way again.

Judah, then, as spokesman for the brothers, has admirably completed the painful process of learning to which Joseph and circumstances have made him submit; the only essential thing he still does not know is Joseph's identity. These revelations of a profound change in feeling shake Joseph. He can no longer go on with the cruel masquerade through which he has been testing his brothers, and so at last he bursts into tears openly in their presence, then says to them, "I am Joseph. Is my father still alive?" (Gen. 45:3). Understandably, they are struck dumb with fear and astonishment, and so he has to ask them to step closer to him (Gen. 45:4) as he repeats his revelation. (The obtuseness of conventional source criticism is nowhere better illustrated than in its attributing to a duplication of sources this brilliantly effective repetition so obviously justified by the dramatic and psychological situation.) "I am Joseph your brother," he announces, now adding the relational term, "whom you sold into Egypt." It is the last hovering moment, perhaps unintended by Joseph, of ominous ambiguity in his address to them, for those words about their having sold him, coming from the all-powerful ruler of Egypt, might well strike terror in the hearts of the brothers. Joseph seems to perceive this, for he continues (Gen. 45:5): "Now, be not distressed or angry with yourselves for having sold me down here. For it was to save life that God sent me ahead of you." He then reveals to his brothers the full extent of his knowledge, telling them of the five years of famine still to come, and repeatedly stressing that it is God who has singled him out for greatness as the instrument of His providential design to preserve the seed of Israel. Joseph sends his brothers back to Canaan laden with the bounty of Egypt, instructing them to return with Jacob and all their households; and finally, after Jacob is vouchsafed a night-vision from God that he should not fear the descent into Egypt, father and son are at last reunited.

All this, of course, makes a very compelling story, one of the best stories, as many readers have attested, that has ever been told. But it also unforgettably illustrates how the pleasurable play of fiction in the Bible brings us into an inner zone of complex knowledge about human nature, divine intentions, and the strong but sometimes confusing threads that bind the two. The consummate artistry of the story involves an elaborate and inventive use of most of the major techniques of biblical narrative that we have considered in the course of this study: the deployment of thematic key-words; the reiteration of motifs; the subtle definition of character, relations, and motives mainly through dialogue; the exploitation, especially in dialogue, of verbatim repetition with minute but significant changes introduced; the narrator's discriminating shifts from strategic and suggestive withholding of comment to the occasional flaunting of an omniscient overview; the use at points of a montage of sources to catch the multifaceted nature of the fictional subject.

All these formal means have an ultimately representational purpose. What is it like, the biblical writers seek to know through their art, to be a human being with a divided consciousness—intermittently loving your brother but hating him even more; resentful or perhaps contemptuous of your father but also capable of the deepest filial regard; stumbling between disastrous ignorance and imperfect knowledge; fiercely asserting your own independence but caught in a tissue of events divinely contrived; outwardly a definite character and inwardly an unstable vortex of greed, ambition, jealousy, lust, piety, courage, compassion, and much more? Fiction fundamentally serves the biblical writers as an instrument of fine insight into these abiding perplexities of man's creaturely condition. That may help explain why these ancient Hebrew stories still seem so intensely alive today, and why it is worth the effort of learning to read them attentively as artful stories. It was no easy thing to make sense of human reality in the radically new light of the monotheistic revelation. The fictional imagination, marshalling a broad array of complicating and integrating narrative means, provided a precious medium for making this sort of difficult sense. By using fiction in this fashion, the biblical writers have bequeathed to our cultural tradition an enduring resource in the Hebrew Bible, and we shall be able to possess their vision more fully by better understanding the distinctive conditions of art through which it works.

9

Conclusion

To WHAT USE can a conscientious reader put the various proposals that have been made in these chapters about the artful workings of biblical narrative? Let me say that in framing my argument I have been guided by an assumption no longer altogether fashionable, and which to some may even seem quixotic—namely, that criticism can provide usable tools, that principles uncovered in the scrutiny of a selection of representative texts may be profitably followed through a broad spectrum of other texts. For the moment, at any rate, it would seem that literary studies at large have branched off into two divergent directions, one involving the elaboration of formal systems of poetics that have only a hypothetical relation to any individual literary work, the other dedicated to performing on the given text virtuoso exercises of interpretation which are in principle inimitable and unrepeatable, aimed as they are at undermining the very notion that the text might have any stable meanings. Throughout this study, I have tried to follow a third path, not really between these two alternatives but rather headed in another, more practical direction, one which I believe is warranted by the nature of literary texts in general and of the Bible in particular.

On the one hand, I have not attempted to provide a comprehensive system of descriptive poetics to explain biblical narrative because it seems to me that the actual operations of these tales are too manifold and too untidy to be contained in any symmetrical frame of formal taxonomies, neatly labeled categories, tables and charts, without distortion. On the other hand, although my exposition has proceeded through the analysis of examples, I have tried to avoid interposing my explications between the reader and the text because I consider it a betrayal of trust to leave him with critical discourse in place of a text. Obviously, my own readings of specific biblical passages assume a certain interpretation, and it will not always be one with which every reader can agree, but I have tried throughout to focus on the complexly integrated ways in which the tale is told, giving special attention to what is distinctive in the artful procedures of biblical narrative, what requires us to learn new modes of attentiveness as readers. Such attentiveness, I think, is important not only for those curious about matters of narrative technique, whether ancient or modern, but also for anyone who wants to come to terms with the significance of the Bible. I do not presume to judge whether a literary text may ever be thought to have an absolute, fixed meaning, but I certainly reject the contemporary agnosticism about all literary meaning, and it seems to me that we shall come much closer to the range of intended meanings—theological, psychological, moral, or whatever—of the biblical tale by understanding precisely how it is told.

In the effort to explain the inventiveness, the subtlety, the luminous depths of various biblical stories, perhaps my comments may have seemed at times to be something of a critical "performance" in their own right, but I should hope that it is a kind of performance that could be repeated, amplified, refined by other readers with other texts, for I have constantly sought to uncover through my analysis the multifaceted artistry of the biblical narratives themselves. In order to underscore the wider applicability of the approach I have put forth, let me briefly summarize the chief distinctive principles of biblical narrative that have been considered in this study. Reading, of course, is far too complex an activity to be reduced to check lists, but it may be helpful to keep certain features in mind, to ask ourselves certain questions, in order to direct the appropriate close attention on these highly laconic, finely articulated tales. Let me propose that for the purposes of synopsis we group what we have been discussing under four general rubrics: words, actions, dialogue, and narration. Here, then, are the kinds of things one might usefully look for in reading a biblical narrative:

1. *Words.* While the verbal medium of any literary narrative can never be entirely transparent or indifferent, the choice or the mere presence of particular single words and phrases in the biblical tale has special weight precisely because biblical narrative is so laconic, especially compared to the kinds of fiction that have shaped our common reading habits. The repetition of single words or brief phrases often exhibits a frequency, a saliency, and a thematic significance quite unlike what we may be accustomed to from other narrative traditions. The one most prominent

device involving the repetition of single words is the use of the *Leitwort*, the thematic key-word, as a way of enunciating and developing the moral, historical, psychological, or theological meanings of the story. What befalls the protagonist of the biblical tale is emphatically punctuated by significance, and the *Leitwort* is a principal means of punctuation. Where the narration so abundantly encourages us to expect this sort of repetition, on occasion the avoidance of repetition, whether through substitution of a synonym or of a wholly divergent word or phrase for the anticipated recurrence, may also be particularly revealing. Repeated words may be relatively abstract, like "blessing" in Genesis, and so point toward a thematic idea, or they may be entirely concrete, like "stones" in the Jacob story, and so serve to carry forward narrative motifs that do not have one clear thematic significance.

When the tale, moreover, is told so tersely, the fact of inclusion or exclusion of any particular lexical item may itself be quite important. There is not a great deal of narrative specification in the Bible, and so when a particular descriptive detail is mentioned—Esau's ruddiness and hairiness, Rachel's beauty, King Eglon's obesity—we should be alert for consequences, immediate or eventual, either in plot or theme. Similarly, when a relational epithet is attached to a character, or, conversely, when a relational identity is stated without the character's proper name, the narrator is generally telling us something substantive without recourse to explicit commentary: Michal oscillates between being the daughter of Saul and the wife of David according to her fortunes in the story, and Tamar, most painfully, is identified as the sister of Amnon when he rapes her.

2. *Actions.* Recurrence, parallels, analogy are the hallmarks of reported action in the biblical tale. The use of narrative analogy, where one part of the story provides a commentary on or a foil to another, should be familiar enough from later literature, as anyone who has ever followed the workings of a Shakespearian double plot may attest. In the Bible, however, such analogies often play an especially critical role because the writers tend to avoid more explicit modes of conveying evaluation of particular characters and acts. Thus, the *only* commentary made on Jacob's getting the firstborn's blessing from his blind father through deception occurs several chapters later in an analogy with a reversal—when he is deceived in the dark and given Leah instead of Rachel, then chided that it is not the law of the land to marry the younger sister before the firstborn.

One kind of recurrence in biblical narrative appears regularly through a long series of events, like the deflection of primogeniture in Genesis, the backslidings of Israel in the Wilderness tales, the periodic intervention

of divinely inspired liberators in Judges; and such recurrence works in
a way akin to the *Leitwort,* establishing a kind of rhythm of thematic
significance, clearly suggesting that events in history occur according to
an ordained pattern. If pattern is decisive in the biblical stress on repeated
actions, concatenation is equally important. There is in the biblical view
a causal chain that firmly connects one event to the next, link by link,
and that, too, accounts for a good deal of recurrence in the narrative
shaping of the events; for analogy reinforces this sense of causal connection. One could say that everything that befalls Jacob flows from the
fatal moment when he buys the birthright from Esau for a serving of
lentil pottage. That event, of course, was itself prefigured in the intrauter-
ine struggle between the twins, and it is followed, both causally and
analogically, by the theft of the blessing, Jacob's flight, his various confrontations with the two rival sisters who are his wives, his contentions
with his wily father-in-law, his wrestling with the angel, and even his
troubles with his sons, who deceive him with a garment, Joseph's tunic,
just as he, masquerading as Esau, deceived his own father with a garment.

The two most distinctively biblical uses of repeated action are when
we are given two versions of the same event and when the same event,
with minor variations, occurs at different junctures of the narrative, usually involving different characters or sets of characters. As a rule, when
we can detect two versions of a single event, it is safe to assume that
the writer has effected a montage of sources, and the question we might
ask is why he should have done this, in what ways do the two narrative
perspectives complement or complicate each other. The recurrence of the
same event—the sameness being definable as a fixed sequence of narrative
motifs which, however, may be presented in a variety of ways and sometimes with ingenious variations—is what I have called "type-scene," and
it constitutes a central organizing convention of biblical narrative. Here
one has to watch for the minute and often revelatory changes that a
given type-scene undergoes as it passes from one character to another.
How, for example, we might ask ourselves as readers, does the barren
Rebekah's annunciation type-scene differ from Sarah's, from Hannah's,
from the wife of Manoah's, from the Shunamite woman's? Occasionally,
a type-scene will be deployed in conjunction with a pointed use of narrative analogy by setting two occurrences of the same type-scene in close
sequence. Thus, the life-threatening trial in the wilderness first occurs
to Abraham's older son, Ishmael (Genesis 21), then to his younger son,
Isaac, whom Abraham seems commanded to slaughter (Genesis 22). The
alert reader can learn a great deal about the complex meanings of the
two stories by studying the network of connections, both in recurring

phrases and narrative motifs, that links them—one a tale of a desperate mother driven out into the wilderness with her son, the other a tale of an anguished father silently obeying the injunction to take his son into the wilderness, in both instances an angel's voice calling out from heaven at the critical moment to announce that the boy will be saved. Even the buffer passage between the two stories (Gen. 21:22–34), the tale of a dispute over a well in the desert, reinforces this network of connections, for it involves obtaining a source of life in the wilderness (as explicitly happens in the Ishmael story) and it concludes with Abraham's making a covenant meant to guarantee peace and well-being for his progeny.

3. *Dialogue*. Everything in the world of biblical narrative ultimately gravitates toward dialogue—perhaps, as I have had occasion to suggest, because to the ancient Hebrew writers speech seemed the essential human faculty: by exercising the capacity of speech man demonstrated, however imperfectly, that he was made in the image of God. This "gravitation" often means that phrases or whole sentences first stated by the narrator do not reveal their full significance until they are repeated, whether faithfully or with distortions, in direct speech by one or more of the characters. It also means that, quantitatively, a remarkably large part of the narrative burden is carried by dialogue, the transactions between characters typically unfolding through the words they exchange, with only the most minimal intervention of the narrator. As a rule, when a narrative event in the Bible seems important, the writer will render it mainly through dialogue, so the transitions from narration to dialogue provide in themselves some implicit measure of what is deemed essential, what is conceived to be ancillary or secondary to the main action. Thus, David's committing adultery with Bathsheba is reported very rapidly through narration with brief elements of dialogue, while his elaborate scheme first to shift the appearance of paternity to Uriah, and when that fails, to murder Uriah, is rendered at much greater length largely through dialogue. One may infer that the writer means to direct our attention to the murder rather than to the sexual transgression as the essential crime.

If, then, the very occurrence of extended dialogue should signal the need for special attentiveness as we read, there is a set of more specific questions we might ask ourselves about the way the dialogue emerges and develops. Is this the first reported speech for either or both of the two interlocutors? If so, why did the writer choose this particular narrative juncture to make the character reveal himself through speech? How does the kind of speech assigned to the character—its syntax, tone, imagery, brevity or lengthiness—serve to delineate the character and his relation to the other party to the dialogue? In looking for answers to this last question, it will be especially helpful to keep in mind the tendency of the biblical writers to organize dialogue along contrastive principles— short versus long, simple versus elaborate, balanced versus asymmetrical, perceptive versus obtuse, and so forth. Finally, we should be alert to the seeming discontinuities of biblical dialogue and ponder what they might imply. When do characters ostensibly answer one another without truly responding to what the other person has said? When does the dialogue break off sharply, withholding from us the rejoinder we might have expected from one of the two speakers?

To the extent that we can reasonably imagine how speakers of Hebrew some three thousand years ago really might have addressed one another, biblical dialogue would seem to exhibit many fine touches of persuasive mimesis, from Esau's crudeness and Judah's desperate eloquence to Hushai's cunning rhetorical contrivance. Virtually everywhere, however, dialogue in the Bible shows the clearest signs of using manifestly stylized speech, and it is always worth trying to see how the stylization makes the dialogue a more elegantly effective vehicle of meaning. Perhaps the most common feature of stylization in these spoken interchanges is the fact that the characters often repeat whole sentences or even series of sentences of each other's speech almost verbatim: A will tell B something regarding C, and B will then proceed to march off to C and say to him, You know, A instructed me . . . and go on to quote A's words. Whenever we encounter this convention—and, of course, there are many variations on the little schematic paradigm of it I have constructed here—it behooves us to watch for the small differences that emerge in the general pattern of verbatim repetition. To be sure, there are times when these differences may be quite inconsequential, as context and common sense should be able to warn us. But frequently enough, the small alterations, the reversals of order, the elaborations or deletions undergone by the statements as they are restated and sometimes restated again, will be revelations of character, moral, social, or political stance, and even plot. Often, such revelations will be matters of piquant or instructive nuance, but sometimes they can be quite momentous. In either case, the reliance on this particular technique suggests how much the biblical writers like to lead their readers to inferences through oblique hints rather than insisting on explicit statement.

4. *Narration.* Perhaps the most distinctive feature of the role played by the narrator in the biblical tales is the way in which omniscience and inobtrusiveness are combined. The sweep of the biblical narrator's authoritative knowledge extends from the very beginnings of things, which he can report down to the precise language and order of the divine

utterances that brought the world into being, to the characters' hidden thoughts and feelings, which he may summarize for us or render in detail as interior speech. He is all-knowing and also perfectly reliable: at times he may choose to make us wonder but he never misleads us. I would suppose that as readers of later fiction most of us tend to associate this sort of emphatic omniscience with narrators like those of Fielding, Balzac, Thackeray, George Eliot, who flaunt their knowledge by stepping out in front of the proscenium arch to chat with or lecture to the audience, making us acutely aware that they are mediating between us and the fictional events. In the Bible, on the other hand, the narrator's work is almost all *récit*, straight narration of actions and speech, and only exceptionally and very briefly *discours*, disquisition on and around the narrated facts and their implications. The assurance of comprehensive knowledge is thus implicit in the narratives, but it is shared with the reader only intermittently and at that quite partially. In this way, the very mode of narration conveys a double sense of a total coherent knowledge available to God (and by implication, to His surrogate, the anonymous authoritative narrator) and the necessary incompleteness of human knowledge, for which much about character, motive, and moral status will remain shrouded in ambiguity.

The practical aspect of all this to be kept in mind as one reads is that the reticence of the biblical narrator, his general refusal to comment on or explain what he reports, is purposefully selective. Why, we should ask ourselves, is a motive or feeling attributed to one character and not to another? Why is one character's attitude toward another stated flatly in one instance, both stated and explained in a second instance, and entirely withheld from us in a third? The Bible's highly laconic mode of narration may often give the impression of presenting the events virtually without mediation: so much, after all, is conveyed through dialogue, with only the minimal "he said" to remind us of a narrator's presence; and even outside of dialogue, what is often reported is absolutely essential action, without obtrusive elaboration or any obvious intervention by the narrator. Against this norm, we should direct special attention to those moments when the illusion of unmediated action is manifestly shattered. Why at a particular juncture does the narrator break the time-frame of his story to insert a piece of expository information in the pluperfect tense, or to jump forward to the time of his contemporary audience and explain that in those days it was the custom in Israel to perform such and such a practice? Why does he pause to make a summarizing statement about the condition of a character, as, for example, in the observation about Joseph's already established viceregal status just as the ten brothers arrive in Egypt? Why at certain points is the regular rapid tempo of narration slowed down to take in details of a kind for which in general no time is allowed?

These various relaxations of reticence are, I suspect, the operation of biblical narrative most resistant to a manageable rule of thumb, but an alertness to their occurrence and a willingness to wonder about their motivation, with the specific contexts as a guide, will help make us better readers of the biblical tales.

In trying to define as I have what one should learn to look for in biblical narrative, I do not mean to suggest that these ancient Hebrew stories need to be thought of as "difficult" works, like the fiction of Kafka, Faulkner, and Joyce, although I do think they involve complexities for which sufficient allowance has often not been made. One might imagine the Bible as a rich and variegated landscape, perfectly accessible to the observer's eye, but from which we now stand almost three millennia distant. Through the warp of all those intervening centuries, lines become blurred, contours are distorted, colors fade; for not only have we lost the precise shadings of implication of the original Hebrew words but we have also acquired quite different habits and expectations as readers, have forgotten the very conventions around which the biblical tales were shaped. Philological research in recent decades has made admirable progress in recovering the likely nuances of many particular words, but that is only a first step. The reconstruction through careful analysis of the literary procedures that govern biblical narrative can serve us, at the immense remove from which we view these ancient texts, as binoculars to bring much that seems hazy into focus.

Let me offer a compact final example of how this sort of focusing through a literary perspective can occur. It is a brief moment of dialogue, introduced and concluded by narrative report, which moves past so quickly that perhaps it might not be thought worthy of special attention, perhaps its terse rendering of an emotion-fraught event might even seem flat and schematic. By asking of the text, however, many of the questions we have just reviewed, I think we shall be able to see how nicely delineated this moment is, how densely suggestive its connections with what has preceded it and with what will follow.

In the latter part of Genesis 29, after Jacob finds himself married against his will to Leah and only afterward to the beloved Rachel, Leah gives birth to four sons in rapid succession while Rachel remains barren. Of the unloved Leah's feelings of vexation we learn a good deal through the little naming-speeches she makes after the birth of each son. Rachel, meanwhile, is not accorded any narrative attention beyond the bare report of her barrenness. Finally, at the beginning of Genesis 30, the narrator turns to the younger of the two sisters.

> 1. Rachel saw that she had borne Jacob no children, and she was jealous of her sister. And she said to Jacob, "Give me sons; if not, I shall die." 2. Jacob was incensed with Rachel and he said, "Am I instead of God, who has withheld from you fruit of the womb?" 3. And she said, "Here is my maid Bilhah. Have intercourse with her so that she may give birth on my knees and I too shall be built up through her." 4. And she gave him her maidservant Bilhah as a concubine, and Jacob had intercourse with her.

This is the sort of seemingly straightforward passage that has not invited much commentary from modern scholars, except for a few explanatory notes on the practice of giving birth on someone's knees as an ancient rite of adoption, and an elucidation of a pun that is quite obvious in the Hebrew, "I shall be built up" (*'ibbaneh*), which plays on *banim*, sons, and so has the sense of "I shall be sonned." The dialogue itself is stark but at the same time, in a characteristic biblical manner, subtle, as I think we shall be able to see by attending to its specific terms and to how it fits into the larger context of the story.

The narrator begins by reporting Rachel's perception—surely not just a flat observation of fact but a bitter conclusion after years of waiting—of her barrenness. Until this point, we have been told absolutely nothing of Rachel's feelings as Jacob her kinsman first embraced her and wept over her at the well, as her father set her aside to make Leah Jacob's first wife, as she received Jacob's love but her sister brought forth his children. Now, to motivate not only the action at hand but also the whole subsequent story of the two sisters and their offspring, the narrator at last gives us access to Rachel's feelings and tells us that she was jealous of her sister. One might note that Leah is not mentioned by name here (verse 1): what is brought to the fore is the primary fact of her identity as sister, and hence the smouldering rivalry for progeny and love between these two daughters of Laban. That rivalry in turn is linked through analogy with the whole series of struggles between younger and elder brothers in Genesis, and the repeated drive of the secondborn to displace the firstborn, as Jacob himself had contrived to displace Esau. Thus, Rachel's jealous rage is both a unique event and something that partakes of the *déjà vu*, the tension between those two contradictory aspects generating much of its depth of meaning.

Conclusion

After the notation of jealousy, Rachel speaks, and we should keep in mind that it is the very first piece of dialogue given to her in the narrative. As such, we might expect that it will be especially revelatory of character, and in fact it immediately shows us a Rachel who is impatient, impulsive, explosive: "Give me sons; if not, I shall die." The brusqueness of this is even a little more emphatic in the Hebrew, where "give," *havah*, is a word often used for peremptory and crudely material requests (Judah begins with the same word when he tells Tamar, who is disguised as a prostitute, that he wants her body), and where the tense of dying is more imminent (literally, "I am dead"). With an alertness to echoes, we might observe that this is the second time Jacob has been confronted by someone who claimed to be on the point of death unless immediately given what he or she wanted, the first instance occurring in the request for lentil pottage by his ravenous brother Esau. The barren Rachel asks for not just a son but sons (the second one she will bear is to cost her life itself). Jacob in his rejoinder says neither son *(ben)* nor child *(yeled)* but instead uses a rather formal locution, the kenning "fruit of the womb." Perhaps he chooses this term because of the theological context—God's withholding from her—of his statement; perhaps, also, it sharpens the rebuke to Rachel by stressing her condition of barrenness through the implied image of the childless woman as a plant that yields no fruit.

This alteration of a single term, a procedure which as I have tried to show is often finely significant in the Bible, is part of a larger pattern here—the familiar technique of definition of character through contrastive dialogue. The writer's easy command of that technique is evident in his ability to bring it into effective play even in so brief an exchange, where Jacob's single utterance is (in the Hebrew) eight words, and Rachel's two statements come to nineteen words. Her speech opens with two short, choppy independent clauses ("Give me . . . I shall die."), rather hysterical in tone; and even in her second utterance, which moves in a longer syntactic chain from intercourse to birth to being built up, the statement is again cast as an impatient imperative. Jacob, by contrast, responds to Rachel's importunity with a rhetorical—and of course sarcastic—question formulated syntactically as a complex sentence. The opposition between the two modes of speech is, roughly, an opposition between expletive franticness and angry control.

It is also worth noting the studied avoidances of response in the dialogue. Rachel does not comment directly on Jacob's rebuke with its suggestion of a divine judgment of barrenness against her, but instead drives forward toward her own practical intention: "Here is my maidservant Bilhah. Have intercourse with her." The narrator, who a moment earlier made a special point of informing us that Rachel's first speech had provoked Jacob's wrath, is now silent on Jacob's reaction to this demand that he take Bilhah as a concubine. The dialogue is abruptly terminated, giving one the impression that whatever Jacob thinks of the arrangement, he sees that Rachel is within her legal rights and that compliance might be the better part of wisdom in dealing with this desperate woman. Without any further report of feeling or speech, Bilhah is given and Jacob performs the required progenitive service. The whole dialogue is a matter of a few lines, but it succeeds in amply suggesting the tangle of emotions—love, consideration, jealousy, frustration, resentment, rage—that constitutes the conjugal relationship.

The widest circle of implication in the scene is defined by its pointed reversal of a type-scene motif. Rachel, as the favored, barren co-wife, is perfectly set up to be the subject of an annunciation. But instead of praying to God in a sanctuary, like Hannah, or being visited by an angel, like Sarah or Manoah's wife, she accosts her husband and asks *him* to give her sons. Jacob's rebuke, then—"Am I instead of God?"—is virtually an explicit reference by one of the characters to the traditional requirements of the type-scene. Rachel is of course theologically wrong in imagining that the conferral of offspring is within the power of husband rather than of God, but at the same time we as readers are reminded, perhaps a little ominously, that as a matter of literary plot, this is not the way things are done in all these stories of barren wives. After Rachel finally manages to conceive a child, her life, as I have already noted, will end prematurely with the birth of her second son; and for all the glory that her firstborn, Joseph, will one day enjoy, the future kings of Israel will spring not from him but from Judah, the fourth son of her sister Leah.

The reading of any literary text requires us to perform all sorts of operations of linkage, both small and large, and at the same time to make constant discriminations among related but different words, statements, actions, characters, relations, and situations. What I have tried to indicate throughout this study and to illustrate by way of summary through this last example is that in the Bible many of the clues offered to help us make these linkages and discriminations depend on a distinctive set of narrative procedures which for readers of a later era has to be learned. It has been my own experience in making a sustained effort to understand biblical narrative better that such learning is pleasurable rather than arduous. As one discovers how to adjust the fine focus of those literary binoculars, the biblical tales, forceful enough to begin with, show a surprising subtlety and inventiveness of detail, and in many instances a beautifully interwoven wholeness. The human figures that move through this landscape thus seem livelier, more complicated and various, than one's preconceptions might have allowed.

This, I am convinced, was at the heart of the authors' intentions: the Hebrew writers manifestly took delight in the artful limning of these lifelike characters and actions, and so they created an unexhausted source of delight for a hundred generations of readers. But that pleasure of imaginative play is deeply interfused with a sense of great spiritual urgency. The biblical writers fashion their personages with a complicated, sometimes alluring, often fiercely insistent individuality because it is in the stubbornness of human individuality that each man and woman encounters God or ignores Him, responds to or resists Him. Subsequent religious tradition has by and large encouraged us to take the Bible seriously rather than to enjoy it, but the paradoxical truth of the matter may well be that by learning to enjoy the biblical stories more fully as stories, we shall also come to see more clearly what they mean to tell us about God, man, and the perilously momentous realm of history.

INDEX

Index

David *(continued)*
 encounter with Ahimelech, 64–67, 70–72
 and Goliath, 35, 64, 66, 71, 78–81, 147,
  151, 152
 and Michal, 115–16, 118–27
 and Saul, 35–37, 64, 66–69, 72, 73, 89,
  101, 115–16, 118–24, 147–48, 150,
  152
 and Solomon's succession, 98–100
 two versions of debut of, 147–53
Deborah, 146
Deuteronomy, 155
Dickens, Charles, 133, 156
Diderot, Denis, 133
Dinah, 18, 161
Do'eg, 64, 66, 70

E, see Elohistic Document
Eber, 63
Ebiathar, 98
Edom, *see* Esau
Eglon, 37–41, 180
Ehud, 37–41
Einstein, Albert, 144
Eisenstein, Sergei, 140
Eissfeldt, Otto, 14
Eli, 82–86
Eliab, 78–79, 134, 149–51, 158
Elihu, 81
Elijah, 73, 90
Eliot, George, 21, 156, 184
Elkanah, 81–84
Elohistic Document *(E)*, 20, 132, 138, 139,
  166
Enuma Elish, 29
Er, 5, 6
Esau (Edom), 42–45, 54, 72, 180, 181, 183,
  186, 187
Esther, 34
Esther, Book of, *ix,* 17, 34
Eve, 27–32, 145–46
Exodus
 Chap. 2
  2:15b–21, 56–58
 Chap. 7
  7:17–18, 90–91
  7:20–21, 90–91

Faulkner, William, 21, 185
Fielding, Henry, 24, 94, 133, 156, 184
Fishbane, Michael, 16, 94
Flaubert, Gustave, 13, 23, 131
Fokkelman, J. P., 16, 54n, 55
Ford, Ford Madox, 126
Formalists, Russian, 62, 79n, 153

Former Prophets, *ix,* 104, 132
 See also specific books
Freedman, David Noel, 14

Genesis, 17, 24–25, 32, 34, 46, 91, 92, 95
 Chap. 1
  1:1–19, 143
  1:27, 146
 Chap. 2, 141–47
  2:1–4, 141–43, 147
  2:10–14, 142
  2:18, 145
  2:18–25, 27–32
  2:46–47, 144
 Chap. 12
  12:1, 59
  12:10–20, 49
 Chap. 16, 49
 Chap. 20, 49
  20:5–6, 43
 Chap. 21
  21:9–21, 49
  21:22–34, 182
 Chap. 22, 181
 Chap. 24, 10–61, 52–55
 Chap. 25, 72
  25:23, 42
  25:27–34, 42–45
 Chap. 26
  26:1–12, 49
 Chap. 27, 45
  27:14–17, 8
  27:18, 37
  27:22, 37
 Chap. 29, 185–86
  29:1–20, 52, 54–56
  29:26, 45
 Chap. 30
  30:1–4, 186–88
 Chap. 31, 120
  31:32, 173
 Chap. 34
  34:31, 161
 Chap. 37, 10, 12, 139, 160, 166
  37:25, 172
  37:26–27, 10
  37:29, 5
  37:32–36, 4–5
 Chap. 38, 3–12, 20, 133, 160
  38:1, 26n
 Chap. 39, 19, 72–73, 107–12, 117
 Chap. 40, 163
 Chap. 41, 163
 Chap. 42, 160–71
  42:20–21, 139
  42:25, 137
  42:27–28, 137–40

192

Index